SCANDAL AT DOLPHIN SQUARE

SCANDAL AT DOLPHIN SQUARE

A NOTORIOUS HISTORY

SIMON DANCZUK AND DANIEL SMITH

The History Press

SD: For Milton and Maurice
DS: For Rosie, Charlotte and Ben

Alas! the devil's sooner raised than laid.
So strong, so swift, the monster there's no gagging:
Cut Scandal's head off, still the tongue is wagging.

David Garrick's 'Prologue' to Richard Brinsley Sheridan's *The School for Scandal*

First published 2022

The History Press
97 St George's Place, Cheltenham,
Gloucestershire, GL50 3QB
www.thehistorypress.co.uk

British Library Cataloguing in Publication Data.
A catalogue record for this book is available from the British Library.

ISBN 978 0 7509 9714 0

Typesetting and origination by The History Press
Printed and bound in Great Britain by TJ Books Limited, Padstow, Cornwall.

Trees for LYfe

CONTENTS

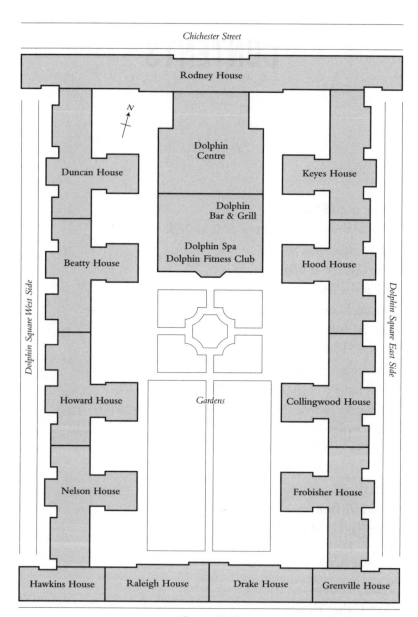

Map of Dolphin Square. (FourPoint Mapping)

INTRODUCTION

> Dolphin Square will, for many reasons, be London's most distin-
> guished address. It will carry the prestige associated with many
> residents notable in public life and society. Members of Parliament,
> people of title, Government Officials and Professional men are among
> those who have been attracted as Residents to Dolphin Square by
> reason of its unique location and exceptional appointments.
>
> Dolphin Square promotional brochure (1935).[1]

When Dolphin Square officially opened in 1936, it was never intended
to be just another block of flats. It was meant to offer a glimpse of
the future – a city dwelling for the modern age. Twentieth-century
living at its most hi-tech and aspirational. Nor was there any pretence
of egalitarian classlessness. These were apartments for the affluent and
the influential, the movers and shakers, the people who ran the country
and made it tick. Sure, you didn't have to be a member of the super-
rich (although if you were, then 'Welcome!') but you needed a certain
standing and a good income to secure a tenancy. (There have only ever
been tenants at Dolphin Square – it has never been possible to buy a
property outright.)

Located in Pimlico, on the north bank of the Thames and just up
the road from Westminster, the Square soon filled with politicians, civil
servants, military figures, lawyers and businessmen, the mix liberally
seasoned with artists, writers, entertainers and other celebrities. There
were a fair few working-class faces too, but they were there to serve

– as caretakers, errand boys, cabbies, tradesmen, shopkeepers and the like, all cogs in the Dolphin Square machine that has ensured life runs smoothly for those who can afford to live there.

The complex has been likened to a citadel. Its tall blocks – forged from reinforced concrete and beautified with brick facades – are indeed imposing as they rise up from the development's calming and beloved gardens. There is a sense of 'the community within' and the foreboding world beyond. Others have likened it to a village, a self-contained hamlet in the city, where the mundanity of everyday life sporadically gives way to gossip, drama and scandal. But Dolphin Square is perhaps more accurately described as a high-rise suburban oasis in the metropolis. A bolt hole for those whose social status relies upon the hurly-burly of 'being in town' but who, when the evening draws in, want some respite from it all. A place where they may put away the public face, hang up the suit, pour a drink and be themselves. For many residents, their apartments have been their main homes, while for others they're but a pied-à-terre. For more than probably want to admit it, Dolphin Square has also been a place to hide away illicit lovers. But for nearly all, it has provided a sense of sanctuary.

Some residents have stayed for decades while others merely pass through. With an ever-evolving cast of thousands, much that has gone on here over the decades is unremarkable, in the way that most lives most of the time are unremarkable to the world at large. But there is always the whiff of gunpowder in the air at Dolphin Square. Sometimes it is just a faint, far-off aroma that you can hardly detect. Other times – bang! – there it goes, the combustible mix explodes, filling the nostrils with smoke and you can only wait for it to clear to see who is okay and who has been caught in the carnage.

Dolphin Square could never be described as a microcosm of the nation as a whole. It is too selective, too much of the Establishment for that. Rather, it is a stage set upon which countless dramas in the nation's life and in the lives of some of its most prominent public figures have played out in miniature (and every now and then as exaggerated, surround-sound, 3D technicolour extravaganzas, too). It has hosted representatives of every imaginable political hue, from the far left to the far right and everything in between. There have been spies and their spymasters, revolutionaries, diplomats and democrats, even armies in exile. Famous love stories have played out, along with monstrous betrayals and sex scandals that felled governments. There have been tragedies, suicides and murder, tales of extraordinary bravery and derring-do, not to mention an enormous dollop of British eccentricity.

It is all to be found in this old place – famous and infamous at the same time – behind the front doors and along the corridors, down in its swimming pool and restaurant, through the shopping arcade and into the gardens. The walls whisper their secrets and sometimes tease with half-truths and lies. Stare into the famous ornamental pool with its elegantly sculpted dolphins, and you may just catch a reflection of our society over the best part of a century. The cultural and political landscape has shifted much over the years, but still Dolphin Square serves as a haven for that class of doers and influencers who mould our lives – a space where the private and the public collides with perhaps unique regularity and consequence. This book, then, unpicks some of the stories that have made Dolphin Square such a notable address – a modern 'school for scandal'. Only time will reveal what other tales we are yet to discover …

1

MOVERS AND SHAKERS

What we now know as Pimlico (its name probably derived from that of the landlord of a popular hostelry over in Hoxton) was for many centuries a stretch of non-descript marshland that came to border an array of desirable neighbourhoods – Chelsea, Knightsbridge, Hyde Park and St James's Park. The land was owned by the aristocratic Grosvenor family who, in the first half of the nineteenth century, partnered with an ambitious builder called Thomas Cubitt, a man of rare vision who would reshape several stretches of the city. It was he who first sculpted Pimlico into a residential neighbourhood catering for an overspill of the middling class gradually shifting west from the centre of London.

Cubitt located his Pimlico works on the site of what is now Dolphin Square, and it remained a hive of industry until his death in 1855. His son then reluctantly took over the family business and gradually the works were turned over to the army, who used it as a clothing depot. As the century rolled by, Cubitt's original vision of a middle-class utopia gave way to something rather more down at heel. In 1902, Charles Booth noted in one of his famous surveys of the city that Pimlico still possessed 'shabby gentility' but showed signs of 'decay' and 'grimy dilapidation'.[1]

Matters eventually came to a head in the 1930s. There were still a few pockets of middle-class domesticity but these tended to have faded, the residents of those neighbourhoods just about clinging on but generally not so well off to be able either to move to a more upmarket area or to ensure the good upkeep of their existing properties. Meanwhile, an increasing number of B&Bs and dosshouses had sprung up, while some streets were so ravaged by extreme poverty that they were little more than slums.

Yet there had been a vast upsurge in the number of people employed as civil servants in the city since the end of the nineteenth century, creating a demand for homes within easy reach of Westminster to suit the desires of this professional class. As things stood, there were simply not enough properties to meet the need. In addition, the army was preparing to relocate its clothing depot from its home in Cubitt's old building works and were keen to stop paying the Grosvenor estate its not insignificant rent. Just as it had been a century earlier, the area was ripe for a shake-up. Cubitt's attempt to turn Pimlico into a destination neighbourhood for London's burgeoning middle class had only been a partial success. Now was a chance to finish the job.

The 'new Cubitt' for a while looked likely to be an American developer called Fred French. He purchased the freehold to the army depot site from Hugh Grosvenor, the Duke of Westminster, with an eye to creating a development modelled on successful projects he had overseen in the US. In particular, he wanted to replicate the success of his Tudor City development. Built in Manhattan in the 1920s, it was a complex that managed to meld the aspirations of the suburban middle classes to city skyscrapers. That was the dream for his Pimlico project, which was initially to be called Ormonde Court. But French soon ran up against a problem – the economic slump on both sides of the Atlantic was straining his company's finances to near breaking point. Unable to secure the necessary finance, he began a desperate search for a building company to partner with.

Eventually, he alighted upon Costains, a family firm with a well-established reputation for speculative projects. They initially agreed to pool their talents but it was not long before French agreed to sell Costains his interest in the project. Costains then brought in architect Gordon Jeeves to revise the plans, while Oscar Faber was employed as consultant engineer. (Albert Costain, a director and brother of the company's managing director, R.R. Costain, would serve as MP for Folkestone and Hythe between 1959 and 1983. That the company straddled the world of construction and politics no doubt helped inform the design of the Square, built in no small part with the political class firmly in mind.) Building began in September 1935 on the first of some 1,200 apartments on the 7.5-acre site. The intention was that Dolphin Square should house some 3,000 people by the time it was finished.

The first completed tranche of the development was officially opened by Lord Amulree on 25 November 1936. Amulree was a barrister and Labour politician who'd served as Secretary of State for Air in Ramsay MacDonald's administration at the beginning of the 1930s. Also in attendance that day was Duff Cooper, the Secretary of State for War and MP for the nearby Westminster St George constituency. As a junior minister several years earlier, it had fallen to him to announce the closure of the army depot on which Dolphin Square now stood. Cooper had a love for a boozy dinner and possessed a liberal attitude to marital fidelity but, as far as we know, the opening went off without a hitch. It would not be long, though, before misbehaving politicians were starting to make their mark at the new apartments.

Although much of Dolphin Square was yet to be completed, it was already easy to see the appeal. The flats themselves benefitted from the latest soundproofing technology and came with such mod cons as fitted kitchens with fridges and self-controlled cookers, while telephones were also installed as standard. There were options to suit a variety of pockets too – you could get anything from a bedsit from £75 per year to a seven-room suite with provision for a maid from £455. But it was the abundance of extra amenities that really set the Square apart. As well as the gardens (which, rather than the buildings, were given a grade II listing in 2018), shops, restaurant and swimming pool (said to be based on the original Paris Lido), there was a library, beauty parlour, theatre booking office, laundry service, on-site childcare provision, a huge underground car park, valeting, shoe cleaning, errand boys and multiple postal collections and deliveries every day. If you so desired, it was quite possible to enjoy an elevated lifestyle without ever having to leave the Square again. It truly lived up to the aspiration expressed in a 1935 promotional booklet that residents might enjoy 'at the same time most of the advantages of the separate house and the big communal dwelling place'.[2] Reflecting the chauvinism of the day, one of the few concerns expressed in the advertising blurb was that 'The Dolphin lady may be spoiled'. With so many of the concerns of domestic life addressed, there was a fear that 'fortunate wives will not have enough to do. A little drudgery is good for wives, perhaps.'[3]

By the time Dolphin Square was completely finished in 1938, there were a total of thirteen Houses, each named after a significant figure from British naval history: Beatty, Collingwood, Drake, Duncan, Frobisher, Grenville, Hawkins, Hood, Howard, Keyes, Nelson, Raleigh and Rodney. These names tied in with the aquatic theme of the development but they also fitted into a wider narrative, one that spoke of British prestige, public service and personal glory. In short, these were the sorts of figures that the residents could look up to, and perhaps even hang a portrait of on the walls. Even if you weren't a military sort, if you were more likely to wear a bowler hat than an admiral's tricorn, there was the sense that within these buildings resided the sort of people who made this island nation great. As a verse published in *Truth* in December 1952 put it:

> Since Admiral's dare watery graves,
> Where'er Britannia rules the waves,
> It's eminently fair
> That theirs is the exclusive right
> To have their names in letters bright
> Displayed in Dolphin Square.[4]

So, who was there among Dolphin Square's early intake? Which names stand out among the lords and ladies, the vice admirals, majors and colonels, the city financiers and captains of industry, the poets and playwrights, the silver screen heartthrobs and West End hoofers?

Arguably, the most significant contemporary political figure in the 1930s was Arthur Greenwood, Clement Attlee's deputy leader of the Labour Party. Greenwood, a tall, rather awkward Yorkshireman and not renowned as a great orator, moved into Keyes House in 1939, just as he was about to enjoy his finest moment in the House of Commons. On 2 September, as Britain stood on the brink of war, Attlee was in hospital for a medical procedure so the responsibility to speak for the party fell to Greenwood. Hitler's invasion of Poland had commenced the previous day – an event set to trigger Britain's entry into the war to defend its ally. But to the disquiet of members on both sides of the House, there was little sign of the Conservative Government putting its military might into action. Prime Minister Neville Chamberlain gave a holding speech in which he dangled the possibility that a negotiated peace might still be achievable, even as German troops swarmed over Poland. Besides, any British action must wait until France was ready to assist. Greenwood got to his feet, encouraging shouts coming from all directions. Notably, Leo Amery, the arch Conservative anti-appeaser, urged him to 'Speak for England, Arthur!' A clearly nervous Greenwood began his address, and soon found his rhythm:

I am speaking under very difficult circumstances with no opportunity to think about what I should say; and I speak what is in my heart at this moment. I am gravely disturbed. An act of aggression took place 38 hours ago. The moment that act of aggression took place one of the most important treaties of modern times automatically came into operation. There may be reasons why instant action was not taken. I am not prepared to say – and I have tried to play a straight game – I am not prepared to say what I would have done had I been one of those sitting on those Benches. That delay might have been justifiable, but there are many of us on all sides of this House who view with the gravest concern the fact that hours went by and news came in of bombing operations, and news today of an intensification of it, and I wonder how long we are prepared to vacillate at a time when Britain and all that Britain stands for, and human civilisation, are in peril … if, as the right hon. Gentleman has told us, deeply though I regret it, we must wait upon our Allies, I should have preferred the Prime Minister to have been able to say to-night definitely, 'It is either peace or war.' Tomorrow we meet at 12. I hope the Prime Minister then – well, he must be in a position to make some further statement. And I must put this point to him. Every minute's delay now means the loss of life, imperilling our national interests … imperilling the very foundations of our national honour, and I hope, therefore, that tomorrow morning, however hard it may be to the right hon. Gentleman – and no one would care to be in his shoes to-night – we shall know the mind of the British Government, and that there shall be no more devices for dragging out what has been dragged out too long. The moment we look like weakening, at that moment dictatorship knows we are beaten. We are not beaten. We shall not be beaten. We cannot be beaten ...[5]

Greenwood had proved the old 'Cometh the hour' adage and Chamberlain was left in no doubt by his whips that the House would brook no further prevarication. Chamberlain declared war on Germany the following day. Rumour has it that Greenwood steeled his nerves with a few drinks in the Commons bar before his speech on the 2nd. One suspects he might have calmed his post-match nerves with a few more back inside Dolphin Square.

Nor would Greenwood have been short of fellow Labourites to consort with. For one, his son Tony was still living with his parents in the Square. The following year Tony married Jill Williams and subsequently they became something of a Labour power couple. She designed the iconic 'Make do and mend' pamphlets during the war and he would go on to hold several ministerial posts in the 1950s and '60s, including Minister of Housing and Local Government, Minister of Overseas Development and Secretary of State for the Colonies. A left-winger, in 1961 he unsuccessfully challenged Hugh Gaitskell for the party leadership. The Greenwoods were also prominent figures in the anti-nuclear Aldermaston Marches and were founding members of the Campaign for Nuclear Disarmament (CND) in 1958.

The MP Josiah Wedgwood, another party stalwart, had taken a flat in Howard House in 1937, by which time he was already into his seventh decade. A descendant of the legendary eighteenth-century potter and industrial giant who shared his name, Wedgwood had been a member of the Liberal Party when he first took a seat in Parliament in 1906 but joined the Labour ranks after the First World War, in which he had seen active service. By the time he arrived at Dolphin Square, he was firmly established among the anti-appeasers in the Commons and was a notable campaigner in the interests of those attempting to flee Hitler's terror on the Continent. He was also a prime example of the sort of 'old money' who could have afforded to live in a much grander, more traditional London abode than Dolphin Square but who had instead bought into the Costains' vision of modern living. Yet even Wedgwood could not avoid a little scandal once a resident of the Square. In January 1938, his wife Ethel was fined £1 for dangerous driving, the judge suggesting down Ethel's ear trumpet that she ought to have a driving test. (When it came to motoring indiscretions, she was in good company. An additional wayward Dolphin Square car owner was Diana Asquith, wife of Michael Asquith and granddaughter-in-law of Herbert Asquith, Britain's Liberal prime minister from 1908 until 1916. She was fined £2 for non-payment of road tax in 1939, an oversight she put down to a bout of illness.)

Whatever his wife's suitability to driving, Wedgwood was able to weather that particular indiscretion and continued with his life of public service. When war arrived, he joined the Home Guard and, in 1942, Churchill elevated him to the Lords, ending his thirty-six-year Commons career. Perhaps tellingly, he died just a year later.

Dolphin Square boasted yet another Labour MP in this period, too. Arthur Henderson shared the same name as his more illustrious father, a bona fide star in the political firmament until his death in 1935. Arthur Snr had been an iron worker by profession and ended up serving three times as leader of the Labour Party over four decades. Moreover, he was the first member of his party to hold a Cabinet position when Herbert Asquith made him president of the Board of Trade in his war-time coalition in 1915. Lloyd George then appointed him minister without portfolio when he took over as prime minister the following year. Further high office was to come when Ramsay MacDonald made him Home Secretary in 1924 after Labour came to power for the first time in its history. With Labour back in power in 1929, he next held the post of Foreign Secretary until 1931. Then, in 1934, to complete a remarkable CV, he was awarded the Nobel Peace Prize 'for his untiring struggle and his courageous efforts as Chairman of the League of Nations Disarmament Conference 1931–34'.[6]

It was quite an act to follow and Arthur Jnr's career never touched quite the same heights but was nonetheless notable in its own way.

In Churchill's wartime coalition, he served as Under Secretary of State for War and, after the conflict ended, he was appointed Under Secretary of State for India and Burma ahead of India's independence. His final government post was as Secretary of State for Air from 1947–51, with responsibility for the RAF.

While it is true that there was a strong Labour flavour to Dolphin Square early on, it was always a bipartisan sort of place. In August 1937, for instance, Lord Burghley took an apartment in Nelson House. Born David Cecil but better known as David Burghley, he was descended from William Cecil, the original Lord Burghley and Elizabeth I's most trusted advisor. But David Burghley was better known to the British public as the Conservative MP for Peterborough and, even more so, as one of the country's finest Olympians. His greatest moment as an athlete came when he triumphed in the 400m hurdles at the 1928 Olympics, an achievement he followed up with a slew of Empire Games titles before adding a silver medal in the 4 × 400 relay at the 1932 Olympics (having been granted time off from his parliamentary duties in order to compete).

A pivotal figure in organising the 1948 London Olympics and a stalwart of the International Olympic Committee, he was immortalised in the 1981 film *Chariots of Fire* as Lord Andrew Lindsay. In real life, back in 1927, he had become the first person to run around the Great Court at Trinity College, Cambridge, in the roughly forty-three seconds it takes the college clock to complete its midnight chimes (a feat traditionally attempted after the college's matriculation dinner). The run was reimagined for the film, however, with Harold Abrahams credited with the feat. Whether Burghley ever tried a similar sprint around Dolphin Square is not recorded, although he was often observed running round the grounds to keep his fitness up.

Other eminent Conservatives included Lord and Lady Apsley. Born Allen Bathurst, Lord Apsley was an Eton and Oxford-educated military man and, since the 1920s, the Conservative MP first for Southampton and then Bristol Central with links to the air industry. Having served with distinction in the First World War, he did so again in the Second World War, when he was a colonel with the Arab Legion in Malta. He died in 1942 after the aeroplane carrying him crashed on take-off from the island. Remarkably, his wife, Violet (commonly known as Viola) then contested and won the by-election for his vacant parliamentary seat, holding it until Labour unseated her in the post-war election.

Viola was always a force to be reckoned with – a nurse and ambulance driver in the First World War, in the 1920s she had gone undercover in the Australian outback with her husband on a government fact-finding mission (and then wrote a book about it), and in 1930 she obtained her flying licence before a hunting accident rendered her unable to walk. In the 1930s, she and her husband aligned themselves with the pro-appeasement lobby and some observers detected a distinct sympathy for European fascism. Lord Apsley was a guest of Hitler at the 1936 Nuremberg Rally, while Viola was given a tour of a labour camp for the unemployed that greatly impressed her at the time. Yet when war was declared, both husband and wife threw themselves into the national effort. While he was in Malta, she headed up the women's division of the British Legion. As an MP, she made her mark as one of very few women in a man's world and also became a noted campaigner for disability rights. Indeed, it was the subject of her maiden speech in the House, which she delivered from her wheelchair and for which she received resounding applause. Honoured with a CBE (Commander of the Order of the British Empire) in 1952 'for public and social services', she died in 1966.[7]

Another of the Square's Conservative contingent was Sir Anderson Montague-Barlow, a barrister by trade and already in his seventies by the time he came to Dolphin Square. A former Minister of Labour, he was still highly regarded enough that in 1938 Neville Chamberlain asked him to head up a royal commission looking at the distribution of the industrial population – a body whose findings would prove highly influential on the post-war 'new town' movement. Then there was the intriguing Clementine Freeman-Mitford, a society figure who would soon marry into the political Establishment. She was a cousin to the famous Mitford Sisters, who'd variously bewitched and scandalised Britain since the 1920s as Bright Young Things whose lustre was prone to tarnish. Another of Freeman-Mitford's cousins was Clementine Hozier, better known as Winston Churchill's wife. Freeman-Mitford was less often to be found among the headlines than her cousins but was nonetheless close to them and was introduced to Hitler by Unity Mitford. She did not, though, develop a passion for the Führer like Unity and a few months before the outbreak of war she married the Conservative MP Alfred Beit, who by then was living in a spectacular mansion property in Kensington Palace Gardens – to which Clementine presumably moved – and had inherited one of the most spectacular private art collections in the country.

Away from political and aristocratic circles, the Square proved an attractive home to figures from the entertainment world, too. For example, Keyes House, and later Beatty House, was the home of Mr and Mrs John Jackson and, by default, headquarters of the 'world famous' J.W. Jackson dancing troupe. It was to Dolphin Square that hopeful applicants wrote to arrange auditions for either the Jackson Girls, the Jackson Boys or offshoots such as the Lancashire Lads. In the 1930s, these represented prized jobs for young dancers intent on carving out a career. Successful applicants might find themselves in cabaret shows, pantomimes and even on screen – the company consistently supplied venues up and down the country and had a good dose of international work too.

The Jacksons' adverts, often to be found in *The Stage*, tell a tale of changing times. Where they were relatively demure in the early days, seeking dancers with expertise in tap and ballet, by the time of the company's final advert in 1963 (Mrs Jackson had died a couple of years earlier) they were competing in a world where dancing ability was often definitely secondary to glamour. 'All Round Good Dancers Wanted,' John Jackson hopefully implored. 'Any Good Girls who are free for a few weeks only may also apply.' Positioned just next to this was a more forthright appeal for 'Exotic Dancers', while an additional ad on the page unapologetically sought girls for a 'Glamour Time Floor Show'. Tap dancing not essential, it did not need to add.[8]

A different production company was located in Howard House, where the flat of actor-director Arthur Hardy doubled as the base for HHH Productions. This was a theatrical management company that he had founded along with fellow director-producer Sinclair Hill, and Edward Hemmerde, a barrister and Liberal MP who also fancied himself as a playwright. If they ever needed a bit of writing muscle, they need not have looked further than Collingwood House, home to the husband and wife writers Margaret Lane and Bryan Edgar Wallace. She was a successful journalist with stints at the *Daily Express* and *Daily Mail* to her name, while he was a crime novelist and occasional screenwriter whose success never quite matched up to that of his father, Edgar Wallace (who boasted career sales of his thrillers approaching 50 million copies and also had a hand in drafting the screenplay for *King Kong*). In fact, Margaret was writing a biography of her father-in-law when the couple moved in to Dolphin Square and barely had time to finish it before she and Bryan divorced in 1939.

She subsequently remarried, putting herself into a chain of social connections that would have seemed entirely other-worldly to the vast majority of the population but somehow was not so out of place for the Dolphin Square set. Her second husband was Francis Hastings, an artist who became the 16th Earl of Huntingdon on the death of his father in 1939 and who would later serve in Clement Attlee's government as Parliamentary Secretary to the Ministry of Agriculture and Fisheries. He had previously been married to Cristina Casati, the daughter of an Italian marquis and his artists' muse wife, herself an heiress. Cristina in turn married Wogan Philipps, an MP for the Communist Party of Great Britain, who eventually became the only Communist Party member in the House of Lords. Philipps, meanwhile, had previously been married to the author Rosamond Lehmann, a regular of the Bloomsbury Set who subsequently took up with the poet Cecil Day-Lewis. A case, certainly, of how the other half live.

As for actors, there was the film director Henry Cass and his actor wife, Nancy Hornsby, who had some success in this period in early made-for-TV movies. Then there was Diana Hamilton, West End star and playwright, who was married to fellow actor and playwright Sutton Vane. Another aspiring actor with digs in the Square was the young Anthony Quayle, long before he found Hollywood success in movies including *Lawrence of Arabia*, *The Eagle Has Landed* and *Anne of the Thousand Days* (for which he would be nominated for an Oscar in 1969). He moved to Dolphin Square with his wife, Hermionne Hannen, a fine actor herself, but the marriage was not to last. Quayle signed up for military service at the outbreak of the war and the couple divorced in 1941. In 1943 he joined the Special Operations Executive (SOE), an undercover arm of the military set up in 1940 and informally known as both 'Churchill's Secret Army' and the 'Ministry of Ungentlemanly Warfare'. As slowly became evident over the years, he was joining what would become a long list of Dolphinites who at one time or another worked on secret operations, in espionage and in counter-espionage.

Quayle was stationed in Albania, where he was involved in various sabotage operations. An official report he posted reveals his distress at witnessing Nazi reprisals against an entire village in the aftermath of a particular SOE-guided resistance operation. He also suffered from jaundice and malaria during his few months in the country. Traumatised by his experiences, he gave expression to them in a novel in 1945, *Eight Hours from England*, which recounted the adventures of one Major John Overton on operations behind enemy lines in Albania in 1943.

By then, he had met his second wife – another figure who transcended the worlds of entertainment and espionage. Dorothy Hyson was American-born but made her name as a performer in England. The daughter of actors, she took her West End bow when still a child and went on to make films with star names including Robert Morley and George Formby. But she also worked as a cryptographer at the code-breaking centre at Bletchley Park, where Quayle became a frequent visitor in the war. At the time, she was still married to a different actor, Robert Douglas, but they divorced in 1945 and she married Quayle in 1947. Quayle's first wife, Hannen, had remarried in 1943 to still another actor, Clifford Evans, who as a conscientious objector served in the Non-Combatant Corps in the war and who in later years was perhaps best known for his work with the Hammer Studios. Quayle, meanwhile, would call upon his wartime experiences for his portrayal of a special operations agent in 1961's *The Guns of Navarone*.

In those very first years, arguably the most glamorous face at Dolphin Square was that of Margaret Lockwood, who was barely in her twenties when she arrived. Her star was truly in the ascendant when she appeared opposite Michael Redgrave in the 1938 British-made thriller *The Lady Vanishes* – the film that made Hollywood sit up and take notice of its director, Alfred Hitchcock. More success was around the corner for Lockwood, too, not least with *The Wicked Lady* (1945), the first British film to take £1 million at the box office.

Her life at Dolphin Square, though, was packed with its own drama. She arrived with her husband, Rupert Leon – the son of a family who had made a small fortune in the steel business – whom she'd married in 1937. Childhood sweethearts, they had wed in secret but their hopes of calm domesticity were interrupted as early as December 1938, when it was reported that Lockwood had received threatening letters from a 17-year-old, demanding: 'It is either your £150 or your life.'[9] While that case was dealt with in the courts, there were other problems closer to home. Lockwood and Leon were already beginning to drift apart, her increasing fame and success apparently putting strain upon them. A child arrived in 1941 – a daughter they referred to as Toots, who would grow up and find fame herself as Julia Lockwood.

Within months of the birth, Margaret was obliged to be back on set, Toots was sent to the country to be looked after and Leon was posted abroad with the intelligence services (he is thought to have been the first man in the ranks of the Allies to learn of Hitler's marriage to Eva Braun, and their subsequent joint suicide). When Margaret found herself back in London, she felt increasingly isolated. Then she met an aspiring actor called Keith Dobson, with whom she embarked on an ill-advised affair. She risked a ruinous scandal, turning up at premiers in his company and even moving him into her Dolphin Square apartment. But the affair eventually ran its course. Dobson's career never really took off and the early passion subsided. It was predictably all too much for her marriage to withstand, and after Leon returned to Britain the pair divorced in 1949.

Incidentally, in 1939 – the year after making *The Lady Vanishes* – Lockwood reunited on screen with Michael Redgrave to co-star in Carol Reed's *The Stars Look Down*. Redgrave, by now in high demand, also starred that year in Herbert Mason's *A Window in London*, in which he played a crane driver who seemingly witnesses a brutal attack through an open window on his commute. Patricia Roc, who in due course would act opposite Lockwood in *The Wicked Lady*, played Redgrave's wife, who happened to be a night-time switchboard operator in … Dolphin Square. The relevant scenes were accordingly filmed in the Square itself, which duly made its silver screen bow.

The Costain family had banked on the fact that Dolphin Square would exert a pull on the great and the good. The more that big-name politicians, matinee idols and the like arrived, the greater the appeal of the Square to others. For a while, it seemed set to be every bit the urban paradise that the advertising people suggested. But just as the cinema – and, dare one say it, the Houses of Parliament – is a place of performance and illusion, it was soon apparent that Dolphin Square should not be taken at face value either. A little scratch of the surface and its dark side soon came into view.

2

THE MIRROR CRACK'D FROM SIDE TO SIDE

Despite the Costains' dreams of creating a utopian haven in the middle of London, crime inevitably quickly came to Dolphin Square, with its tenants cast as both victims and perpetrators. Of course, there would be break-ins and bag snatches, bicycle thefts and petty thieving, muggings, drunken fisticuffs and the like. Such events are inevitable in any city setting, but some of the residents' own brushes with the law were more spectacular. Lady Apsley and Lady Asquith's run-ins quickly paled in comparison.

Take, for instance, the curious story from August 1939 of Harry Wells of Beatty House, who was hauled up in court for allegedly defrauding a Miss Henrietta Bennett of Kensington out of a number of Chinese antiques and artworks. It was an elaborate ruse, involving possibly entirely fictional antiques dealers in Paris, but most intriguingly, the question was raised as to whether the artworks, which included painted silks and scrolls, were not in fact indecent and obscene. When probed on the witness stand, Miss Bennett was adamant that the various female forms were merely 'medicine figures … used by Chinese doctors'.[1] There was a definite sense that Bennett was attempting, not entirely successfully, to blind the defence counsel with (Chinese medicinal) science. In any event, Wells was found guilty of defrauding her and given a six-month sentence.

A year before, it had been the turn of Hardinge Giffard, the 2nd Earl of Halsbury and owner of a flat in Nelson House, to appear in the dock. He'd succeeded to his title in 1921 on the death of his father, the

1st Earl and a man who had three times served as Lord Chancellor. The 2nd Earl had followed him into the law but in the mid-1930s swapped his wig and robes for life as a city investor. He arrived at the Square just as his new career was coming off the rails, and in March 1938 he was found against in a complex legal action centred around his various company directorships. He was then declared bankrupt the following month but by then he had fled to Paris, never to face his creditors or return to Britain again. The pitiful denouement to the story was Halsbury's death in an internment camp in German-occupied France in 1943.

Another of the more tragic Dolphin Square miscreants in this period was Bertha Verrall, whose clashes with the law suggest she was likely her own biggest victim. Verrall was the daughter of a successful businessman and now, in her early forties, was widowed and of independent means. Having enjoyed some success as a jockey, she was focussing her energies on training horses.

Her troubles first caught the attention of the press when it was reported in 1937 that she had been fined £5 for galloping a racehorse on Rotten Row in Hyde Park, almost taking out a perambulating pensioner in the process. In December, she was at it again, this time charged with being drunk in charge of a horse in the same location. When approached by an officer, she reportedly told him, 'I want to see my fair policeman; I like him.' The implication was clear: Verrall was a regular offender who relied on the understanding of friendly officers. But she was not in luck that day. In court she would reveal that the horse she'd been supervising was called April 4th, a half-sister to Derby winner April 5th. The arresting officer attested to the fact that she had been riding at 'a similar speed to what one would expect in the Derby'. But Verrall was adamant that she had not been drunk and had merely taken an odd-smelling nerve tonic. The doctor who'd examined her contradicted her, asserting she'd been 'maudlin drunk'. A further £5 fine was decreed by the judge. Verrall cut quite a figure in the dock on that occasion, dressed in a short leopard-skin coat over a green dress, accessorised with green scarf, black hat and veil.[2]

It was some short time after these events that she moved into Raleigh House in Dolphin Square, but the new locale did little to bring her the stability she seems to have lacked. In October 1938, she was fined another 30s (plus 15s costs), this time for 'riding a horse dangerously at the junction of Knightsbridge and Albert Gate on August 26th'. That day, she told the arresting officer, 'Do not make things worse. I came very closely across. Surely that is not furious riding.'[3]

From then on, her offending became more serious. In July 1939 she was sued for non-payment of fees owed to a woman charged with looking after several horses. Then two months later, she was accused of threatening to cut the throats of jockey Leonard Lund's three children. Undoubtedly an empty threat and one she claimed to have no recollection of making, it seems likely she uttered it while either under the influence or in a red mist of anger – a professional disagreement apparently behind the atrocious exchange.

It was noted at one of the 1939 trials that she was experiencing 'bad financial circumstances' and it was not long before she had moved out of the Square. However, her legal troubles continued – she was back in the papers when she was fined £20 for allowing suffering to a horse, then, in 1942, a further £25 penalty for similar offences. We now lose track of her as she departs the scene, unable to pay despite pawning her jewels and furs and pleading that she was 'most awful broke' and had been having a 'grim time'.[4]

If some of Verrall's behaviour was deeply troubling, it turned out that there was another woman living in Dolphin Square at the same time whose historical charge sheet was significantly worse. At the end of March 1937, it was reported in the newspapers that Lady Edmée Owen, resident of the Square, was embroiled in a legal case with a woman whom she accused of trying to defraud her over the sale of some furniture. Essentially, the woman had arrived at a location where Lady Owen was storing some of her property with a list of items that she had paid for, but Lady Owen held that she had expanded the list to include several items to which she was not entitled. When Lady Owen appeared at Marylebone Police Court to give her evidence, few realised that she was already very familiar with the inside of a courtroom.

Lady Owen was born Edmée Nodot in France in 1896. Leaving school at 16, she came to England with a view to learning the language and soon set herself up as a teacher. She then met Theodore Owen, a tea and rubber magnate with a family from an earlier marriage, and the couple wed in London in 1915 when she was still just 18 and he was 60. The marriage was unhappy – she was repeatedly unfaithful to him – and they went their separate ways five years later. However, seemingly in the hope of avoiding scandal, they did not formally divorce so when Owen was knighted in 1926, Edmée was able to take the title Lady Owen. By then, she had moved back to France, where she was attempting to make it in the movies as Edmée Dormeuil. Marketed as an established British starlet about to be unleashed on a lucky French public, in truth her career had amounted to little more than a few minor stage appearances in London and Oxford and a role in a 1919 film that was likely financed by her husband and which sank without trace.

A few months after his knighthood, Owen died and his estranged wife inherited his fortune. Yet for all her wealth, Owen struggled to find happiness, embarking on a series of doomed love affairs. When one dalliance came to an end in 1929, she visited a weight-loss specialist by the name of Dr Gataud, and promptly started a passionate (at least on her part) affair with him. She lavished gifts and money upon him and even feigned a pregnancy in the hope of winning his devotion, but the married doctor seems never to have intended leaving his wife for her. Just a few months into the affair, he called a halt to it. But the drama was only just beginning.

Owen purchased a gun and drank a considerable volume of alcohol before going to the doctor's house and shooting his wife, Léonie, a total of four times. The woman survived but Owen was arrested and charged with attempted murder. Her arrival at trial raised eyebrows as, sporting a peroxide-blonde hairdo, she posed for the cameras on her way into court as if she were the film star she longed to be. It was said that she even sent invitations to journalists encouraging them to attend the trial and pleaded with the press 'not to mention my weight gain'.

The jury found her guilty of attempted murder and Owen was imprisoned for five years, although she was free in three. She lived in Paris for a while but then returned to London, ostensibly to find some peace. But the calm she desired proved elusive. She was successfully sued in 1934 by her late husband's two children, who claimed she had failed to provide them with their rightful inheritance. (The son's wife, Ruth Bryan Owen, had by then been elected to the US House of Representatives and a year earlier had become the first woman to be appointed a US ambassador when President Roosevelt named her ambassador to Denmark and Iceland.) In the same year as she lost that criminal action – and perhaps not unrelated – Owen courted more controversy when she published a racy account of her life under the provocative title *Flaming Sex*.

She also developed a gambling habit and in November 1936 was declared bankrupt. Within just a few months, she was to be found in severely reduced circumstances, but still able to rent at Dolphin Square and chasing £20-worth of goods she claimed she'd been cheated of. How long ago it must have seemed since she was the aspiring screen siren, starring in films bankrolled by her ageing husband and, later, the heiress showering holidays, gifts and cash on a string of paramours.

Owen's story contained strands of tragedy, but not so many as in that of 31-year-old Lynda Woods, whose life came to a premature end in her flat in Drake House in 1938. On Wednesday, 19 October she was found lying on a bed of green silk cushions, clasping a toy dog, a suicide note addressed to her father lying on a nearby table. She was dead from gas poisoning. As evidence given to the coroner would reveal, Woods was in all major respects an ordinary young woman whose life was overcome by events beyond her control. Hers was a pitiful story that spoke of the everyday secrets and the intense human dramas that are normally restrained but which sometimes erupt to devastating effect in contained communities. For Dolphin Square, it was one of the earliest sagas to propel the address into the headlines and represented a significant early dent in the estate's veneer of respectability and contentedness.

The story was picked up by the *Daily Mirror*, which splashed it across the front page. The very first paragraph set the scene, hinting at a salacious subplot: 'Lynda Woods, beautiful and mysterious dance hostess, died yesterday in a gas-filled room of her £145-a year luxury flat overlooking the Thames, after she had confessed to a friend that she was being blackmailed.'[5] Here was the promise of wealth and glamour, sexuality, confidentialities, indiscretions and crime.

It would in due course emerge that the woman was the daughter of a retired army major and had attended a convent school. She had then married a shipping agent (an age gap of half a century was suggested by someone purporting to be her uncle) but was widowed in 1932. Finding herself alone in the world and in need of an income, she started working at Romano's, a famous eatery on the Strand that, until destroyed in the Blitz, was a society institution. Before he became King Edward VII, the Prince of Wales was among its notable clientele and it appeared in fictional form in W. Somerset Maugham's 1915 classic *Of Human Bondage* and in the stories of P.G. Wodehouse. The entertainments there were the stuff of legend and, in particular, it became associated with the Gaiety Girls – the chorus girls who originated at the Gaiety Theatre up the road, and who were given preferential prices when they dined there after a show.

How the young widow Woods felt about working there is not clear, although the *Daily Herald* described her knowingly as 'well known in West End restaurants and night clubs'.[6] We do know that until a short while before her death, she cohabited with a man at Dolphin Square who was known as Mr Woods but who was not in fact her husband. The evidence suggests that this relationship broke down and Lynda then took up with a different man of whom she was very fond. But then things had turned nasty and a former beau (presumably the enigmatic 'Mr Woods') threatened to share intimate correspondence with her new boyfriend if she did not pay £100.

The story of an apparently respectable life undermined was grist to the mill for the journalists telling the story. Much of the coverage adopted a suggestive tone. It was even said in some reports that she had been a dance partner and potential business partner of one Brian Sullivan, whose name had been linked to the discovery of a headless torso in Gloucestershire earlier in the year after he himself committed suicide. In that particular case, the headless victim was never conclusively identified, Sullivan's potential involvement in the death never proven, and Woods' connection to Sullivan only rumoured at.

Nonetheless, it was used as additional colour when recounting Lynda Woods' wretched demise.

Her death was, in truth, a sad but not entirely uncommon story. The premature culmination of a life that had not gone according to plan. The result of a delicate individual succumbing to pressures that others, and perhaps even she in different circumstances, may have weathered with comparative ease. The intervention of a vengeful former lover in a new relationship is never longed for, but more often than not it is ultimately navigated past. But her death is a motif of sorts for Dolphin Square, an early calamitous example of how the tensions between an outwardly respectable life and the potential exposure of behind-closed-doors secrets can have devastating consequences.

It is possible that the strain between public and private accounts for the mysterious death of another of the Square's earliest female tenants – one who had a significantly higher profile than Lynda Woods. Ellen Wilkinson, or 'Red Ellen' as she was popularly known – both for her politics and her hair colour – was a prominent Labour MP with a firebrand reputation and a flat in Hood House. She'd been born in Manchester in 1891 into a family that understood what it was to be poor and recognised education as a path to better things. With a voracious appetite for work, she won a place for herself at her home city university and came to politically align herself with the trade unions as well as the women's suffrage movement. The Russian Revolution was initially an inspiration to her and for a while she was a member of the Communist Party of Great Britain, before winning a seat in Parliament with the Labour Party as MP for Middlesbrough East in 1924. A stalwart of the General Strike in 1926, she came to her greatest public prominence ten years later when (as MP for Jarrow by then) she joined the Jarrow March. She was adamant that she must show support to the 200 or so people who walked almost 300 miles from Jarrow in the north-east of England down to London to protest the intolerable poverty and labour conditions that had beset the town when its major employer, a shipyard, was closed. Wilkinson was at her most brilliant, telling a crowd in Hyde Park, 'Jarrow as a town has been murdered … What has the Government done? I do not wonder that this cabinet does not want to see us.'[7]

She also ventured to Spain several times in the decade to witness at first hand the impact of the civil war there, then held several junior ministerial posts under Churchill during the war. Nor could anyone accuse Wilkinson of being out of touch with the ordinary people in those years. The flat she shared in Dolphin Square with her sister Anne was bombed out twice in the Blitz.

After Attlee succeeded Churchill as prime minister in 1945, he appointed Wilkinson his Minister of Education. But her life was to end in tragic circumstances just two years later when she was discovered unconscious in her apartment on 3 February 1947. Although still only in her mid-50s, she had suffered from asthma since childhood and her health had been in a poor state for some while, exacerbated by long-term overwork and a heavy smoking habit. She had collapsed when visiting the Czechoslovak capital, Prague, the previous year, and in January 1947 she'd attended an outdoor function in Bristol that brought on a bout of pneumonia.

After she was discovered in her flat, it was determined she'd taken an overdose of barbiturates. She'd been long-term medicating to counter not only her respiratory problems but insomnia too. Taken to St Mary's Hospital in Paddington, she died three days later on 6 February. Her death was recorded as accidental, the cause 'heart failure following emphysema, with acute bronchitis and bronchial pneumonia, accelerated by barbiturate poisoning'.[8] There was no substantial evidence to suggest that she had hoped to hasten her own death. Nonetheless, it subsequently emerged that she'd been engaged in a long-term affair with the married wartime Home Secretary Herbert Morrison, and was only reluctantly reconciled to the fact that he was unlikely ever to abandon his wife for her. In addition, there were rumours that her job was under threat in a proposed Cabinet reshuffle. What effect these additional strains placed on her already stressed physiology has been a subject of enduring conjecture.

Ellen Wilkinson's death, dreadful of itself, was also a further link in a growing chain of events at Dolphin Square that raised as many questions as they answered. There was a sense that things went on within this citadel by the Thames that were not all they appeared. It was a reputation quickly earned and one yet to be shifted to this day, fuelling a mini-industry in conspiracy theories. Sometimes, ultimately, it is all a matter of perspective. Who can be sure when an overdose is accidental and when it's a suicide? And who gets to judge what is a work of art and what is merely a dirty picture? In such grey areas, it is inevitable that something wholly innocent can be cast in a bad light, just as some awful things may be hidden away.

3

THE GATHERING STORM

Although the first residents moved into Dolphin Square in 1936, it was only in March 1939 that the development was reported as fully let. It would be just six months before the country was locked into another world war, but the reality was that the threat of conflict had lingered over Dolphin Square almost from the moment that people started to live there. If Fred French and then the Costains had believed a depressed economy was the greatest challenge they faced at the outset, the possibility of a second global conflict – less than two decades since the last one – cast a much longer shadow over the new community.

In March 1939, 25-year-old Miss C. Lewis, described as resident of 'a luxury flat' in the Square, was interviewed by the weekly *John Bull* magazine. She was asked her opinions on National Service and her response gives a sense of that tension between wanting to carry on as normal and preparing for what might be to come:

> I want to be a woman with a career. The time I have for studying art is all too little as it is. I cannot put my name down for National Service without giving a little time to it – and, really, I can't afford to do that. If war did come there would be emergencies no Government could contemplate at the present moment … I think there should be another National Service register, which could be signed by people to whom nothing in the present handbook appeals, but who want to serve if war should come.[1]

There were steadily growing reminders of the seriousness of the threat. Within a few weeks of Lewis's interview, Dolphin Square hosted a demonstration of how deep air raid shelters might be used for speedy evacuations of the London populace. Then, in July, it was announced that the Square's large basement would be one of five such areas in the city designated as major casualty depots in the event of war. No one could fail to notice the gathering clouds.

For a few, the prospect of another bloody slaughter was too much. There was a desire to avoid war at almost any cost. It is easy to condemn the British Government's policy of appeasement in the 1930s that was meant to prevent war but served only to embolden Hitler. Yet it cannot be forgotten that vast swathes of the population were still traumatised by the last round of bloodshed. But in Dolphin Square, there were a number of prominent figures for whom this understandable fear combined – whether reluctantly or willingly – with an admiration for what Hitler was doing in Germany. It was a trend that had found particular traction among the nation's elite and tended to end in ignominy.

Take, for example, the formidable Ethel Snowden – or more properly, Viscountess Snowden – who came to Dolphin Square in 1937, shortly after the death of her husband, the former Chancellor of the Exchequer, Philip Snowden. While he had been the household name, she was a significant political force in her own right. A committed socialist from a young age, she had forged early associations with the Fabian Society and the Independent Labour Party, was a prominent campaigner for votes for women, demanded a negotiated peace during the First World War and – to the disappointment of many of her colleagues on the Left – warned of the dangers of the Soviet system after a visit to the nascent USSR in the 1920s. Whether speaking publicly or writing in the press, she was fearless – a trait that sporadically lost her friends and attracted controversy.

She'd married Snowdon in 1905 and he won a seat in the Commons the following year, rising to become Chancellor in Ramsay MacDonald's landmark, though short-lived Labour administration in 1924, and again from 1929 until 1931. Ethel enjoyed her own career peak in a similar period, serving on the BBC's board of governors (the corporation's unimpressed director general, John Reith, referred to her as a 'poisonous creature'[2]) from 1926 until 1932.

By the time she stood down, Philip was in poor health. He had required prostate surgery in 1931, which effectively marked the end of his front-line political life. He was, though, granted a viscountcy, while she continued to write and campaign on various issues. But life was hard for them in the 1930s. What money there was came from journalism now that their political appointments had disappeared – he was a particularly noted critic of his once-ally MacDonald. But by 1936 his failing health was overtaking them. They struggled to cover the bills for his care and the upkeep of the family home, Eden Lodge in Surrey. By the time the coronation came around in May 1937, he was too ill to attend so Ethel went alone. He was dead within days and she effectively transplanted her life to Dolphin Square, Eden Lodge having lost its appeal for her.

In the September, she went to Nuremberg to cover Hitler's rally for the *Sunday Chronicle*. Like others of her class in that decade, the Führer captured her imagination. He was, she wrote, 'a simple man of great personal integrity'.[3] Harsher criticism was reserved for British guests at the rally who declined to salute him. She was not alone among the residents of Dolphin Square – and beyond – in flirting with the idea that Hitler had something to teach Britain's own leaders. But at the same time, she was putting herself on a collision course with several of her neighbours for whom the Führer was already an immensely troubling and threatening presence. Her words for the *Chronicle* did not age well and by 1939 she was adamant that the Nazi threat must be confronted. But those earlier pro-Hitler sentiments were not easy to escape. That said, though, they did not leave her entirely out in the cold. Queen Mary, the Queen Mother, was among those who had visited the viscountess at Dolphin Square for tea in 1938.

If the prospect of war failed to bring out the best in some, others discovered previously untapped reserves of bravery and ingenuity amid that stifling atmosphere of uncertainty that pervaded the second half of the decade. Over in Howard House were two sisters in their thirties who were much more than they at first seemed. Neither Ida nor Louise Cook had ever married and they'd lived in the family home in south London prior to getting a flat together in the Square. Louise worked as a secretary in the civil service, while Ida – previously a typist – discovered a penchant for writing romances. Under the pseudonym Mary Burchell, she wrote well over 100 titles for Mills & Boon, earning good money in the process. This came in useful as the sisters shared a passion for opera, regularly travelling to the Continent for concerts and performances.

In modern parlance, they were something like opera groupies, regularly writing to their favourite stars. In 1934, they went to Salzburg to attend the city's celebrated opera festival and while there they made the acquaintance of the conductor Clemens Krauss and his wife, the celebrated Romanian soprano Viorica Ursuleac. Krauss and Ursuleac were already concerned about the plight of the Jews in Hitler's Germany and it was suggested to the sisters that they might check up on a friend who had recently travelled to England.

So began the Cooks' remarkable contribution to assisting the flight of a great many refugees (mostly Jews but political dissidents, too) away from the grasp of the Nazis. Initially, their role was principally to smuggle the treasures of Jewish refugees, who at the time were free to leave Germany but not to take their wealth with them. An operation typically consisted of the unprepossessing sisters flying from Croydon Airport on a Friday night into Germany or Austria on the pretext of attending an operatic event. Krauss would sometimes arrange performances specifically to give the Cooks a reason to be at a particular location on a given weekend. They would enter the country in their everyday, nondescript attire and leave on the Sunday via a different exit point (to avoid unnecessarily drawing attention to themselves), wearing expensive furs and dripping in jewellery – stores of capital that would be reunited with their real owners once safely transported to England.

Often the ruse worked without any problem but, as time passed, the sisters had ever more close shaves. They developed various techniques to avert exposure. Ida recounted how surprisingly easy it was for 'two nervous British spinsters'[4] to get away with claiming that they did not trust their families at home so always travelled with their valuables. And on at least one occasion, she pinned an ornate diamond brooch to an otherwise very plain jumper in the hope that anyone who saw it would assume that it must be a cheap knock-off rather than the real thing. The plan worked perfectly. Moreover, the pair were always back in London in time for Louise to get to the office on Monday morning.

But the sisters were not merely experts in smuggling. Their Dolphin Square apartment also served as a refuge for escapees recently landed in the country. Ida and Louise served as go-betweens, too, passing on messages and developing a network of contacts who could provide the testimonials, financial guarantees and job opportunities necessary to meet the tests for immigration.

It is thought that around thirty refugees found a safe haven with the Cooks in Dolphin Square, some for quite significant periods of time. In later years it also provided a roof for various opera professionals down on their luck, and became a focal point for the sisters' fundraising activities. In 1964, it even hosted an event at which Maria Callas was guest of honour. The sisters stayed loyal to the Square, keeping the flat for decades – after Ida's death in 1986, Louise maintained it till she too passed away five years later. There is something of the Ealing Comedy to the two slightly awkward-looking sisters embroiled in undercover work of international importance, but theirs is really a story of the highest heroism – the heroism of ordinary people who had the courage to do extraordinary things. As Ida would note years later, 'The funny thing is we weren't the James Bond type – we were just respectable Civil Service typists.'[5]

James Bond they might not have been, but another major figure in the Square in this period had a much more direct connection with that archetypal spy. His name was Knight ... Maxwell Knight. From a series of apartments in the Square, he operated one of the most significant espionage networks in the country – an operation that went into over-drive in the immediate pre-war years.

Born in Mitcham, Surrey, in 1900, Knight served in the navy in the First World War. Come the 1920s, he had aligned with the hard right in British politics, working against what he regarded as the leftist threat of socialism, the trades unions and the Labour Party. An employee of the pro-free trade Economic League, he subsequently joined the British Fascisti – the country's first major, overtly fascist political organisation

– and was soon head of its intelligence wing. It was a role that saw him not only gathering information on figures identified as enemies of the group but also undertaking counter-intelligence work – for instance, inserting spies into left-wing movements. But all the while, Maxwell was also reporting to the Security Service, Section 5 of the Directorate of Military Intelligence, better known as MI5. He had been recruited by its director, Vernon Kell, at a dinner party in 1925.

By 1930, Knight was sufficiently well regarded at MI5 that he was given charge of section B5(b), a secretive sub-department concerned with political subversion. He built up a crack network of agents, many of whom he recruited from his far-right contacts. He was also noted for his particular skill at spotting and nurturing female agents, an ability that over time revolutionised British spy craft. His web of operatives was sometimes referred to as Knight's Black Agents, a nod to Macbeth's 'black agents of the night'.

In 1925 he'd married, for the first time, a wealthy and glamorous redhead called Glawdys Poole, but the relationship was unhappy and she died of an overdose in 1934. In 1937 he married again, this time to one Lois Coplestone, with whom he lived in a property on Sloane Street. However, within a very short space of time he began to rent what was effectively a bachelor pad in Hood House, leasing a flat previously let to his brother-in-law, Anthony Coplestone. By now, Knight had a reputation as one of the Security Service's leading lights, and among his colleagues was Ian Fleming. When Fleming came to write his James Bond novels years later, 007's boss was known by the same single-letter identifier as Knight: 'M'.

To the world at large, Knight seemed nothing so much as an old-fashioned English eccentric. Tall and ungainly, he routinely dressed in tweeds that had seen better days. A moderately successful thriller writer and a keen musician who sometimes played drums with a jazz band, he was also a keen naturalist who populated his living quarters with all manner of pets and wild animals, including bears, lion cubs and monkeys. It was the perfect distraction from the secret life he was leading. In fact, such was the level of secrecy that he liked to maintain, he persuaded his MI5 bosses to let him run B5(b) from Dolphin Square itself, away from the prying eyes of even his fellow spooks. It was from here, for instance, that he instigated the infiltration of the so-called Woolwich Arsenal communist spy ring in 1938, and where he entertained informants and agents like the Communist MP, future Labour Party chairman and KGB operative, Tom Driberg.

As war approached, Knight's focus inevitably moved away from communism towards the threat posed by fifth-column fascists – including several who regarded Knight as a kindred spirit. It was around this time that his path crossed with that of Joan Miller, who for most of 1939 was working for the Elizabeth Arden cosmetics company. But when war was declared, she looked to do something of more immediate service to the country and through a friend was given an introduction to MI5. On her first day, she was directed to take a bus to the notorious Wormwood Scrubs prison in west London, where the Security Service had recently relocated.

There she was directed to the office (which was, in fact, a cell) of the head of MI5's transport division, Lord Cottenham. Cottenham – also known as Mark Pepys and a distant descendent of the diarist Samuel Pepys – was, by chance, also a resident of Dolphin Square. Known primarily as a racing driver, road safety campaigner and writer, he had endured an unpleasant divorce earlier in the year following his wife's adultery with his cousin, the Earl of Devon. Miller worked for Cottenham only briefly but soon found herself employed at Dolphin Square itself and reporting to Knight instead.

The exact nature of her relationship with Knight is moot but seems to have amounted to a grand affair in all respects other than it was not consummated. As the war progressed, Knight extended B5(b)'s reach in the Square, taking properties in Keyes, Nelson and Rodney Houses and also, seemingly, in Collingwood House. According to Miller, when he came into possession of this latter property, Knight sent her a note: 'You see, I really need to have you close. Otherwise I don't think I can carry on with this nerve-straining work. You take my mind off things.'[6]

Miller duly moved into the flat and recalled the long walks she'd regularly make from Victoria to Dolphin Square, a route upon which bag snatches were not uncommon. She was in the Square's restaurant one day when Labour's deputy leader, Arthur Greenwood, called her over and expressed his concern for her. He then demonstrated a valuable defensive technique he had apparently picked up in the Gorbals to ward off prospective assailants, 'Put pennies between yur fingers – like this – and hit *hard*.'[7]

It is possible to see Miller as a sort of super-fuelled Miss Moneypenny to Knight's 'M'. She was always much more than the admin girl. He trained her, for instance, to infiltrate the Right Club, a fascist and anti-Semitic organisation run by Archibald Ramsay, a Scottish Unionist MP who was suspected of being a German agent. It was, unsurprisingly, opposed to Britain's entry into war with Germany. At significant personal risk, Miller sensationally uncovered a spy ring there that stretched to the US Embassy in London and onwards to Berlin and Moscow. Miller's work directly led to the arrest of Tyler Kent, a cypher clerk at the US Embassy who had been stealing confidential documents (including wires between Churchill and Roosevelt), and his fellow Right Club member, Anna Wolkoff, who was passing information to Berlin. After an in camera trial at the Old Bailey, Kent was sentenced to seven years in prison and Wolkoff to ten. Kent also provided Ramsay with sensitive materials that it was believed the MP intended to leak. As a result, Ramsay was interned in May 1940 – the only serving British MP to suffer that fate.

All the while, the lines between Knight and Miller's professional and personal relationship blurred. As she told it, by 1943 he had effectively moved into the flat he'd earmarked for her in Collingwood House and most of those who knew them assumed she was his mistress (his second marriage was to all intents and purposes over by this time). Yet still there was no sexual relationship. She would suggest many years later that he blamed it upon her inexperience in the bedroom, but in time she concluded that he was in fact gay (a status that would have immediately ended his career with MI5 if it came to light and which was then still an imprisonable offence). His marriages and his relationship with her, she came to believe, had merely been a cover.

Knight's active service with MI5 continued into the 1960s, by which time a generation had grown up to know him not as a spy master but as avuncular 'Uncle Max', a popular nature writer and prolific broadcaster. The tales of his life in Dolphin Square – doubtless an exquisite landscape in which to explore the nature of the human species – took much longer to seep into the public consciousness. As late as the mid-1980s, the British Government did all it could to prevent Joan Miller lifting the lid on the secret side of his extraordinary life, taking legal action to block the publication of her memoirs. But by Knight's efforts, Dolphin Square played a pivotal role in the nation's defence in the pre-war era and far beyond. Indeed, his work in the 1930s and during the war itself would have a very direct and public impact on two of his nearest neighbours in the Square.

4

THE SQUARE AT WAR

The Phoney War might have extended from September 1939 until May 1940, but the war got real enough for many residents of the Square during this period. The earliest known Dolphinite to be killed was 29-year-old Pilot Officer Anthony St Croix Rose of Rodney House. He perished on 11 September 1939, barely a week after the declaration of war, when his Gloster Gladiator crashed while on manoeuvres in Surrey. Several more fatalities followed in the coming weeks and months as the armed services readied their personnel for live combat.

In April 1940, for instance, 23-year-old Lieutenant Victor Marryat of the Royal Marines died when the aeroplane that he was training in (again, it was a Gladiator) crashed in Wiltshire. Just the previous July, he had been convicted for driving under the influence. His barrister had pleaded for leniency on the basis that, in common with other members of the Fleet Air Arm, Marryat had been under intense pressure. Officers, he'd said, 'have to get about all over the country and have a lot to do. In these perilous times I urge that no difficulty should be put in this officer's way.'[1]

Dolphin Square offered many advantages to those who could find their way to a tenancy, but the war was a great leveller. Its community suffered loss and grief just as any other town, village or neighbourhood in the country. Indeed, the presence of so many military families, not to mention government officials and assorted secret agents – coupled with its position at the heart of the national capital – ensured that no one could accuse its residents of sheltering away from peril. The sons of the Square – young men like Marryat and Rose – were asked to shoulder onerous burdens when they ought really to have been revelling in their youth, equally as much as the sons of anywhere else. The horror at once again sending a generation into the uncertainty of conflict, with the inevitability that many would not return, was palpable.

Within days of the German invasion of France on 10 May 1940 – a marker denoting the end of the Phoney War phase – there were reports of the death of one of the Square's many feted young men. On 15 May, 32-year-old Lord Frederick Cambridge, resident of Beatty House and a captain in the Coldstream Guards (not to mention, the Vienna-born son of the Marquess of Cambridge – previously the Duke of Teck – and a nephew of George V's wife, Queen Mary), was killed in action in Leuven, Belgium. Proof, if necessary, that the war would be no respecter of social position.

As the conflict rolled on, the newspapers were increasingly littered with notices of Square residents, or the 'dearly loved' sons of residents, who were killed, presumed dead, missing in action or being held as prisoners of war. One such report of May 1944 related the death in action in Burma of 22-year-old Captain John Lawrence Smyth. He was the son of Collingwood House resident Brigadier John G. Smyth, who had endured a wretched war. A veteran of the First World War, in 1915 the brigadier was awarded the Victoria Cross for 'the most conspicuous bravery' when serving as a lieutenant in the Indian Army. According to his citation:

> With a bombing party of 10 men, who voluntarily undertook this duty, he conveyed a supply of 96 bombs to within 20 yards of the enemy's position over exceptionally dangerous ground, after the attempts of two other parties had failed. Lieutenant Smyth succeeded in taking the bombs to the desired position with the aid of two of his men (the other eight having been killed or wounded), and to effect his purpose he had to swim a stream, being exposed the whole time to howitzer, shrapnel, machine-gun and rifle fire.[2]

Come the Second World War, Smyth briefly served in France with the British Expeditionary Force but returned to India in March 1941 as a colonel and then an acting major general. In February 1942 he was blamed for a disaster in Burma, when some two-thirds of the division he was commanding became stranded on the banks of the Sittang River during a retreat, rendering them prey to the advancing Japanese forces. The Japanese were subsequently able to press on and take Rangoon. Smyth was relieved of his command and returned to England. Over the proceeding decades, he convincingly argued that he had suggested a strategic withdrawal several days before the tragedy but that his plea was rejected by his corps commander, General Hutton.

Smyth somehow recovered from the trauma of it all to build a new career for himself in the post-war period, entering politics and winning the parliamentary seat of Norwood for the Conservatives in 1950. He was made Baronet Smyth of Teignmouth in Devon six years later and retired from the Commons in 1966, to date, the last VC holder to sit in the House. But what a price he had paid.

In autumn 1940, London itself became a target for the Luftwaffe, and Dolphin Square found itself squarely on the front line. When the Blitz arrived, the Square marketed itself as 'Supreme in the Blackout'. The design of the development certainly gave the impression of resilience and its chief engineer, Oscar Faber, had the foresight to use reinforced concrete liberally in the building process, which increased the sense that the Square was 'tougher' than many of the city's other landmarks in the event of aerial attack. Nevertheless, it took a battering, both structurally and in terms of damage to human life – but it did stay standing.

The destruction started on 22 September 1940 when a 500lb bomb landed on Hawkins House, killing seven and injuring a further thirty-two. Five days afterwards, a 250-pounder fell on Grenville House, but thankfully there were no casualties. The Square and its immediate environs would be hit again on 11, 15 and 16 October. Then, on 5 November, a massive 2,000lb bomb wreaked extensive structural damage and killed four people. There were a further two deaths in May 1941 when a bomb exploded close to Hawkins House, again.

Joan Miller recorded her own vivid recollections of those months when her home was under attack. One night in September 1940, she and Maxwell Knight went on to the roof of Collingwood House to survey the city stretched out before them. 'The East End was ablaze,' she wrote. 'I watched the docks burning. The sky, in which white vapour trails from warring aircraft were a common sight, was lit with an unearthly glow. The heat and the smoke were appalling.'[3]

Another spy would have an even more direct experience of the Blitz. In late 1940, a Cambridge graduate and civil servant called John Cairncross moved into the Square. He would later reflect:

Dolphin Square was something of an innovation in conservative London. There was a certain aura of freedom from strait-laced society. I remember a skit at the Great Theatre in which an innocent maiden was about to be seduced and murmured, 'Oh Dolly this is Folly', while the sly young man uttered, 'O Rupert this is stupid'. He is finally assaulted by an entertaining lady who drives home her appeal with the cry that 'this is Dolphin Square where women are desperate'. It was not often my luck to run into such cases of despair.

But Cairncross's stay there was brief, after his apartment found itself a direct target of the Luftwaffe. 'I heard the plane overhead, the bomb dropping, and the falling debris in the room next door,' Cairncross wrote in his memoirs. 'When I looked around, there were no walls, but the staircase was sound, and I climbed down the four floors to safety wrapped in a blanket.' Shortly afterwards, he moved out to live with his brother elsewhere in the capital. During the war, Cairncross worked with the code breakers at Bletchley Park but, unbeknown to his colleagues, he was also spying for the Soviets, feeding information to Moscow that materially affected the progress of several battles, most notably the Battle of Kursk in 1943. It has been estimated that he provided the Kremlin with over 5,000 documents during the course of the war. Much later, in 1990, he would be confirmed by a Soviet double agent, Oleg Gordievsky, as the fifth member of the notorious Cambridge Spy Ring that fed intelligence to the Soviet Union during the Cold War.

Back in Pimlico in August 1940, the nearby Church of the Holy Apostles had been bombed, although fortunately the nuns who were sheltering there escaped unharmed. It was one of twenty-five churches hit in London that night and Rev. E.M. Hadfield entered the bombed-out building to rescue its Ciborium (a vessel used in the Eucharist), cycling it to a place of safety in Westminster Cathedral. The following day, he was approached by a group manning the ambulance station at Dolphin Square, who suggested that he might perform mass there while the church was unusable. It was an offer he gratefully accepted and the basement served as the stage for masses until May 1942.

The Square's underground shelters were divided sensibly enough into three types – one for snorers, another for non-snorers and a third for pet owners. In this latter division, there was the expected array of cats, dogs and budgies, but much else besides – not least snakes and a notorious parrot with an uncanny ability to mimic the sound of a falling bomb before crying out, 'Coo, that was a close one!' On one memorable occasion, there was even a lion cub down there – one suspects that Maxwell Knight was likely nearby.

The texture of daily life changed noticeably and quickly. For instance, there was a dramatic upsurge in the number of women porters after a great many of the men who had previously filled those roles signed up to fight. Down in the Square's basement, meanwhile, a decontamination centre was built (though it never saw active use) and a shooting gallery, too. There were some distinctly 'Pimlico' touches as well. For example, each day six very large milk churns were filled with water in case the regular water supply should be compromised. These were kept down in the car park and on one occasion a resident arrived with a cut-glass claret jug that they wanted filled. Somehow the jug was smashed in the process, leading to the unveiling of a new sign: 'Everyday vessels only. No antiques served.' A similarly 'only at Dolphin Square' moment came when a nudist publication called *Bare Facts* began campaigning hard for the gardens to accommodate a nudist colony. Whether this would have encouraged the putting up or tearing down of blackout curtains in the surrounding apartments is uncertain.

While the war undoubtedly brought the majority of Londoners together as they faced common adversity, the Blitz also ushered in a surge in crime across the capital. Dolphin Square certainly witnessed its own crime wave. Enforced blackouts, bombed-out buildings and the disruption to social norms all played into the hands of criminals, while desperation and a boom in the black market (fuelled by the imposition of rationing) often provided additional motivation to commit offences.

Most of the crime reported in the Square was, thankfully, petty. Small-scale theft was not uncommon, nor the handling of stolen goods (the goods, in some instances, having been stolen from the miscreants' near neighbours). There was also a spate of disputes stemming from the selling on of various second-hand goods – typically, the seller would accuse a third-party agent of pocketing more than their agreed share of the sale price, or there would be disagreement as to the legitimate ownership of a particular item. Meanwhile, the design of the flats inadvertently offered an advantage to the wily burglar – most had rubbish hatches built in just by the front door, about the right size for a smallish intruder to gain ingress.

Unattended bikes were also a common object of the thieves' attention. But other crimes were more brazen, such as a 1942 robbery in which one of the on-site shops lost around 90,000 cigarettes and cigars worth £400. The perpetrators of much of this low-level offending were never caught, but when a suspect did find themselves in the dock, their stories were often laced with a good dose of pathos – such as that of a labourer of previously good character who was found to have stolen several bikes from the Square in order to pay for treatment for his ulcerated stomach.

Nor was the temptation to stray from the rules confined to any single class. The desire for an extra bit of bacon over and above the ration, or for a pair of nylons, could drive the least likely candidates into the realms of illegality. Among the most surprising Dolphin Square characters to find himself up before a judge was Charles Berger, the managing director of the internationally successful Berger Paints (the company had been founded in the eighteenth century by Lewis Berger – born Louis Steigenberger – and Charles was the last in the family line to manage it). Berger had a branch in Belfast and another in Dublin, where supplies of linseed oil necessary for the mixing of paint were in chronically short supply. Berger employed an agent to buy up spare stock of the oil in Northern Ireland and then had it transported to the Irish capital. While the judge recognised the smuggling was small scale and done only for the maintenance of the company's Dublin operation,

Berger was nonetheless convicted of illegally exporting goods and fined £500.

Back in July 1941, Westminster Police Court heard evidence in another of the more curious robberies of the period. Robert McGuire, a 22-year-old general labourer, was accused of trying to steal the contents of a trinket box from a flat in Hood House. But rather than breaking in, he was said to have been at the flat as a guest before he shoved the flat's legitimate resident out of the front door, which he then locked. The victim collared a nearby police constable, the pair returning to Hood House to find McGuire still there but empty-handed as the box contained nothing of value. The real mystery, though, was why McGuire was at the apartment in the first place.

According to Robert Wilton, a member of the Auxiliary Five Service whose flat it was, he had spotted McGuire earlier in the day in the subway at Piccadilly Station. Wilton testified that he had warned the other man that he risked being arrested for drunkenness and that he could come back to his flat for tea. However, on arrival, McGuire was promptly sick and then fell asleep for somewhere between two and three hours, while Wilton wrote some letters. After eventually waking McGuire, Wilton said, he encouraged him to leave, at which point he was shoved out of his own flat while McGuire allegedly rummaged around. Wilton could see what he was up to by peering through one of those conveniently placed rubbish hatches. McGuire, meanwhile, suggested Wilton had followed him at Piccadilly Circus. He hoped, he continued, that his pursuer might take himself off into a café but he didn't and when he invited him to his flat, he accepted. The evidence of both men left questions hanging in the air. Is it typical behaviour to find a stranger in a railway station in a suspected state of inebriation and invite them to one's home in case they get picked up by the police? And is it usual to instantly move from feeling pursued by a stranger in a public place to accepting such an invitation?

That certain sections of the press seized upon the story – a criminal non-event in truth – suggests that those journalists felt that the real story was not that which was voiced in the courtroom. The reporting of this particular crime did not point any fingers or make explicit accusations but for those willing to see it, the subtext was obvious. The real, unstated, interest was in whether this was, as appeared likely, an encounter in which at least one of the parties was gay. Those suspicions seemed to be confirmed four years later when Wilton, now described as a film extra living in the Square, faced trial at Bow Street for 'importuning men for immoral purposes' in the neighbourhood of Piccadilly Circus. Wilton denied the charge, claiming he had consumed five or six drinks and was simply meandering home to kill time, and that nothing improper had entered his mind. His testimony was to no avail, though, and he was sentenced to three months' imprisonment.[4]

It was in such moments that the outside world was able to peep into the citadel of Dolphin Square, to speculate about what its residents, upright pillars of society, were getting up to in their private lives. Such instances all played into a narrative that behind the veneer of respectability, secrets abounded in the Square. In years to come, as we shall see, the associations between Dolphin Square and Piccadilly would intensify with far more serious consequences.

Everyday life was not merely impacted by the war, but fundamentally moulded by it. Nonetheless, there was still room for a normality of sorts and even, every now and again, some old-fashioned joy. One such occasion came in January 1944 with the announcement of the engagement of navy Captain Philip Roberts and Collingwood House resident Primrose Hope-Osborne. She was the widow of Major Anthony Hope-Osborne, who had been killed in action the previous year, but prior to her first marriage she had been something of an 'It girl'. As Primrose Salt, she not only had the name of a Wodehouse-ian creation, but the appearance, too. With sculptural cheekbones and a pixie cut replete with kiss curls, she had been named 'Debutante of the Year' in 1933. She looked just the sort of girl with whom Bertie Wooster might have had a short-lived and ill-fated engagement, but in fact it was with King George II of Greece that she was linked in the 1930s. In the end, though, she found love rather closer to home, and in the process brought a little light to the frequently dark days of wartime Dolphin Square.

Hers was not the only society wedding of the era, either. In August 1942, *Tatler* eagerly announced the marriage of Lord Sandhurst to noted beauty Ann Fielder Johnson of the Square (though the marriage would end in divorce in 1946).[5] Then, in 1943, another Dolphinite, Margaret Woodburn Davidson, married Richard Prichard-Jones, who hailed from a famous retail dynasty. His father was John Jones, who had risen up through the department store business to become chairman and partner of the Regent Street store Dickins, Smith & Stevens, which was later renamed Dickins & Jones. And in November of the same year, Rosemary Hickling married Anthony Griffin Griffiths. Rosemary was the daughter of Dolphin Square's Captain Harold Hickling, who would be a pivotal figure in the planning and execution of the D-Day landings that occurred just a few months later in June 1944. He was Naval Officer in Charge of Mulberry 'B', one of the two prefabricated portable harbours so crucial in the operation, and would end his career with the rank of vice admiral. Griffiths, meanwhile, rose through the ranks too, serving as Controller of the Navy in the 1970s before a stint as chairman of British Shipbuilders.

Just as the war could not entirely put a brake on happiness, nor did it call time on the many types of personal dramas and crises that have a habit of enduring regardless of war or peace. Although, in certain cases it is probable that everyday stresses and tensions were elevated by the additional strains of the war until nerves frayed beyond repair. There is the suspicion that this was true in the case of Keyes House resident Elizabeth McNiele in March 1943. According to her husband, Flight Lieutenant Hugh McNiele, his wife – who worked at the Admiralty – had suffered with severe headaches for several years, which in turn brought on depression and frequent loss of temper. On one occasion, he said, she had threatened to throw herself into the Thames before he talked her out of it. But his mother, who had recently stayed at the Square, seems to have been a particular source of contention between the couple.

On the night in question, he had dined with his mother and then returned to the third-floor flat he shared with his wife to find her in a particularly ferocious mood. An argument erupted and, Mr McNiele said, she'd stormed into their bedroom, slamming the door behind her. Still the argument raged until suddenly he heard the sound of a window 'being flung open and then silence'. Bursting through the door, he ran to the window and saw his wife's body lying prone in the garden below. The verdict of the inquest into her death was 'Suicide with the balance of her mind disturbed'.[6]

The coroner overseeing the case was, incidentally, Bentley Purchase, something of a legend in the medico-legal field. He led somewhere in the region of 20,000 inquests over his long career, counting among the cases he covered several notorious homicides, including those perpetrated by John Christie (of Rillington Place infamy) and John Haigh (the Acid Bath Murderer). But around the time he was review-ing the circumstances of Elizabeth McNiele's demise, he was heavily involved in assisting one of the most audacious counter-espionage operations of the war. He was responsible for providing a cadaver for use in what was called Operation Mincemeat, in which the body of a 'John Doe' was dressed as a British naval officer and parachuted into Spanish waters. Equipped with forged documents, the ambition was that this fake intelligence would be communicated to the German authorities, thus misdirecting them from the genuine military plans of the British, who were preparing for an attack on Sicily. The operation proved to be one of the outstanding Allied undercover operations of the entire conflict.

Bentley Purchase had also been the coroner for an earlier puzzling death, that of 35-year-old Dolphinite Gregory Hicks Haye, whose drowned body was discovered on the foreshore of the Grosvenor Road embankment in March 1940. According to the evidence of his family, several acquaintances and the pathologist, he was a young man in good health with no known romantic or financial difficulties. His body was found fully clothed and in his pockets were several pounds that seemed to have recently been withdrawn. With robbery thus probably not the motive, and the area where he was discovered an unlikely spot for an accidental fall, the coroner was left somewhat perplexed and recorded an open verdict of 'found drowned'.

While the sad demises of McNiele and Haye marked lives tragically foreshortened, in October 1943 the Square was the setting for another passing. This time, though, it was a natural – if sadly early – ending of a life that had been rich and full, that of author Radclyffe Hall. Although she only moved into Hood House a couple of months prior to her death from cancer, in certain respects she epitomised the Dolphin Square ethos as a free thinker and social influencer striving to balance her public and private personas.

Born in 1880, Marguerite Antonia Radclyffe Hall had a tempestuous childhood. Her rich but philandering father left the family home when she was an infant but did bequeath her a hefty inheritance. Her mother, meanwhile, suffered with her mental health, causing a rupture in the mother–daughter relationship that only worsened when she married a man that Marguerite could not stand.

Economically independent thanks to her father and unfettered by any self-imposed pressure to please her mother or find a husband to provide financial security, Hall fearlessly explored her own identity and, in the process, trod around the very edges of what was socially acceptable for the time. By her twenties, she was actively pursuing relationships with women and dressing in typically masculine attire – wearing trousers and suits and often sporting a monocle and traditionally male headwear. Yet, the question of defining her sexuality is complex. In line with the latest thinking of turn-of-the-century sexologists, she considered herself a 'congenital invert' – broadly speaking, she believed herself to be a man trapped inside a woman's body as opposed to a lesbian (what sexologist Richard von Krafft-Ebing memorably described as 'the masculine soul, heaving in the female bosom').

When she was in her late twenties, Hall met and fell in love with a singer, Mabel Batten, almost a quarter of a century her senior. They set up home together and Batten encouraged the younger woman to explore her literary potential. She was also responsible for nicknaming Hall 'John' on account of her resemblance to one of her ancestors – a name Hall subsequently adopted for the rest of her life. Batten died in 1916, by which time Hall had met and fallen for Batten's cousin, Una Troubridge, moving in with her in 1917.

A talented author, Hall's most famous book was *The Well of Loneliness*, published in 1928 – considered a landmark portrayal of lesbianism, it was the subject of a highly anticipated obscenity trial. A roll call of the era's literary alumni was prepared to take to the witness stand to defend the book on the grounds of its political and social importance and the inalienable right of free speech. It became a symbol of something much greater than itself, with several of the witnesses privately doubting the work's literary merits (Virginia Woolf acerbically described it as a 'pale tepid vapid book which lay damp & slab all about the court' while another scion of Bloomsbury, Lytton Strachey, considered it 'pretty frightful').[7] In the event, these and other eminent writers were denied the right to testify after the magistrate ruled that while they might be considered experts in the artistic merit of the book, they could not be deemed expert in what constituted obscenity. In the end, the court found against the book and it was pulped. A review in the *Sunday Express* encapsulated the moral panic it prompted: 'I would rather give a healthy boy or a healthy girl a phial of prussic acid than this novel. Poison kills the body, but moral poison kills the soul.'[8]

Troubridge moved into Dolphin Square with the ailing Hall, nursing her till the end. It was not an easy time. Hall was desperately ill and impatiently awaiting the relief of death. Troubridge, meanwhile, was fighting to secure her position as guardian of her lover's reputation. Her rival to this end was a Russian nurse called Evguenia Souline. In 1934, Troubridge had been ill with enteritis and Souline was employed to care for her. She and Hall then embarked on a passionate affair that endured through to the latter's move to the Square. Troubridge could not bear the situation and did not hide the fact. At the end, though, she persuaded Hall to make her the principal beneficiary of her will, proof in Troubridge's mind that she had won the day. After Hall died on 7 October 1943, Troubridge reflected on seeing her partner – 'You were all mine when you went' – laid out:

> Ivory clear and pale, the exquisite line of the jaw, the pure aquiline of the nose with its delicate wing nostrils, the beautiful modelling of eyelids and brow. Not a trace of femininity, no one in the right senses could have suspected that anything but a young man had died.[9]

Although Hall's literary reputation was secure as a result of her seven other novels and several volumes of poetry, *The Well of Happiness* would only be published in her homeland in 1949. But in 1974, the book received the ultimate gesture of acceptance, being selected as a BBC Radio 4 *Book at Bedtime*.

Death and love and loss, dramas minor and major, personal triumphs and cruel tragedies – the war changed everything and life went on as it always did.

5

'M' IS FOR MOSLEY

In late 1939, with the Phoney War in full swing, Dolphin Square had acquired a pair of new tenants who happened to be two of the most divisive figures in the country. They were Oswald Mosley, leader of the British Union of Fascists (BUF), and his wife Diana (of the famous Mitford clan), and they moved into two adjacent flats on the seventh floor of Hood House. Just three years earlier, in October 1936, the couple had secretly married in the drawing room of Hitler's chief propagandist, Joseph Goebbels, with Hitler himself among the assembled guests. That was quite some baggage to carry around in a London at war.

Their journey to this point had been long and winding. Oswald Mosley was born in 1896, the son of a baronet, and, after fighting in the First World War, he entered Parliament in 1918 as a member of the Conservative Party. Then, in 1920, he married Cimmie Curzon, the daughter of Lord Curzon, former Viceroy of India and at that time Foreign Secretary. It was one of the society weddings of the year, with King George V and Queen Mary (along with assorted European heads of state) in attendance. Mosley seemed to have it all: youth, position, family, money and a considerable brain. For a while, he was a shining light in Parliament – someone several of his colleagues believed might not only make it to the top but could set the country on a sure path into the future.

Much of his politics was influenced by a profound desire never to return to the sort of seemingly endless and destructive war from which Europe had only just emerged. But he soon found himself politically homeless, at odds with his own party over the question of how to handle the Irish Problem. He then sat as an independent, defending his seat at the elections of 1922 and 1923, and the following year he joined Labour, aligning himself with the economic left of the party. When Labour won the election of 1929, Mosely was named Chancellor of the Duchy of Lancaster and tasked with tackling the problem of spiralling unemployment.

He laid out his vision for the country's economic future in what became known as the 'Mosley Memorandum' – a radical and wide-ranging manifesto that leaned heavily on the economic theories of John Maynard Keynes. Mosley argued for industrial nationalisation, large-scale public works to generate jobs, protective tariffs and a new economic model that melded state, workers and commerce into a coherent unity. But Labour was not yet ready to take on such a comprehensive programme of reform, so when the Cabinet rejected his proposals, he resigned from the government.

Against the advice of some of his closest confidantes, he next set up his own party, the New Party, but failed to gain much traction in local or national elections. After its poor performance in the 1931 general election, Mosley found himself increasingly drawn to Europe's fascist movements, who in those early years of the decade appeared to be getting much done and quickly. After a fact-finding trip to Italy, he became convinced that Benito Mussolini had the right idea, and in 1932 Mosley established the BUF, an organisation committed to protecting the British economy and warding off the threat of communism, but also one steeped in nationalism and authoritarianism. Before long, echoing fascist European counterparts, the party established a paramilitary wing popularly known, on account of its uniform, as the Blackshirts.

Mosley was one of the outstanding orators of his generation, a man who could cast a spell with his words. While many stood opposed to all the BUF represented – a fact attested to by the famous Battle of Cable Street in 1936 when a BUF march ended in chaotic clashes with an alliance of anti-fascist groups in London's East End – plenty were attracted to Mosley and his party. Attendances in the tens of thousands were recorded for some rallies. Certainly, the BUF caused sufficient concern in the corridors of power that MI5 was carefully monitoring its leader from at least 1934.

Mosley had already started his affair with Diana Mitford when Cimmie died suddenly in 1933. He had met Diana at a garden party the previous year, at a time when she was still married to Bryan Guinness of the Irish brewing dynasty – although they would be divorced by the end of the year. In 1933, Diana travelled to Germany with her sister, Unity, where they attended that year's Nuremberg Rally. While Unity became utterly infatuated with the Führer, Diana was marginally more circumspect but nonetheless fell under his sway. A friendship developed via Unity that saw Diana personally invited by Hitler to future Nuremberg rallies and to the Olympic Games in Berlin in 1936. By then she was on friendly terms – along with Mosley – with many prominent figures within the German hierarchy.

Mosley had invested a significant part of his personal wealth into the BUF by the time the couple moved into the Square in 1939 with their infant son, Alexander. A second child, Max, followed in April 1940. Many decades later, in 2008, Max – then the head of the world motor racing governing body, the Fédération Internationale de l'Automobile (FIA) – found himself the focal point of a new controversy when he sued a Sunday newspaper for alleging that he had taken part in a sex orgy while dressed in Nazi uniform. He won his case (and became a notable campaigner for tighter privacy laws), but still the shadow of his parents' legacy endured.

Within a few months of arriving at Dolphin Square, the fate of the Mosleys was a vexed question for those at the heart of government. Oswald Mosley was continuing to push hard for a negotiated peace with Germany, his underlying desire to avoid war combining with his sympathies for fascism and admiration for its leading adherents. The political and legal situation was delicate, though. While Mosley was clearly politically aligned with (and personally friendly to) figures generally understood as enemies of the British nation, he avoided making any pronouncements that might legally be deemed treachery.

Certainly, in the early months of 1940, Home Secretary Sir John Anderson did not believe him to be an active threat to British interests and considered it unlikely that the BUF would actively assist a German invasion. However, as German forces advanced through Denmark, Norway, the Netherlands, Belgium and into France in that spring of 1940, others were more worried. Among them was Maxwell Knight, whose MI5 desk was on the floor below the Mosleys' accommodation in Hood House. The recent Tyler Kent saga and the Knight-orchestrated infiltration of the Right Group – investigations featuring a long list of characters with links to the BUF – convinced him that Mosley and his party were potentially very dangerous foes already on home soil in the event of further German aggression. In May 1940, he met the Home Secretary, Vernon Kell (the head of MI5) and General Sir Alan Brooke (Chief of the Imperial General Staff) to lay out his concerns. He made his argument with enough power that Anderson was sufficiently taken aback to review his position.

By the following evening, the Home Secretary passed on his concerns at a meeting chaired by Churchill. Legislation allowing for internment had been enacted in 1939 but now the Cabinet passed an amendment – secret for the time being – that allowed for the detention without trial of individuals suspected of being members of political groups thought to be under foreign influence. If Knight had been instrumental in driving the amendment through, it seems another Dolphinite also had a significant role. When Clement Attlee and Arthur Greenwood were sounded out a couple of weeks earlier about the possibility of joining a coalition, they had consulted with Labour's National Executive Committee. The historian Hugh Ross Williamson suggested the key issue they discussed was 'whether or not the Labour Leaders had made the arrest and imprisonment of Mosley a condition of their entering government. The general feeling was that they had – or at least, that they ought to.'[1]

The day after passing the amendment, 23 May, the police began to pick up members of the BUF. A game of cat and mouse ensued between the police and the Mosleys that day. The police had gone to Dolphin Square in the morning, but found no one there so had then driven to the family's property in Buckinghamshire. In the meantime, though, Oswald and Diana had started on a planned journey to their Pimlico flat. When they arrived at the Square, Diana remembered seeing four men waiting outside, 'staring into space'.[2] One of them, an Inspector Jones, presented her husband with an arrest warrant and promptly took him off to Brixton Prison. Diana, however, was allowed to go free. Meanwhile, back in Buckinghamshire, the police recovered a list of political contacts, along with several firearms.

That Diana was not arrested alongside her husband was not, it turns out, because she was regarded as a lesser threat. In fact, quite the reverse. In MI5 documents dating from the period, it is stated:

> Diana Mosley, wife of Sir Oswald Mosley, is reported on the best authority, that of her family and intimate circle, to be a public danger at the present time … [She] Is said to be far cleverer and more dangerous than her husband and will stick at nothing to achieve her ambitions. She is wildly ambitious.[3]

Another MI5 document acknowledged: 'Before the outbreak of war Lady Mosley was the principal channel of communication with Hitler. Mosley himself has admitted she had frequent interviews with the Fuhrer [*sic*].'[4] While she was free to come and go for the time being, she was nonetheless under surveillance and a person of deep interest to the authorities. Nor would her liberty last much longer.

Having decided that staying at Dolphin Square was not now viable, she moved with the children to a friend's property in Oxfordshire. On 29 June, the police arrived to inform her that she was under arrest. Max was only around ten weeks old and breastfeeding, so Diana was understandably unsure how best to handle the situation. One of the officers told her to pack just enough for a couple of days as it would only be a temporary detention. She decided to leave Max in Oxfordshire, confident of soon being reunited with him. In fact, she was about to start a three-year detention at Holloway Prison in London. Oswald would soon be permitted to join her there to see out the rest of their internment together – a confinement for which responsibility could be laid squarely at the door of their near neighbour, Knight.

During their internment, the couple nonetheless kept on their apartment – only in 1951 did they let it go. In February 1942, Lady Mosley even gave evidence in court at the trial of a 33-year-old electrician called Francis Johnson. She had received information, she explained, that their flat had been broken into and items stolen including cutlery, a watch, silk stockings and a white silk bedspread (valued at £10). Johnson, it emerged, had been responsible for the upkeep of electrical apparatus in the Square and was of previous good character. He did, however, admit to sometimes buying items from 'men employed cleaning debris etc.' and was sentenced to four months imprisonment for receiving the bedspread.[5] It was an unusual case in which not only the perpetrator faced incarceration at its end, but the victim too. Diana Mosley was returned to Holloway.

After the war, Oswald Mosley came closer than he perhaps realised to being squirrelled away from the Square for a second time. This time it was the so-called 43 Group – an anti-fascist organisation established by Jewish ex-servicemen in the aftermath of the war – who wanted him. In the memoirs of one of its founders, Morris Beckman, it is related that a team of young members had come up with a scheme to kidnap Mosley, strip him naked and dump him in Piccadilly Circus. A Jewish textile exporter had told them where his flat was and what his movements were, along with intelligence that he was usually accompanied by a pair of burley bodyguards. The kidnap team decided they would block his car with a taxi before bundling him into a saloon and taking him to Piccadilly, where they had lined up photographers from the press. The plan was only aborted when the group's legal advisor got wind of it and warned of the potential prison sentences they might face.[6] If the Mosleys had hoped Dolphin Square might offer their family some peace away from their public lives, they were mostly to be disappointed.

Over in Germany, meanwhile, an old associate of Mosley, Lord Haw-Haw, was broadcasting his propaganda to English listeners and on one occasion gleefully predicted the destruction of Dolphin Square specifically. Yet, Haw-Haw (or William Joyce, as he was really called) ought really to have felt more kindly towards the place. He had indirect history with the Square, given that he had become close to Maxwell Knight when the two were both associated with the British Fascists in the 1920s. Knight cultivated him as one of his informers and although the spy master was alert to the danger Joyce posed by the time war came around, he allowed his sense of personal loyalty to override his oath of duty to his country on this occasion. Aware that Joyce was a prime candidate for internment in 1939, Knight had tipped him off and Joyce promptly left the country for Germany.

With hindsight, though, interment might have been Joyce's better option. Having used the airwaves to undermine Allied spirits, Joyce was picked up after the war and tried for treason. His defence counsel argued that Joyce – American-born, raised in Ireland and a naturalised German – was not a British citizen at all. The British, though, contended that, as a British passport holder (despite gaining the passport by lying in his application) he owed allegiance to the Crown. Joyce lost the argument and was executed, the last person in the UK to suffer that fate for the crime of treason. Perhaps Knight had not done him such a favour after all.

6

DOVES, HAWKS, HEROES AND A GOVERNMENT IN EXILE

Dolphin Square was never more of a melting pot than during the war. Sharing corridors and sometimes separated by nothing more than the width of a dividing wall could be found individuals with vastly different outlooks and experiences. There were fascists and anti-fascists, appeasers and anti-appeasers, decorated war heroes and secret agents, refugees, home-front heroes and no doubt a few draft dodgers too – all rubbing shoulders on a daily basis. The extent of the political spectrum spanned by residents before and during the war is neatly encapsulated in the stories of two men: the anti-fascist Stephen King-Hall and right-wing journalist and editor Henry Newnham.

The enigmatic King-Hall, who lived in an apartment over in Hood House, had been elected to Parliament as the National Labour Member for Ormskirk in Lancashire in a 1939 by-election, although he was soon sitting as an independent. Born in 1893, he had acquired quite a record of achievement before ever setting foot in Parliament. A retired naval commander, he had, for example, developed a highly success-ful sideline as a playwright. In particular, he co-wrote a naval comedy, *The Middle Watch*, which enjoyed a long run on the stage before being adapted for no fewer than three movies between 1930 and 1958. He was also employed post-navy as a researcher at the Royal Institute of International Affairs at Chatham House and, from 1930–37, became something of a star of the wireless as host of a weekly current affairs talk on BBC *Children's Hour*.

Then, in 1936, he founded a regular current affairs newsletter that became the subject of international tension as war with Germany threatened in 1939. When King-Hall issued the first of the missives in the summer of 1936, he had a modest 600 subscribers around the world, each paying an annual subscription of 10*s*. In return, he offered them a summary of major global events and his own incisive commentary upon them. The newsletter's popularity grew steadily– there were 2,000 subscribers by the end of the year, 13,000 by the end of 1937 and 55,000 in 1939.

Buoyed by this success, between June and August 1939 he sent a series of newsletters to German citizens that aimed to address anti-British misinformation emanating from Joseph Goebbels' Ministry of Propaganda in Berlin. King-Hall hoped for nothing less than that his efforts might play a part in averting war. Instead, they enraged Nazi officials, who reprinted large chunks of the letters in the German press in a bid to ridicule them. Goebbels himself wrote a 4,000-word repudiation of some of the charges laid against his country and critiqued various aspects of British 'civilisation' (as he put it with deliberate irony), including its history of slave trading. Moreover, it was suggested that the letters were not really the work of King-Hall at all but of Lord Halifax, the Foreign Secretary. This claim spooked the Foreign Office, as did letters from British Ambassadors in Germany and Italy who believed King-Hall's words were actively undermining their diplomatic efforts at that sensitive time.

Nonetheless, King-Hall was not to be deterred and went to extraordinary ends to ensure his letters' safe passage, disguising them in a variety of different envelopes and having them posted into Germany from locations around Europe. The German secret police were meanwhile liaising with their national postal service in a bid to block delivery. Goebbels then claimed that the diatribe he had written had been ignored by the British, which prompted King-Hall to personally pay for its publication in the *Daily Telegraph* so as to dodge accusations of censorship.

By September, the letters had ceased but their impact had not. After Hitler rejected Neville Chamberlain's ultimatum to withdraw from Poland, prompting the declaration of war on 3 September, the Führer's subsequent address to his people was sent to London, the last official peacetime communiqué between the nations until 1945. Attached to it was a memorandum containing the following passage:

> The intention communicated to us by order of the British Government by Mr King Hall, of carrying the destruction of the German people even further than was done through the Versailles Treaty is taken note of by us, and we shall therefore answer any aggressive action on the part of England with the same weapons and in the same form.[1]

While King-Hall's efforts to change hearts and minds may have failed resoundingly, the cause of democracy remained dear to him. His next major effort to promote its values in the face of fascism and dictatorship elsewhere in Europe was markedly more successful – and was orchestrated from his flat in the Square.

King-Hall had long suspected that Hansard – the official, verbatim record of parliamentary debates – was a much underused and under-valued resource. Indeed, it was the subject of his maiden speech in the House. If it could be disseminated more widely, he argued, it would promote the wider cause of democratic freedom by revealing just how the system worked and how it protected fundamental democratic principles when elsewhere they were under deep threat. So, in 1944, he hit upon the idea of establishing the Friends of Hansard, and went straight to the top in search of allies. One August day that year he strode into the Common's Smoking Room, where he saw Churchill and the deputy prime minister, Clement Attlee, sitting together. He seized his moment to outline his ambition. Churchill was immediately impressed by his pitch. 'How much do you want to start this up?' he asked.

'One pound from each of you if you approve the idea, and you will be the first Friends.'[2]

The two giants of the political scene dipped into their pockets and, with their seal of approval secured, it was not long before the informal circle of 'Friends' was reconstituted as a fully fledged society, attracting donations from an array of public figures including members of the royal family. Administered from Hood House in those early days, its impact was immediate. By the early part of 1947, Hansard was enjoying some 12,000 sales of its weekly edition and 5,000 of its daily edition – a situation that led the Ministry of Information to contemplate a paper shortage should sales continue on such a trajectory.

King-Hall died in June 1966, six months after he had been made Baron King-Hall of Headley in the County of Southampton. The society he founded, though, has continued to thrive, describing itself now as 'the UK's leading source of independent research and advice on Parliament and parliamentary affairs'.[3]

King-Hall's fellow Dolphinite, Henry Newnham, however, was cut from very different cloth. He was the editor of the periodical *Truth* when, in the summer of 1941, he was sued for libel for an article he had written for it. *Truth* had been founded in the late nineteenth century by Henry Labouchère, a diplomat and member of the Liberal Party, but by the 1940s it was considered a mouthpiece of the right. By then, the proprietor was Major Joseph Ball, a former MI5 agent who in the 1930s emerged as a skilled media operator promoting a pro-fascist and anti-Semitic agenda. Co-ordinating vitriolic attacks on those who demanded an aggressive anti-Nazi stance, he rose to become an advisor to appeaser-in-chief Neville Chamberlain in No. 10.

Under Newnham's guiding hand, *Truth* eyed up an assortment of political opponents including the likes of Churchill and Anthony Eden. But it waged a particularly vicious campaign in the early stages of the war against the Jewish Secretary of State for War, Leslie Hore-Belisha. Newnham did little to disguise his antisemitism in this period. There were editorials, for instance, berating 'the Jew-controlled sink of Fleet Street',[4] and he was a friend of John Beckett, the former Labour MP who subsequently became embroiled with Mosley's Fascists before leaving to set up the National Socialist League alongside William Joyce, Lord Haw-Haw, prior to being interned.

In August 1940, Newnham ran an editorial prompted by reading the official list of British casualties resulting from the fighting in France. He wrote:

I noticed, among the names of other members of the 'ruling class' those of the Duke of Northumberland, the Earl of Aylesford, the Earl of Coventry, Lord Frederick Cambridge – all killed in action. I did not notice any names like Gollancz, Laski, and Strauss, from which I draw the conclusion that what happened in the last war is being repeated in this. The ancient families of Britain – the hated ruling class of the Left Wing diatribes – are sacrificing their bravest and best to keep the Strausses safe in their homes, which in the last war they did not don uniforms to defend.[5]

Almost exactly a year later, Neville Laski – a much-respected silk, a future judge and a son of the celebrated Laski family (alongside his brother Harold, a Marxist political theorist) – was awarded £525 in damages against Newnham and *Truth* on the grounds that it had suggested he was cowardly and had sought to avoid service in the last war. In fact, he had served in Gallipoli, Sinai and France, achieving the rank of captain before being invalided out, suffering from shell shock. Newnham may have lost that particular battle but he would continue to wage his ideological war through the pages of his magazine. One can only wonder whether the likes of Newnham and King-Hall, Mosley and the Cook sisters worked hard to avoid each other when in residence, or whether politeness dictated that such disparate figures would nod their 'hellos' and 'how are yous?' in the stairwells, at the shops or down by the swimming pool.

For Arthur Greenwood, Attlee's deputy in the Labour Party, the war proved something of an anticlimax professionally. If his stock was never higher than after taking Neville Chamberlain to task at its outbreak, he showed his mettle again in May 1940 as a staunch ally of Churchill, supporting him even as pressure grew for the prime minister to seek a way out of a war that many were beginning to suspect Britain had little chance of winning. But his stint as minister without portfolio in Churchill's administration was otherwise disappointing and he resigned in 1943, although he retained national significance as the nominal leader of the opposition (while Attlee was serving as deputy prime minister) until the war's end.

His determination to tackle the Nazi threat rendered him a wanted man in Berlin. His was one of the roughly 2,800 names included in the *Sonderfahndungsliste GB* (Special Wanted List for Great Britain)

– a directory of 'undesirables' pre-selected for rounding up and incarceration prior to what Hitler was convinced would be his country's inevitable overrunning of the British mainland. Principally the work of the SS general, Walter Schellenberg, the list was dominated by Jews but also included prominent non-Jewish public figures and those who Schellenberg in his paranoia determined were members of a class-bound ruling elite. Mysteriously, Greenwood was listed in the directory as a Jew (he was not). His suspected address was given as Old Queen Street, SW1, but it would not have taken long for German invaders to have tracked him to Dolphin Square had the war taken a different course. Instead, thankfully, Greenwood emerged from the war with his liberty intact, whereupon he was drafted into Attlee's post-war Labour Government as Lord Privy Seal and, later, Paymaster General.

While the likes of King-Hall, Newnham and Greenwood attracted significant publicity, others in the Square were involved in activities that, literally, went under the radar. Raymond Harries, for instance, emerged from the war as a highly decorated flying ace who boasted upwards of twenty individual victories against German aircraft, most achieved in the cockpit of his trusty Spitfire. But Dolphin Square, with its spy masters and secret agents in residence, was also the backdrop for scenes in some of the conflict's most extraordinary tales of espionage.

One of these involved a Dolphinite called Major Monty Chidson, although it would not be until after his death in 1957 that word of his most daring exploits became public. Born in Brentford, Middlesex, in 1893, he had been a pilot in the First World War – one of the first to engage enemy aircraft over British territory. In 1915, though, he was shot down over enemy lines and spent the next three years as a POW.

In 1919, once more a free man, he married a Dutch national, Marie De Brijn, and embarked on a career with MI6, the British foreign intelligence service, serving variously in Vienna and Bucharest until, in 1936, he was posted to The Hague in the Netherlands. Fluent in the local language, he was assigned to the Passport Control Office as cover for his secret work.

On 10 May 1940, the German invasion of the Netherlands began – an aggression that prompted two British-based Dutch diamond traders, Walter Keyser and Jan Smit, to suggest a daring scheme to the British

Government. Amsterdam, they pointed out, was a city full to bursting with diamonds. Should these stocks fall into German hands, not only would they significantly swell the Nazi coffers but Berlin would also have access to vast quantities of industrial-grade diamonds to bolster their war production capabilities. So, Keyser and Smit asked for assistance in being smuggled in and out of the country, confident that with their connections they would be able to bring a significant haul of Amsterdam's diamonds back to Britain.

The British agreed to the plan and attached Chidson to the operation. They also supplied an ageing First World War destroyer, HMS *Walpole*, to take the men into Dutch waters, where they would be dropped a little way from the coast. The voyage was perilous and undertaken in blackout conditions while trying to dodge both British and German minefields. There was a near-miss with another vessel too, which turned out to be transporting the Dutch royal family to safety as their homeland was being overrun.

Nevertheless, the trio were landed off the coast and made their way into the city, where they were provided with a local guide and driver. All the while, German troops were advancing across the country towards the capital. Keyser and Smit were quick to leverage their contacts, talking trader after trader into entrusting them with their high-value commodity. Many of the dealers were Jews who needed little persuading that there was no point keeping the stones in the city for the Germans to seize in a day or two. But there was a problem. A large stash of industrial diamonds sat in a vault of the Amsterdam Mart that operated on a clock timer – in other words, it could not be opened before the timer had run through a set period of time.

Keyser and Smit carried their cases laden with gems and made their way back to the *Walpole*, effectively hijacking a tugboat for the last stretch of their return journey to the vessel. Chidson, though, stayed in the city, hidden in its bowels awaiting his opportunity to break into the vault once its clock had timed out. He spent many fretful hours there, only finally seizing his treasure as German paratroopers swarmed into the building above him. With just moments to spare, he effected his escape and all three of the British-sponsored agents made it safely back to England. The diamonds seized by Keyser and Smit were subsequently stored in London for the war's duration, while Chidson's haul was reunited with Holland's exiled Queen Wilhelmina. Meanwhile, Chidson returned to life in the Square, his neighbours entirely oblivious to his extraordinary act of daring and nerve.

Another long-hidden espionage operation with Dolphin Square connections involved a former Welsh police inspector, Gwilym Williams. Williams' career in the police was largely unremarkable (after twenty-nine years of service with Swansea Constabulary, he had a single commendation – for stopping a runaway horse) and he then worked as a private detective, mostly focussing on divorce cases. However, he had clearly developed a passion for adventure and the stomach for danger over his many years on the front line – traits that were about to prove invaluable.

At the start of the war, Major Nikolaus Ritter – a German spy master – asked one of his British-based spies, Arthur Owens (who was in fact a double agent) to recruit a Welsh nationalist spy – a figure, he hoped, who would be opposed to the Westminster Government and interested in destabilising it. But when MI5 learned of the plan from Owens, they decided to provide the Germans with a man of their own to go undercover. Their man, it turned out, was Williams, who had the added advantage of having picked up a good deal of French and German during his military service in the First World War. Williams agreed to take on the role and duly visited MI5's head of transportation, Lord Cottenham, at his Dolphin Square flat to sort out travel arrangements. He then travelled to Belgium to begin his mission of infiltrating the German intelligence services, and it was not long before he managed to convince his Nazi handlers that he was indeed the fanatical nationalist they were looking for to assist them in undermining British efforts.

Ritter was intent that Williams and his 'nationalist network' should sabotage British aerodromes, factories and the like. Instead, the German was fed a diet of false information to distract and confuse. Moreover, Williams was able to feed information back to his MI5 overlords and alert them to potential plots in the offing. Among the schemes he obstructed was one employing a German U-boat to land explosives in a remote spot on the Welsh coast, another aimed at poisoning a reservoir and even an audacious attempt to steal a Spitfire. It was immensely dangerous work, with Williams well aware that exposure would likely result in a painful death. Nonetheless, he carried out his tasks with remarkable aplomb. In fact, so effective was he that for a time John Masterson – chairman of the Twenty Committee, which ran the Double-Cross (XX) System within MI5 that managed double agents – considered him his most valuable asset.[6]

In contrast to Chidson and Williams' stirring stories of derring-do, Lady Carolyn Howard cut a much sadder figure in the Square. The only daughter of George Howard, the 11th Earl of Carlisle, and his first wife, Bridget (eldest daughter of Major General Walter Hore-Ruthven, 10th Lord Ruthven of Freeland), Carolyn was only 20 years old at the onset of the war. She served in the Auxiliary Territorial Service (of which her mother was Senior Controller) and the First Aid Nursing Yeomanry but it was clearly a miserable phase in her life, during which she was effectively an alcoholic.

In May 1944, for example, she pleaded guilty at Bow Street Magistrates after being found drunk – a result, her defence counsel suggested, of a 'weakness of will' brought on by ill health. She was put on probation on condition that she seek psychological help, but was back before the court within four months. Having been diagnosed with a dental complaint, she'd been allowed to leave the home under whose care she'd been placed to visit a dentist in London. But she had then failed to return to the home and was subsequently fined and returned to the institution.

There is the sense that Carolyn was one of those unenviable people who seemed to have so many advantages in life but was yet to find her own place in the world. Her parents would divorce in 1947 on the grounds of her mother's adultery with Sir Walter Monckton, who had risen to national prominence as one of Edward VIII's key advisors during the abdication crisis of 1936 and then as Solicitor General in Churchill's wartime government. He and Lady Carlisle subsequently married. Then, in 1956, she inherited from her father the lordship of Ruthven of Freeland in Scotland – an honour that entitled her to a seat in the Lords from 1963 after a change in regulations. With her husband having been created Viscount Monckton of Brenchley in 1957, the highly unusual situation arose of a husband, wife and her son (the new Earl of Carlisle following the death of his and Carolyn's father) all sitting in the Upper House.

But was there more to Lady Carolyn's story than met the eye? During the war, the Cambridge spy Kim Philby sent a report to his Russian handlers alleging the existence of an outrageous espionage racket designed to provide Germany with intelligence about the RAF. According to Philby, an attaché at the German Legation in Dublin was in the habit of sending drugs to London in return for information and deserters. It was said that the drugs – marijuana, cocaine, morphia – were parachuted into Ireland from Germany and then smuggled to England by a platoon of Welsh fishermen. They were then distributed out of assorted London clubs to officers who, 'under the influence of drugs, alcohol, sex orgies or Black Mass are induced to part with information. An important side-line is blackmailing officers, getting them into debt at crooked chemin-de-fer parties.' Immediately after this assertion, Philby wrote, 'Personalities mixed up in the racket are: Lady CAROLYN HOWARD, drug addict, always with RAF men.'[7] Quite what this spy network amounted to and exactly how Lady Carolyn was involved is unclear. But certainly, she appears to have been a vulnerable individual whose life in London, based out of Dolphin Square, had spiralled far further out of control than anyone had quite imagined.

While aspects of Lady Carolyn's story are hazy, the history of the Free French Forces at Dolphin Square is often equally elusive, as if hidden in a fog of Gauloises smoke. Free France was the government in exile established by Charles de Gaulle in London to co-ordinate French resistance against the German occupation after June 1940, when the nation was placed under the nominal control of the Nazi puppet Marshal Pétain.

Following a broadcast from London in June 1940, the initial response to de Gaulle's call to arms was limited – only a few thousand men and women signed up in those early weeks. But by 1944, the movement had united many of the disparate underground resistance groups within France and secured support from across France's colonial territories, so that its forces now numbered somewhere in the region of 400,000. It was, then, an organisation that needed some serious administrative heft. De Gaulle was granted various accommodation in London, most notably at Carlton Gardens but also at Dolphin Square. In 1942 the British Government formally transferred Grenville House over to use by the Free French Forces, although the evidence suggests the forces had been operating out of there for a while already.

In December 1941, for instance, there were notices in the press that mail for the Free French Forces overseas should be sent to the headquarters at Grenville House, from where it would be distributed. But it was likely that they were there even earlier – a Czech member of the Free French, Serge Vaculik, spoke in his memoirs of those he ironically referred to as 'heroes' fighting 'gallantly behind a big desk strongly entrenched on the first floor of some big block of offices in Dolphin Square or some similar place' as early as January 1941.[8]

What de Gaulle's people got up to at the Square was necessarily shrouded in secrecy, with strict security in place and special passes required for entry to the block. It is also rumoured that de Gaulle himself spent some time living there, though there is no known documentary proof. Nonetheless, when the actor Peter Finch took an apartment at the Square in the 1960s, he was assured it was the one where de Gaulle had previously lived. We can be more certain that the shops at the Square – always well-known for aiming to please the locals (it was rumoured that Clementine Churchill especially detoured to the greengrocers because of the exceptional quality of their cauliflowers) – made particular efforts to accommodate the tastes of the new French residents, although when the bakery took to producing croissants, the results were generally considered pretty disappointing.

One prominent member of the Free French was Louis Burdet, a hotelier by trade, who operated before and after the war in London. During the war, he was the Free French military delegate for the Marseille region. In that role, he was a pivotal figure in the Resistance, who assisted the Allied landings in southern France in August 1944 that sent the German forces into retreat and protected Marseille from being razed by the departing troops. Burdet, who was sometimes known as John Brown, died a resident of the Square in March 1969.

André Gillois, a writer and broadcaster who worked with the French programme at the BBC and for a while served as a spokesman for de Gaulle, remembered a distinct feature of 'le quartier de Dolphin Square': the girls (in fact, he used a term that may also be interpreted as 'prostitutes'). In his *Secret History of the French in London*, he described how these 'girls' were in the habit of visiting soldiers in barracks in the vicinity of the Square 'to revive the sentries in their huts'.[9]

Another memoirist who related a little of life at the Square was Jacques Barchilon, a member of the French Resistance in Tangiers before finding his way to the Free French in London, where he worked as a driver. He recalled:

January 1st, 1944 is an unforgettable date for me. With three or four other comrades, we emerge from the Waterloo railroad station. It was raining and we made our way slowly through the slippery London streets; on our young shoulders, we balanced the heavy British duffel bag. We arrived at Dolphin Square, Grenville House. S.W.1 in the Victoria Station-Belgravia district. We had to register at the office of the Free French. I was not told then, but through other drivers, I learned that the young female drivers were no longer assigned to work with the French officers, and that they (the French officers) were especially forbidden from going to their rooms to wake them up, for obvious reasons.

Male drivers were a safer choice. We were moving between the garage and the headquarters of General de Gaulle at Carlton Gardens. The officer in charge of the chauffeur service surprised us, pleasantly. He told us that in over-populated London there is no room for military barracks for foreign soldiers. This is why we had to be lodged and take rooms among the civilian population. We were given 25 shillings each for renting rooms. This can seem somewhat surprising, like a special favour, but in reality, our lodging endowment did not allow us to be lodged in an apartment. We could only be in a room, there was no great luxury. For the noon meal we had a free Dolphin Square canteen. For every other meal we had to make do on our own. We didn't have much money and looked for cheap meals for students.

Our work was at once serious and important. At seven in the morning we had to pick up our service cars in the garage of Dolphin

Square, on the edge of the river. We were to pick up various officers in their apartments and drive them to Carlton Gardens, or elsewhere according to their assignments. In the basement of Carlton Gardens there was a waiting room for drivers on duty. After six p.m., we had to return our little service cars to the garage; these were either requisitioned service cars or camouflaged Renaults or Peugeots. When we were on night duty, driving was difficult in the black-out (no headlights to guide us in the black night). I remember in the obscurity of a certain evening, a tall and distinguished looking gentleman in civilian clothes asked me to wait in a parking lot of a building I didn't know. This was General François Astier [commander of the French Forces in the UK and a key figure in preparations for the Allied invasion of France]. He guided me slowly to a parking spot and asked me to wait. After 45 minutes I saw him on top of a stairway shaking the hand of a man, round and smiling dressed in a kind of mechanic's outfit. It was Winston Churchill.[10]

A few months before Barchilon's arrival, another mysterious figure came to the attention of the Free French. His backstory left both the British and French authorities wondering if he wasn't a German spy. His entry into the country was anything but orthodox – at around 1 p.m. on 29 March 1943, a Royal Navy patrol boat spotted a figure in a canoe a few hundred yards from Dover Breakwater. When they picked him up, they saw that he was exhausted so escorted him to Dover, where the Security Services waited for him to recover a little before interrogating him. He had, he said, been rowing for over thirteen hours.

Once he'd revived, the story he told his rescuers was literally incredible. He claimed to be called Claude Henri de la Fere and that he came from an aristocratic French family descended from the sixteenth-century king, Francois I. He said he had been raised for some time in Indo-China and was extravagantly wealthy, owning chateaux and numerous cars. Recently, he insisted, he had been working with an underground resistance organisation in France, aiding the escape of individuals being sought by the German authorities. He had, though, set his heart on coming to England to join the Free French. He then described an extraordinary trip across occupied France by, variously, foot, horse and cart, and train. He'd eventually arrived at Boulogne, where he held a series of menial jobs, having lost his wallet containing all his money before being reunited with it and buying a canoe. This he had rowed, undetected, from Boulogne all the way to the waters around Dover where he had been picked up.

His initial interrogators did not know what to make of it all, so he was sent to the Security Service's special interrogation centre for suspected foreign agents, Camp 020, in South London. Under further questioning, he eventually admitted to making up virtually all the biographical details but insisted the story of his escape across the sea was just as he'd said. The truth, so it seemed, was that he was illegitimate and had manufactured a cover story to hide his shame. His interrogators concluded that he was 'either a lunatic or a spy, or possibly both'.

Within a few weeks, the British suspected that their captive was not called de la Fere at all, but was likely one Henri Ferriere, who was keen to escape his troubled family past and start anew in England. The Security Service was also by now convinced that he was not working for the enemy and that the details of his escape were probably true. They noted, for instance, that he described how he had got his canoe down the beach at Boulogne with the help of an invalid on crutches – a detail so seemingly ridiculous that it was hard to countenance anyone manufacturing it for a cover story. The British therefore decided, after some six months of holding him, that it was safe to hand him over to the Free French Forces.

La Fere formally signed up with the Free French (presumably at the headquarters in Dolphin Square) but was then interrogated by French officials as to his treatment over the prior six months. What had the British asked him about? Which French personnel had he encountered who were working with the British? When he refused to divulge any information – in accordance with the pledge he had made to the British – his new interrogators suggested they were not convinced that he wasn't a German agent after all. Nonetheless, he was told to sign further paperwork tying him to the Free French and refusal would result in further incarceration.

Unimpressed by his treatment, he almost immediately went into hiding. With the help of the British, he secured a position at the BBC, where his skills as a multi-linguist were put to good use. However, when the BBC made enquiries about him with the Free French, they received a response that made it impossible for the organisation to retain him. He made it clear to the British that he was not prepared to work for the Free French (and the British considered the forms that he'd signed with them were not binding) but said he would be interested in joining the British forces or else doing some other useful war work. It then seems he was put forward as a candidate for Special Operations Overseas but was deemed by his interviewer there as 'a most unsuitable candidate' and a 'hypersensitive bastard who in order to conceal the fact of his illegitimacy had invented a wholly fictitious story of his early life'. As of May 1944, we know that de la Fere was living in Hood House, perhaps hiding in clear sight of the Free French in Grenville House. He was sharing a flat with a Miss Natalia Korel-Katzin, a South African-born British citizen some eighteen years his senior. The nature of their relationship is unclear but that month, de la Fere's solicitor, Theodore Goddard (a prestigious name in the legal field who represented Wallis Simpson in her divorce and advised her during the abdication crisis of 1936), wrote to the Metropolitan Police to complain about an impromptu interview at the apartment. A plain-clothes officer and a uniformed policewoman arrived unannounced and conducted an interrogation, during which both interviewees were questioned as to their domestic set-up. The plain-clothes officer also accused Korel-Katzin of 'harbouring and encouraging' the Frenchman, whom he said was of 'weak character'. The officer demanded of her, 'Can you imagine anyone of Jewish blood helping the Nazis?' – suggesting that was what she herself was doing.[11]

We know little else of the elusive de la Fere, although he seems to have worked with the United Nations Relief and Rehabilitation Administration in the war's aftermath. He is, in many ways, the perfect embodiment of the Square in this period and beyond – a figure of mystery, where fact and fiction collide and truth remains just out of reach, there to be moulded by whoever can maintain even a partial grip on it.

But before leaving the war behind, there is one further character with distinct ties to Dolphin Square who ought to be noted for his rare sense of selflessness, courageousness and desire to do good. His name was Michael Hargrave and he was the son of one Wing Commander William Bowen Hargrave and his wife, who lived in Beatty House (after the war, Michael would in fact take over the lease from his parents and spent the early part of his married life there before he was called up for military service in East Africa). In 1945, Michael was a student of medicine at Westminster Hospital when he volunteered, along with ten fellow students, to go to Holland to assist in a famine relief programme in a part of the country still awaiting liberation. At the eleventh hour, though, these eleven were told that they were instead to go to Germany, to the just-liberated Bergen–Belsen concentration camp. Hargrave, just 21 years old, was about to walk through the gates of hell.

He joined a large team of medics systematically cleaning and disinfecting the huts of Camp One and turning them into makeshift hospitals, where the camp inmates were treated and prepared for their return to freedom. The news footage of Belsen that was shown in cinemas across Britain came as a jolting shock to a populace that might have thought itself inured to whatever new atrocities the war could conjure up. Hargrave, though, was one of the few to see at first hand the misery wrought in that camp. Moreover, he kept a diary of his experiences, a record that has emerged as an invaluable historical artefact. Here, for instance, is the entry for Thursday, 3 May 1945:

> The first thing that struck me was the amazing bleakness. Everything was grey or slate brown. The next thing was the dust, then the internees: they looked thin, brown and dirty and they shuffled along in a purposeless sort of way in their blue and white striped slave clothing. They were not in the least interested in anything and took no notice of us.
>
> We went into the hut and were almost knocked back by the smell. The sight that met us was shocking. There were no beds and in this one room were about 200 people lying on the floor. In some cases they wore no clothes at all.

One or two patients were quite literally just a mass of skin and bones, with sunken eyes which had a completely vacant look. We went back to the other end of the room, followed by weak cries, or at least whines, of 'Herr Doktor, Herr Doktor'.[12]

What effect Hargrave's words had on those prominent Dolphin Square residents who had once campaigned for rapprochement with Hitler and, in a few cases, voiced undiluted admiration for the Führer, can only be a matter of conjecture.

7

LIFE RESUMES

In 1949, Dolphin Square resident Catherine Black, a nurse in her early seventies, died and left an estate of just over £1,700. She was by no means a well-known name, but her death notices might just have rung a bell with some who read them. Her passing, though, had a deeper symbolism – Black had led an extraordinary life but one rooted in a world that was fast disappearing.

Born in County Donegal in 1878, she'd come to London to train as a nurse. The journey across the Irish Sea to work in caring or domestic jobs was not an unusual one. Even into the 1930s and '40s there were still plenty of the wealthier Dolphin Square residents placing adverts in Irish papers to recruit staff. Black's first job was working at the Royal London Hospital in the capital's East End when the First World War broke out. After a stint treating injured soldiers returned to England, she subsequently went out to both Belgium and France to nurse the sick and wounded there, too. Then when the war ended, she returned to private practice and in 1928 was employed as nurse to King George V, remaining with him through to his death on the night of 20 January 1936. A moment, we now understand, when the king's doctor, Bertrand Dawson, decided to hasten the king's departure – a decision that Black was said to have strongly opposed. King George was, it is true, dying as a result of cardiorespiratory failure but the doctor's diaries, uncovered many years later, reveal that he prescribed his royal patient a deadly combination of morphine and cocaine. He did so, in part, to reduce the length of the king's suffering, and that of his family, but there were other considerations. For one, he was keen that the announcement of the king's death appeared in the morning papers instead of the 'less appropriate … evening journals'. Nurse Black, meanwhile, is believed to have been the recipient of the king's last words, uttered as she injected him with a final sedative, 'God damn you!'[1]

Having enjoyed accommodation on site at Buckingham Palace while engaged with the royal family, it is easy to see why Dolphin Square – just a twenty-minute walk away, and with its amenities and a certain class of tenant – was an attractive proposition for Black's retirement. A place where she could reflect discreetly and in some comfort on a life lived in the fast lane of the first half of the century. Hers was an existence moulded by international politics and conflict, and experienced alongside the most powerful in the land. But it largely played out in a version of England that, though still fresh in the mind, had already all but been left behind by the time she died.

In 1954, the death of Commander Oliver Locker-Lampson, a naval officer and for thirty-five years a Conservative MP, was another one of those moments that seemed to signal a passing of the ages at the Square. Having first entered the House in 1910, Locker-Lampson received a commission with the navy early in the First World War, where he was charged with establishing an armoured car division. In common with Black, he served in France and Belgium, before being sent to Russia, where he soon found himself embroiled in its tumultuous domestic politics. He claimed, for example, to have been invited to join an assassination plot against Rasputin in 1916, and he'd then developed an escape plan to smuggle Nicholas II out of Russia following the Tsar's abdication in 1917 – a scheme, needless to say, that ultimately failed. Vehemently opposed to the revolutionaries, Locker-Lampson is also thought to have been attached to an unsuccessful military counter-coup later in the same year.

His Russian experience ensured that he was a committed anti-communist, determined to see off any leftist threat in Britain after the war. Chancellor of the Exchequer Austen Chamberlain appointed him his parliamentary private secretary in 1919, in which role he attended that year's Paris Peace Conference as the European powers strived to establish a post-war settlement. But back at home, his distrust of Bolshevism set him on a path that brought him, seemingly inadvertently, into the arms of fascism. Security at his anti-communist rallies was often provided by members of the British Fascisti and by 1930 he was writing articles that expounded the potential of Hitler. Then, in 1931, he established the paramilitary 'Sentinels of Empire' (also called the Blue Shirts) with the stated aim of peacefully fighting Bolshevism and 'clearing out the Reds!' While the organisation was largely ineffectual and soon fell apart, it did find a fan in the prominent Nazi strategist and myth-maker Alfred Rosenberg. The two men dined together at the Savoy in 1931, after which Rosenberg presented him with a gold cigarette lighter.

But by then, Locker-Lampson was beginning to see European fascism for what it was. Appalled that he might be considered an advocate of its ideology, he now redirected his energies into anti-fascist action. In 1933, for instance, he introduced a Private Member's Bill intended to grant British citizenship to the increasing number of Jews fleeing Nazi persecution (the Cook sisters would have surely appreciated his efforts). Moreover, he personally assisted in the flight and resettlement of a great many individuals – among them, Albert Einstein, for whom he provided a temporary home in Norfolk after he was subjected to death threats on the Continent. In addition, he campaigned for, though was unable to win, British citizenship for Sigmund Freud, and assisted Ethiopia's Emperor Haile Selassie when he sought refuge in Britain after the Italian occupation of his country in 1936.

Too old to fight in the Second World War (he was 58 at its outbreak), Locker-Lampson joined the Home Guard and retired from Parliament at the 1945 election. Like Nurse Black, his was a life lived fully but one whose greatest moments belonged to a chapter of history that was now drawing to a close. The times were changing quickly. With the end of the war came a hunger to move forwards, to build a new world where conflict and poverty did not loom eternally, where the technological advancements of the time might actually start to deliver the higher quality of life that they had long promised but failed to produce for the masses.

Of course, for most people, the new dawn still lay some way off. This was a time of rationing and austerity, of tallying the true cost of the war both materially and in terms of Britain's place in the world order, and of individuals and families adapting and adjusting after years of disruption to their normal lives. Those longing for a brave, shiny new world were more often faced instead with drear and make-do. Yet Dolphin Square was not most other places. Populated by enough people of money and position, it was at the vanguard of the march towards modernity. The post-war period would deliver more glitz and stardust here than in virtually any other postcode in the nation. Life in the Square was frequently shiny, exciting and exuberant. At long last, it seemed capable of delivering the lifestyle that the Costains had promised back in the 1930s, before that dream was waylaid by war.

Embodying the early post-war razzle-dazzle of Dolphin Square were half the members of the Crazy Gang – arguably the country's favourite entertainers in their prime – who had decided to make their home here. But there was a sense that even they were at the tail-end of something and that a changing of the guard was in the offing. The Gang were undoubtedly still beloved and about as famous as they came just then. With their roots in the grand old tradition of music hall variety, they had subtly adapted it to the tastes of a mid-century audience, but they were mining an increasingly old-fashioned seam of cheeky-chappy gags, slapstick, sentimental songs and general nostalgia. Somehow, it all seemed a little steeped in the past (even then) to feel like a perfect fit for the Square, with its aspirations for modernity and looking forward.

But if their presence seemed anachronistic, it was still not difficult to see why so many of the Gang chose to live there. While their shows may have seemed anarchic, they were really co-ordinated performances of military precision – everything was tried and tested, rehearsed to within an inch of its life, designed to please. And please they certainly did, commanding fans from all walks of life right through to the heart of the royal family (the Gang were a particular favourite of George VI and his children, performing in countless royal command performances). In truth, the Gang were not really 'crazy' at all – their shtick was skilled and polished and had become part of the social fabric, part of the Establishment even. Moreover, several of them had London running through their veins. And while they may have left the mean streets of their childhoods behind, Dolphin Square allowed them to remain in the heart of the city – close to the theatres that had birthed them and which had made them famous and rich – living a life of comparative comfort and ease.

Most famous of them all was Bud Flanagan, who lived with his wife Anne (always known as 'Curly') in a flat in Raleigh House (as well as having another property on the south coast). Bud was born in 1896 in Whitechapel, in the heart of the East End – an area he would describe as 'a patchwork of small shops, pubs, church halls, Salvation Army hostels, doss houses, cap factories and sweat shops'.[2] His parents were Jewish émigrés from Poland and they named him Chaim Weintrop. He anglicised his name as a child to Bud Robert Winthrop and started finding work in a local music hall when he was around 10. He later chose Flanagan as his stage surname to cock a snoot at an old army nemesis from the First World War, a Sergeant Major Flanagan who had made Winthrop's life hell, not least because of his Jewish roots. Bud vowed to exact revenge someday by making the senior officer's name a laughing stock.

As well as finding a new name in the war, he also discovered among his comrades in Flanders the professional partner with whom he would rise to stardom – Chesney Allen. However, fame took some time to arrive. It was not until the mid-1920s that they established themselves as a headline act, notably at the Holborn Empire. Their songs and skits became the stuff of legend, and their unofficial anthem, 'Underneath the Arches', was a touchstone for a generation. By the time Bud wrote it in 1932, Flanagan and Allen were not only a duo but had also been integrated into the Crazy Gang, whose classic line-up consisted of the pair of them and two other established double acts (Jimmy Nervo and Teddy Knox plus Charlie Naughton and Jimmy Gold) as well as solo artist 'Monsewer' Eddie Gray. Come the war, the Gang and its composite acts were vital figures in keeping up national spirits – in their stage performances, on the big screen and through songs that mocked the enemy such as 'We're Going to Hang out the Washing on the Siegfried Line'.

Flanagan and his beloved Curly made a comfortable life for themselves in the post-war period. The business had been kind to Bud and he decked out their flat in furnishings supplied by Harrods. 'I like it here,' he would tell the press in the 1950s. 'The view of the river from my study, the tugs and the barges, they sort of inspire me.' And, of course, he was surrounded by old friends, too. From the Gang, Jimmy Nervo (born in London in 1898 into a circus family), Teddy Knox (who grew up in the north-east and started out as a juggler) and Glasgow-born Jimmy Gold all had apartments in the Square.

For Flanagan, the man whose very name was a retort to an antisemite, there must have been an element of irony in making a home in a place that had counted the likes of Henry Newnham and Oswald Mosley among its residents. But he found contentment here, hosting loved ones and famous friends – not least Charlie Chaplin, who Bud knew from an unsuccessful attempt to make it in America in his youth. He is also believed to have welcomed Harold Macmillan in the period, giving the politician acting lessons so that the notoriously stiff and awkward statesman might better 'perform' in whatever political or social setting he might find himself.

Flanagan was also able to exercise his passion for gambling here, especially on the horses. He claimed that his success with the book-ies was down to arming himself with insider knowledge, courtesy of an extensive network of racing contacts that he had built up through his showbiz connections (he reckoned to be making somewhere in the region of £5,000 per year from gambling in the early 1960s). In particular, each morning a sheet was delivered to his flat with all the day's races and riders listed in order of form by one of his trusted turf experts.[3]

But Flanagan's life was not without its sadness during his time in the Square. Most cruelly, in 1956 Bud and Curly's son, Buddy, died from leukaemia. Buddy, just 29 years old, was in Los Angeles at the time, attempting to achieve the Stateside success that had eluded his father. Flanagan was devastated by the loss but found refuge in his work, con-tinuing to perform with the Crazy Gang in their famous Victoria Palace Theatre residencies and occasionally reuniting with Allen as a duo too (Allen had gone into partial retirement at the end of the war). One of Flanagan's last jobs was to sing the theme tune for the sitcom *Dad's Army* – the piece, 'Who Do You Think You Are Kidding, Mr Hitler?', a loving pastiche of the sorts of songs that had made Flanagan and Allen superstars. Flanagan died in 1968, a few months after that recording, although Curly would keep their flat on for several years to come.

The Square in the 1950s was also home to assorted other stars from this golden age of British variety – an age slowly coming to an end, its gentle rhythms a nod to the past but increasingly out of kilter with the younger, edgier forms of entertainment that the 1960s would bring. But for now, its leading exponents remained major players – performers who continued to amuse and entertain the parents and grandparents, even as their grip on the youth was slipping. Arthur Askey, for example, had a place in Grenville House, and Tommy Trinder lived in Beatty House. Then over in Nelson House was Vic Oliver, who successfully mixed a natural feel for comedy with his spectacular musicianship to establish himself as a mainstay of the entertainment scene on both sides of the Atlantic (as an entertainer of Jewish descent, he'd also won a place – alongside fellow Dolphinite Arthur Greenwood – in the Nazis' 'black book' of undesirables). Oliver lived in the Square with his wife, Natalie Conder, whom he married in 1946 and who herself had leased an apartment in the complex since 1943. Back in 1942, Oliver had become the first guest to appear on the BBC radio show *Desert Island Discs*, created and presented by Roy Plomley, who for a while in the 1950s was also one of his neighbours in the Square.

Another of Flanagan's circle – they regularly shared a bill – was Bert Bernard, who found fame as part of mime-dance act The Bernard Brothers. He lived in the Square with his wife, Zoe Gail, a well-regarded actor who nonetheless had the dubious honour of starring in a 1948 British gangster flick called *No Orchids for Miss Blandish*, a film often cited as among the worst ever made. Bernard and Gail had married in 1951 and then honeymooned in the south of France, where she suffered serious leg injuries in a car accident. Dolphin Square thus served as a convalescent home for the early stages of their married life.

While there had always been entertainers and performers in the Square, it was now awash with them. The character actor Thorley Walters was among the most enduring Dolphinites, keeping up an association from the 1940s until his death in 1991. He was equally as much a fixture of the British film industry, perhaps best-known today for his work with the likes of Peter Sellers and Terry Thomas, and for his run of *St Trinian's* movies. Hugh Griffith, meanwhile, had a flat in Rodney House in this period. He formed a powerhouse double act opposite Richard Burton in a Broadway run of *Legend of Lovers* early in the decade, and in 1959 enjoyed his finest moment when he starred in *Ben-Hur*, a role that earned him an Oscar. The previous year, he had been up for a Tony for playing opposite Anthony Perkins in New York in *Look Homeward, Angel* and there were plenty more plum movie roles to come too, including in *Mutiny on the Bounty*, *Tom Jones* (which got him another Oscar nomination) and *Oliver!*

Not everyone, though, appreciated the ease with which Dolphin Square and showbiz went together. In May 1950, for example, John Rankin, a shipping manager of Beatty House, divorced his wife, Angela, on the grounds of adultery with the actor Hugh McDermott – a professional golfing champion as well as prolific actor on stage and screen. But it would not be long before a more famous example of thespian shenanigans overtook the Square.

Peter Finch was born in London in 1916 but spent a large part of his childhood in France and India before moving to Australia when he was about 10. He discovered a talent for acting and by the late-1940s was a star of Australian radio and a stalwart of its burgeoning film industry. However, his life was to change in 1948 when Sir Laurence Olivier and his wife, Vivien Leigh, were touring Australia and caught Finch in a play. The Oliviers were at that point the undisputed king and queen of stage and screen in Britain. Among their many honours, she would count two Oscars (for *Gone with the Wind* and *A Streetcar Named Desire*), while he received four (for *Henry V*, two for *Hamlet* and one honorary award).

Olivier was suitably impressed by what he saw in Australia so he urged Finch to relocate to London. Finch did just that and, over the next few years, Olivier acted as a mentor to him, helping to establish him on both the stage and in the movies. Finch would end his own highly decorated career with five Baftas, a couple of Golden Globes and, in 1977, a posthumous Oscar for his role in *Network*.

Finch had married ballerina Tamara Tchinarova in 1943, and in October 1949 she gave birth to a daughter, Anita. Not long afterwards the family moved into Dolphin Square. These were exciting times for the Finches, with his growing reputation as a heavyweight actor, liked by critics and audiences alike. In 1951, he played Iago opposite Orson Welles in a West End production of *Othello* directed by the American. Early in the run, the Finches hosted a party at the Square. Finch himself arrived from the theatre when the party was already in full swing. To his surprise, among the guests was a friend from his childhood in Sydney, who had also relocated to London. It was Paul Brickhill, who was just then enjoying great acclaim for his two most recent books, *The Great Escape* and *The Dam Busters*. They raised a glass to each other, toasting 'Success! Success!' But this dream life in the Square was already on borrowed time.

It was around two o'clock on a cold January night in 1953 when the doorbell of the Finch flat rang. And rang again, and again and again. Tamara found a robe to put on and sleepily made for the door. She opened it just enough to see who was there. It was Vivien Leigh. She wore a dress of translucent white and a long mink coat and was talking in a highly animated way. Tamara let her in, then went and got her husband. The three of them sat in the living room while Leigh commended Finch's recent turn as Mercutio at the Old Vic. Then she came to the point. She was soon to start filming a movie called *Elephant Walk*. It was about a tea grower and his wife in Ceylon (Sri Lanka). She was signed up but Olivier was too exhausted to star as planned. Nor had it been possible to get Marlon Brando, Ralph Richardson or Clark Gable to stand in for him. So, she wanted Finch for the part.

Within a few weeks, Finch and Leigh were on an aeroplane headed for Ceylon. Professionally, it was a disaster from the start. Leigh was in the grip of an episode of what we now know to be bipolar disorder. Her behaviour on set was highly unpredictable and almost as soon as the cameras started to roll, she was forced to pull out. Elizabeth Taylor was brought in at short notice to replace her. But there was something going on between Leigh and Finch – a chemistry that neither was able to resist. Finch recognised that he owed a large part of his career to Olivier, but on this trip he embarked on an affair with Leigh, and they weren't particularly discreet. The press were soon on to it, and both cuckolded spouses were aware of what was going on. But the newspapers did not go public about the relationship for the time being, which just seemed to spur them on. Rather than the fire burning out, it raged stronger as 1953 turned into 1954, and 1954 into 1955. Leigh would ring Dolphin Square, leaving messages if Peter was out. She'd send cars around, too, squirrelling him off for illicit weekends away at Notley Abbey, the spectacular Olivier home in Buckinghamshire. There were more of the late-night visits to Pimlico, too. Peter would tell an obviously upset Tamara not to answer the door. Sometimes Leigh would shout and holler before finally giving up. Over Christmas 1955, Finch and Leigh even holidayed together in the south of France, while their partners remained at home.

That, however, was really the last straw. Olivier was not prepared to endure any more of the semi-public humiliation. When they were all back in England, Finch was summoned to the abbey to thrash things out. In the end, Olivier fought off his protégé's challenge. In Finch's mind, it was always an inevitability – Lady Olivier was never going to settle for giving up the title and the lifestyle to become plain Mrs Finch. But neither marriage would endure. The Oliviers parted ways in 1960, by which time the Finches had been separated for four years and divorced for one. A grand passion set alight in Dolphin Square had ended in charred remains.

Another of the Square's actors, and a friend of Olivier from the time when they were both embarking on their careers, was Nelson House resident Marjorie Fielding. She came to prominence in the West End before making a name in the movies, starring in a succession of hits from the late 1930s into the early '50s (among them, the Ealing classic, *The Lavender Hill Mob*). In early 1956, though, her name was in the papers after she fell victim to a fraudster who swindled her out of a considerable sum of money by spinning a series of hard-luck stories. A man in his forties (said to have been working with unknown confederates) was sentenced to three years for the crimes. What effect the trauma had on Fielding is not certain but she was, nonetheless, dead by the end of the year at the age of 64.

Away from performers, the post-war years also saw Dolphin Square consolidate its credentials as something of a literary salon. Angus Wilson took a lease on a one-bedroom apartment in Frobisher House in late

1948, living there with his partner, Tony Garrett. A veteran of the code-breaking operation at Bletchley Park, Wilson was always noted for his flamboyant style of dress (usually incorporating a foppish bow tie) and was open about his homosexuality both during and after the war – traits that set him apart in those grey days of awkward uprightness. But while a gay couple living openly in the Square no doubt raised eyebrows among some residents, even by then the estate was garnering a reputation for being rather more free and easy than much of the rest of the country.

In a profile piece published in *The Paris Review*, Wilson's flat was described as 'small, comfortable, tidy, uneccentric; there were books but not great heaps of them; the pictures included a pair of patriotic prints from the First World War ("The period fascinates me"). For Wilson it is just a place to stay when he has to be in London …'[4] His biographer, Margaret Drabble, saw it rather differently though, describing it as the 'height of chic' where he was able to find 'peace, privacy and independence'[5] – three attributes that surely explain the attraction of the Square to so many of its residents down through the years.

It was while he resided within the walls of Frobisher that Wilson made most of his biggest steps towards becoming a leading figure in the mid-century English literary world. An employee of the British Library by day, he published his first collection of short stories, *The Wrong Set*, in 1949, and subsequently wrote the three novels that made his name: *Hemlock and After* (1952); *Anglo-Saxon Attitudes* (1956); and *The Middle Age of Mrs Eliot* (1958).

Other leading literary lights of the day seeking that same 'peace, privacy and independence' included C.P. Snow, a physicist by training and a senior civil servant by profession (and yet another of the locals to be listed in the Nazis' 'black book'), best known for his *Strangers and Brothers* cycle of novels, several of which he wrote while a Dolphinite. One of Snow's friends and civil service colleagues, Harry Hoff, also took a flat, although he is better known by his pen name, William Cooper. In particular, his 1950 novel, *Scenes from Provincial Life* – with its naturalistic dissection of Britain's social and class constructs – proved a seminal influence on several of the Angry Young Men authors who moulded the literary landscape in the 1950s and '60s, among them Kingsley Amis and John Braine.

Catherine Gaskin, meanwhile, was an aspiring 25-year-old romance novelist when she moved into the Square with her sister in 1955, but did not have to wait long before she was the toast of the London publishing world as her novel, *Sara Dane*, sold some 2 million copies after it was released that year. Three years prior to her arrival, a resident of Hood House – the German-born photographer Felix H. Man – had found himself at the centre of a landmark trial as to the very question of what could be considered art. Man had helped pioneer the discipline of photojournalism, particularly in his work with the *Picture Post*, and over his career photographed countless leading political and cultural figures, including Mussolini, Clement Attlee, Henry Moore and Evelyn Waugh. In 1952, he sued a painter for selling a canvas he had created that took inspiration from one of Man's photographs. Man claimed his copyright had been infringed, but the judge found for the defendant, arguing that the two works were sufficiently different that the painting could not be regarded as a copy. During the trial, Professor Rodrigo Moynihan of the Royal College of Art scandalised Man by stating in evidence, 'After all, a photograph is not a work of art.'[6] It was a tough trial for Man, but offered further evidence that the Square was a significant location in terms of the cultural zeitgeist.

Then there was Quentin Crewe of Hawkins House, who cut a memorable figure and left a slightly unexpected but nonetheless enduring imprint on the nation's literary landscape. The flat where he lived was leased by Crewe's father, a career diplomat. Crewe's deceased mother had been the daughter of the Marquess of Crewe, and his half-brother was Terence O'Neill, who would serve as Northern Ireland's prime minister for much of the 1960s. Quentin, though, was a thoroughbred rebel. Having been diagnosed with muscular dystrophy as a child, he was subsequently expelled from Eton and sent down from Cambridge. Then, as a young man in London, he embarked on an affair with Sarah Macmillan, daughter of Dorothy Macmillan (herself the daughter of the Duke of Devonshire) and the future Conservative prime minister, Harold Macmillan (although the rumour mill has always wondered whether Macmillan's Tory colleague, Bob Boothby – a man no stranger to scandal, not least through his association with the Krays and his decades-long affair with Lady Dorothy – was actually her father).

By the age of 29, Crewe was wheelchair-bound as a result of his long-term illness and in 1956 he embarked on the first of his three marriages. A journalist of some reputation, arguably his greatest contribution to the field happened by lucky circumstance. In the 1960s he was working for *Queen* magazine when one day a half-page needed filling at short notice. Crewe saved the day by filing a review of the lunch he'd just had at a place called Wilton's in St James's. He took the opportunity not simply to critique the food but to dissect the establishment itself and all that it offered. Among his observations was that the clientele largely consisted of aristocratic types happy to eat the same sort of food they were once fed in nursery, all served up by waitresses dressed like their nannies. He also memorably likened Wilton's prices to death duties. A new style of culinary criticism was born.

In her memoirs, the writer and historian Lady Antonia Fraser recalled a party of Crewe's she attended at the Square in 1953. At the time, she was Antonia Pakenham, the daughter of Lord Longford, who gained notoriety for his representations on behalf of, among others, Myra Hindley, the 'Moors Murderer'. Fraser recalled as a young girl seeing her father lying in bed at their Oxford home in May 1936, nursing his bruised and injured body. He had, she came to learn, been beaten up by a posse of Oswald Mosley's Blackshirts at a meeting at Oxford's town hall. According to Longford, as he was attacked, Mosley watched on from the platform 'like Napoleon on a hillock while the battle proceeded on the plain'.

It was a crime against her father that his young daughter could not shrug off. Then, around the time that she came to London after graduating from Oxford, she found herself at one of Crewe's 'genial and generous' soirees, which he was co-hosting with his brother Colin. There, she was appalled to find Oswald and Diana Mosley, she 'with her terrifyingly perfect beauty', sat on a sofa in the living room. Discreetly but firmly, Pakenham refused any engagement with the man she remembered from her childhood causing her father so much pain. But when Mosley came to leave, he cornered her. 'Ah yes, Miss Pakenham,' he said with a twinkle in his eye. 'I'm so sorry we didn't talk. As your father said to me at lunch today … we were having lunch at the Ritz. Did you know?' Pakenham immediately decoded his words – her father, who so publicly preached on the themes of mercy and forgiveness, had long ago made peace with the bogeyman of her infancy.[7] It should perhaps not have come as a great surprise, given that Longford was the most famous advocate for penal reform of the age and the Mosleys had spent three years in controversial detention during the war.

The scene that Fraser recalled speaks of both the lightness and darkness that have been permanent facets of life in the Square. And while the 1950s as a whole saw the light in Pimlico begin to overcome the shadows of its earlier decades, there were still plenty of dim and shady corners in which murkiness reigned.

8

IN THE SHADOWS

Russel Braddon was an alumnus of the 1950s Dolphin Square literati. Born in Sydney, Australia, he'd served in Malaya during the war and spent much of his early twenties held as a POW and working on the notorious Thailand–Burma Railway. In common with many others who suffered as POWs in that region, the experience had a huge impact on his psychological well-being and he eventually attempted suicide. Seeking a new beginning, he moved to England in 1949, where he enjoyed some notable success as manager of The Piddingtons – a husband and wife mind-reading act. Braddon and Sydney Piddington had been prisoners together in the Changi POW camp in Singapore, and Braddon helped develop the act that in time topped the bill at the London Palladium. Then, partly as a means of therapy, he wrote an account of his experiences as a POW, which was published in 1952 as *The Naked Island*. It sold a million copies and set Braddon off on a notable literary career. He also happened to be gay and it is in that context that an account of a mugging he was subjected to in 1955 should be considered.

In November of that year, he had been lecturing in Wolverhampton and was in the environs of the railway station at around midnight when he was set upon by two men who stole a watch, some personal papers and his wallet containing £15. They left him with cuts to his face and head that required hospital treatment. According to Braddon, he had been at the station enquiring about trains but given the late hour of the day, that seems doubtful. Perhaps more likely was that he had gone to the station to seek companionship. In common with countless other gay men of the time, Braddon knew that his sexuality left him vulnerable to both the law and the opprobrium of others. Physical peril and the threat of exposure were daily burdens.

Engineering covert sexual encounters with strangers thus became an unavoidable feature in the lives of countless gay men. But the danger in such action was palpable, as the earlier case of Robert Wilton had proved. Even by the time that Braddon died in 1995, forty years after his mugging, the stigma of being gay remained sufficiently strong (despite the decriminalisation of homosexual consensual acts in 1967) that his obituaries largely avoided the fact that he was gay, even including one written by the man who had been the first of his three long-term partners.[1]

Throughout its history, the Square had been a battlefield between champions of social progressiveness and personal liberty and those of a rather more conservative bent. The tension between doing what one wants to do and what one is expected to do has run like a thread through the decades, its frayed ends sometimes coming to the surface and unravelling. Occasionally, as we have already seen, personal lives at the Square spiralled out of control with devastating consequences.

In 1947, for example, there were celebrations for the extravagantly named Sir Vivian Tyrell Champion de Crespigny, who had a flat in Keyes House. The occasion was his remarriage to his first wife, Helen Whitehead (née Dobb), whom he'd originally wed in 1930. They'd had a daughter together, Fleur (born in 1937), but had divorced in 1940 and each made an unsuccessful second marriage before deciding to give things a second go with each other. The joy, though, was short-lived. They divorced for a second time in 1951 – it was alleged that she had committed adultery with an army major – and he committed suicide the following year, aged just 44. A military man, de Crespigny was discovered in his room in the officers' mess on Pulau Brani, an island off Singapore. He had been due to face a court martial a few days later on charges of drunkenness.

Another resident of the Square, Commander David Clark of the Royal Navy, found it was his turn to have his private life unpicked in May 1952, when he was embroiled in a court action that must have caused him acute embarrassment and served as a cautionary tale to others. It was a classic case, repeated in essence many times over the years, of a man relying on the privacy offered by the Square to behave indiscreetly, only to find that his behaviour had rendered him vulnerable. In the case of the commander, he found himself the victim of a serious fraud worth several hundred pounds committed by a woman, Ann Bardsley, with whom he was conducting an affair, and her accomplice, a variety artiste called Derek Hollies.

In evidence, Clark admitted that he had been intimate with Bardsley on and off since 1937, at her flats in Brighton and London and also in Dolphin Square. In the course of their association, he said, he had given her many presents. Bardsley, who the press noted had arrived at court 'wearing 6in. high heels and nylon stockings', had some fifty convictions for prostitution and, it would emerge, was on intimate terms with the prosecution's three star witnesses.

Bardsley and Hollies seem to have come up with a ruse whereby he impersonated her solicitor, ringing Clark during his working day at the Admiralty and convincing him to transfer sums of money to cover, for instance, her mortgage or stamp duty payments due on her Brighton property. Clark admitted to feeling ill at ease with this sort of extracurricular contact at his place of employment. Both defendants were found guilty and imprisoned, but Clark no doubt paid his own heavy price as the details of his private life were laid bare in the public arena.[2]

In the same year, another resident, Edyth Frediewide, was revealed as the victim of an even crueller deception. She had been manipulated since 1946 by a man – a Canadian electrical engineer – who persuaded her that they were in love and that she should leave her husband for him, which she duly did. He then proceeded to defraud her of several thousand pounds on false pretences, before eventually his crimes were exposed and he was sentenced to three years in prison. She, meanwhile, was left to try to reassemble the fragments of her life.[3]

The newspapers of the period suggest that criminality of many different types was a consistent spectre in the Square. There had been a particularly nasty incident in February 1947 when a Captain Brye and his wife, of Hawkins House, interrupted a late-night burglary at their flat. Returning from an evening out, they noticed their front door ajar and so the captain retreated downstairs in order to phone the police. As he did so, a man emerged from the apartment carrying a fur coat and assorted jewellery, and armed with a jemmy and a razor. He and the captain met in the stairwell and a fight ensured that had them rolling down the stairs. In the melee, Brye received a long cut to the left side of his face that narrowly missed his eye before the thief made good his escape.[4]

An altogether stranger affair was reported in 1948 when it emerged that Group Captain Leonard Cheshire – a celebrated Bomber Command pilot who received the Victoria Cross after his participation in the dam-buster raids and who was Britain's designated observer when the atomic bomb was dropped on Nagasaki in 1945 – had sold two Mosquito aircraft to a Harold White of Dolphin Square. Cheshire could not get the aircraft certified airworthy by the Ministry of Civil Aviation but seems to have kept 'one for work' and the other for 'spares' before opting to sell them on. The saga attracted the attention of the papers, not least because the ministry no longer had any idea where the aircraft were. Although, not even the expansive Dolphin Square car park had room enough to park up a pair of Mosquitos without some-one noticing.[5]

Then, in the autumn of 1950, there was a one-man crime wave when Scotland Yard revealed their belief that a lone individual was responsible for a spate of twenty-seven burglaries in the Square within a five-week window. It was suggested that this slickest of thieves could empty a four-bedroom apartment of its valuables in two minutes – a level of dexterity that ensured he evaded capture even after the Met's appeal for help in finding him. A less-accomplished criminal was the window cleaner sentenced to six months in 1953 for various petty thefts, including £10 stolen from the Australian test batsman Arthur Morris – a member of Don Bradman's 1948 'Invincibles' – who was staying at the flats during that year's Aussie test series.[6]

Another case of interest occurred in 1952, when 49-year-old Clive Ley of Nelson House appeared on charges of fraud in relation to a company of which he was a director.[7] The fascination, though, was more to do with the defendant's father than Ley's own legal troubles, since he was the son of the Honourable Thomas Ley, a former Minister of Justice in New South Wales – and a man with whom the tag 'honourable' did not rest easy.

Ley Snr was born in Bath in 1880 and moved with his mother to Australia when he was about 8. He began a career in local politics while in his twenties and quickly climbed the slippery political pole, heading up the New South Wales justice ministry in 1922. Three years later, he won a seat in the Federal Parliament but was accused of bribery by his opponent, Frederick McDonald. Here is where the intrigue really begins. McDonald subsequently disappeared, prompting rumours that Ley – popularly known as 'Lemonade' Ley for his advocacy of temperance – had a hand in his murder. These allegations were, it should be said, never proven in a court of law. But there was further talk that other rivals had also fallen foul of him. Firstly, an outspoken legislator called Hyman Goldstein was found dead in 1928 at the foot of a notorious suicide spot in Australia. Then Keith Greedor, who had once been on reasonable terms with Ley but who had then been hired to investigate his business practices, drowned when he mysteriously fell overboard from a boat.

After electoral defeat in 1928, Ley decided it was time to return to England, which he did in the company of his lover Maggie Brook, with whom he'd had an adulterous affair for the best part of a quarter of a century. His wife, meanwhile, remained in Australia. Back in Britain, Ley made a small fortune from various dubious ventures but it did not prove a recipe for happiness. In 1946, he became convinced that Brook was engaged in an affair with a barman called John Mudie. With the help of two associates, who were persuaded that Mudie was a blackmailer, Ley murdered his love rival and threw the body into a Surrey chalk pit. The case, known in the press as 'The Chalk-Pit Murder', caused a sensation and Ley, along with one of his accomplices, was sentenced to death at the Old Bailey in March 1947. He was, however, subsequently declared of unsound mind and sent to Broadmoor Asylum for the Criminally Insane instead. He died the same year from a cerebral haemorrhage, having supposedly acquired the dubious honour of being Broadmoor's wealthiest ever inmate. One effect of his unhappy legacy was to ensure that his son's criminal exploits five years later seemed rather half-hearted in comparison.

Dolphin Square also suffered at least two mysterious instances of 'bodies in the bath' in the 1950s. The first occurred in December 1953, when the body of 30-year-old RAF officer Flight Lieutenant John Leslie Walrond Innes was found in the bath of the flat belonging to his father-in-law, Air Vice Marshal Sir Conrad Collier. After a distinguished RAF career, Collier had served as an air attaché in Moscow and was knighted in 1947. Innes had married Collier's daughter, Elspeth, some eight years earlier but she was at the flat they shared elsewhere in London at the time of her husband's death.

A second bath death was reported in May 1956, involving Clarissa Barrow, a retired civil servant and by all accounts a quiet and unassuming woman, who was discovered dead in her Hawkins House flat, her body still clothed. It was thought that she had lain in her bath for some six weeks before she was discovered. A post-mortem concluded that she died from natural causes, although the pathologist was reported to have said that he could not rule out foul play. Her neighbours were also questioned, with the police refusing to dismiss the possibility that she had been murdered.

But perhaps the most intriguing criminal drama connected to the Square in this era played out in 1957, when one of its most prominent political figures, Hartley Shawcross, found himself caught up in what had the potential to become a fully fledged public scandal. He was at the time the Labour MP for St Helens in Lancashire and was a barrister by profession. He had been a prosecuting counsel at the Nuremberg Trials, where his precise, forensic style was widely celebrated. 'There comes a point,' he famously told the court, 'when a man must refuse to answer to his leader if he is also to answer to his own conscience.' He also served as Attorney General from 1945 to 1951, overseeing many significant trials, including that of William Joyce, Lord Haw-Haw.

In 1957, a south coast doctor, John Bodkin-Adams, faced trial for murdering one of his patients – a legal action that captivated the nation. There were strong suspicions that this was but the tip of the iceberg and that Bodkin-Adams was in fact a serial killer. He has long been suspected of killing an unspecified number of patients by lethal injection, many of whom left him gifts in their wills – those who believe him guilty have suggested the number of his victims was likely in three figures. The question of the extent of his crimes (and, indeed, his guilt) remains a hotly debated subject, but it is possible that Bodkin-Adams had no murderous rival until the crimes of Harold Shipman were exposed in the late 1990s. Yet while some experts are convinced that he was a cold-blooded murderer and fraudster, others have instead questioned his competency or suggested he was an 'angel of death', dispensing eternal sleep to those already dying – much as George V's doctor had done. But the very thought that an avuncular doctor, the type people literally trusted their lives with every single day, was taking it upon himself to end the lives of his patients caused a minor earthquake in British society.

In the event, Bodkin-Adams was controversially acquitted on that single count of murder at his Old Bailey trial in 1957. But Shawcross's part in the drama occurred at a committal hearing in Lewes back in the January of that year. At a hotel in the town, the MP and former Attorney General had lunch with the Lord Chief Justice, Lord Goddard (who it is widely suggested also lived in Dolphin Square, although the authors have been unable to verify the fact) and a former mayor of Eastbourne, Sir Roland Gwynne. The trouble was that Gwynne was at the time the subject of rumours shared both with the local police and a *Daily Mail* journalist that he was the doctor's lover. The pair certainly had a close relationship, seeing each other daily and holidaying together. Gwynne was also Chairman of the Magistrates but stepped down from the committal hearing on the grounds of conflict of interest.

The former mayor was involved in a car accident after the hotel lunch, which brought the gathering to the attention of police and raised questions as to why a local grandee (and potential lover of a mass murderer) was meeting with the Lord Chief Justice and a former Attorney General at such a delicate stage in proceedings. In due course, Goddard pressed the trial judge to grant Bodkin-Adams bail should he be acquitted on the first charge of murder and then charged with any further deaths – a highly unusual move given that no one else facing trial for murder had ever been bailed in British judicial history. It was even more surprising given that Goddard had the reputation of being a Hanging Judge – his clerk even suggested that when passing a death sentence, Goddard had a habit of ejaculating so that it was customary for there to be a spare pair of trousers in court on such days.[8]

Whatever the truth of what was discussed at that lunch – and it seems unlikely we shall ever know – it had the effect of playing into a narrative that there was inappropriate interference in the judicial process, perhaps driven by the fear of an exposé of homosexuality in public life or by a wish to avoid such a potentially damaging blow to the reputation of the still nascent NHS. Moreover, it helped foster those links between Dolphin Square, powerful public figures and criminal cover-ups that came to haunt it in the decades to come.

9

CHAMPAGNE AND PRINCESSES

By the second half of the 1950s, life in the Square was really hitting its straps. The big-name Old Guard were still a distinct presence, but a more youthful glamour was beginning to take over. Alongside the entertainers and actors, the writers and artists, there were also a number of significant musicians to add a touch of cool. Among them was Harry Hayes – a stalwart of the British jazz scene in the period – who lived in the Square with his wife, Primrose, a singer. As an alto saxophonist, he had played with many of the giants of American jazz, among them Louis Armstrong, Oscar Peterson, Benny Carter, Lester Young and Ella Fitzgerald. Throughout the 1940s, he was regularly to be seen in one major London venue or another, either as a bandleader in his own right or playing with Geraldo's legendary dance band. Into the 1950s, he remained a man in demand, not least as an integral part of the Kenny Baker Dozen, and had strong associations with the Churchill Club in particular. (Incidentally, many years later, in 1977, a Dolphinite called Leslie Botibol was the licence holder for Churchill's. He was charged with knowingly allowing the club to be 'the habitual resort of reputed prostitutes'.) Yet Hayes was not the only jazz aristocrat in residence. Nat Temple, the celebrated clarinettist and saxophonist – who would be described by *The Guardian* on his death in 2008 as 'the last of the great British showmen bandleaders and the closest to being the British Benny Goodman' – also had an apartment. Among his many notable achievements, he was the first British musician to play the famous clarinet intro to George Gershwin's 'Rhapsody in Blue', in a concert at the Royal Albert Hall conducted by Malcom Sargent. For the time being, these were the sort of figures who continued to provide the soundtrack to London's nightlife, with rock 'n' roll still yet to entirely take over.

One can imagine how exciting an evening at the Square's restaurant or cocktail bar would have been in this period. Which celebrities might be passing through? Might one or two even offer up some informal entertainment – a song or a skit to delight the crowd? All set against the Square's spectacular backdrop, its art deco grandeur adorned with delightful artwork – such as the 90ft-long and 7ft-deep swimming pool mural depicting the Thames from Hampton Court to Woolwich, designed in 1937 by the celebrated artist and designer Edward Halliday (a favourite of the queen, whom he painted; he counted among his other sitters Churchill and Edmund Hillary). There were two more murals by him in the milk bar and cocktail bar, too, depicting 'Seaside Today and Yesteryear', alongside other work by talented if lesser-known artists like Robin Mackertich. Halliday had also been responsible for the uniforms of the house dance band, who entertained guests with a classy musical roster that included the specially written 'Dolphin Waltz'.

In January 1956, a dose of royal sparkle was thrown into the Dolphin Square mix. Nineteen-year-old Princess Beatrix of Hohenlohe-Langenburg and 22-year-old Princess Christina of Hess, both nieces of Prince Philip, the Duke of Edinburgh, took an apartment in the Square – one that their uncle had prepared with furnishings from Windsor Castle.

Their presence sparked excitement not only among the other residents but in the press too. It was also a signal of a desire within the British Establishment to move on from the turmoil of the 1940s and to heal some war wounds. Beatrix's mother was Princess Margarita of Greece and Denmark, elder sister of Prince Philip. Her father, though, was Gottfried, Prince of Hohenlohe-Langenburg, who had been a German officer on the Russian Front (although, to his credit in the eyes of the Allies, he was subsequently implicated in an albeit failed attempt to assassinate Hitler in July 1944). Christina's mother, meanwhile, was Philip's sister, Princess Sophie of Greece and Denmark, while her father was Prince Christoph Ernst of Hesse, nephew to

Kaiser Wilhelm II and an SS officer until he was killed in a plane crash in 1943.

Where ten years previously it would have been unthinkable that the two princesses could come to London to set up home, they were now warmly welcomed, their family histories hardly mentioned. They arrived as students, Beatrix of dressmaking and Christina of art history – rich, well-connected students, admittedly, but young women engaging with London life on their own terms. However, it was soon evident that they did not intend to be at their books all hours.

In April 1956, it was reported that Christina had become engaged to Yugoslavia's exiled Prince Andrej, with the wedding scheduled for August.[1] In the meantime, as was required for the marriage to go ahead, she was accepted into the Serbian Orthodox Church in a formal ceremony at the Cathedral of St Sava in Bayswater in the May. (The marriage, sadly, proved unsuccessful and culminated in divorce in 1962. Christina was accused of adultery with Dutch artist Robert van Eyck. Custody of her two children was awarded to their father, Andrej.)

Then, on 24 June 1956, the *Sunday Pictorial* ran a story on Beatrix's twentieth birthday party, held at her flat:

> Girls in satin jeans and low-necked sweaters canoodled with bearded students on antique furniture from Windsor Castle at a party thrown by Princess Beatrix. The nineteen-year-old princess … kicked off her red sandals and lay on a divan surrounded by boyfriends in her flat in Dolphin Square. Students in anything from swim suits to riding kit jived through the three rooms. Gate-crashers were thrown out by three Muscle-Men. A party of Teddy Boys and their girlfriends from Fulham were thrown out after a skirmish. But they started a rival party across the corridor … Doors banged, bells rang. Porters were bringing complaints from tenants of other flats …[2]

There was also a rumour that the royal pair had a hand in filling the swimming pool with detergent on one occasion. The Princesses of Pimlico had made their mark.

Donald Campbell brought a different kind of style, and a distinct sense of danger, when the speed record breaker took up residence in

Duncan House, also in 1956. He followed in the supersonic steps of his father Malcolm, who had held a slew of land and water speed records in the 1920s and '30s. By the time Donald moved on after three years in Pimlico, he had three world water speed records to his name, earned in his famous *Bluebird K7*. A superstitious fellow, he'd been upset by his Dolphin Square door number when he arrived. It was 805, the digits of which add up to unlucky 13, so he was granted permission to have it renumbered as 811. It seemed to do the trick for a time, as he went on to break a total of eight world speed records and, in 1964, became the first and only person to break the land and water records in the same year. But his good fortune tragically ran out on 4 January 1967 when, during another record attempt, *Bluebird* crashed and sank on Coniston Water in the Lake District and Campbell was drowned.

Two tenants who moved in as the decade drew to a close proved that not all princesses are born to their station; some claw their way up from the streets and earn their tiaras the hard way. One such example was Shirley Bassey, who had a flat in Rodney House as of January 1959. It was an exciting time for the 'Girl from Tiger Bay' – Cardiff's notoriously rough docks neighbourhood from where she hailed. At the time she joined the ranks of the Pimlico elite, she was enjoying her first Number One single, 'As I Love You', which spent four weeks at the top of the charts. At the same time, another of her tracks, 'Kiss Me, Honey Honey, Kiss Me', was also scaling the hit parade, and the songs would soon occupy two of the top three slots.

Yet it was not all champagne and adulation. Also in that January, Bassey was given a £2 fine – easily covered by the royalties rolling in just then, it can be presumed – after her beloved miniature poodle, Beaujolais, was found to have fouled the streets on a trip to Leicester.[3] But there was rather worse to come. The following month, Bassey returned one night to her apartment in Dolphin Square to find it ransacked, the phone line cut, and a passport, furs and jewellery worth £1,000 missing. The police, it was reported, were unable to find any sign of forced entry, but there was good reason for this. The thefts were committed by her private secretary, David Gilmour, who had stolen the goods in order to pay off a blackmailer who was threatening to reveal his homosexuality. He was subsequently arrested and charged but when he appeared at Bow Street Magistrates, the judge commended Bassey's generosity for agreeing to retain the services of Gilmour and even to pay his costs.[4] (As a side note, in 1964, Bassey would split from her then husband, Kenneth Hume, after she had an affair with the by-then ex-Dolphinite, Peter Finch. Finch would be cited as a co-respondent in her divorce the following year. Small world.)

Another of the era's pre-eminent British 'glamour-pusses' also moved in to the Square in 1959. Diana Dors took a six-room apartment with her then new husband, Dickie Dawson. Dors, still only 27 years old, was already a veteran of the British entertainment scene, and one who had undergone several reinventions. In the early part of the decade, she had been sold as 'Britain's Marilyn Monroe' ('Until I appeared,' Dors recalled in 1979, 'sex was a dirty word and the most cinema audiences had seen was [former Dolphinite] Margaret Lockwood and some very ample cleavage in *The Wicked Lady* ...').[5] Although Monroe-esque levels of international stardom always eluded her, she was nonetheless a figure of enduring fascination for the British public, and 1959 was one of those years that marked the turning of a new page in her career.

Born as Diana Fluck in Swindon in 1931, Dors started her movie career as a 15-year-old, going on to appear in a string of mostly unremarkable movies. But with her striking looks and sound acting skills, not least in comedy, her star was on the rise – she received good notices not only for her work on the screen but on the stage, too. Then, in 1951, on the set of a film called *Lady Godiva Rides Again*, she met Denis Hamilton. After a whirlwind romance, they were married within weeks and he gradually assumed control of her career. He was intent on turning her into the next Monroe, but he was a volatile personality with questionable judgement and their relationship strayed into the region of abusive co-dependency.

In 1956, Dors enjoyed one of her greatest critical successes in *Yield to the Night*, in which she played a character with echoes of Ruth Ellis – the last woman to be hanged in Britain after shooting dead her lover in 1955. (Curiously enough, Ellis had appeared very briefly in *Lady Godiva Rides Again* four years earlier.) Now Dors at last got the call from Hollywood. She and Hamilton went over to America but things soon went seriously awry. After making the movie *I Married a*

Woman for the RKO film company, she signed up for a further three movies. The first of these was *The Unholy Wife*, which she was due to start filming (with Rod Steiger as the male lead) before the end of 1956. But as she attempted to get a foothold in Los Angeles, she and Hamilton appeared incapable of remaining faithful to each other. In fact, Dors now counted Steiger among her lovers, to Hamilton's utter fury. There was a PR disaster, too, when Dors was accidentally pushed into a swimming pool at a meet-the-press party after a surge by the assembled photographers. Hamilton responded by grabbing the nearest photographer and beating him up. Meanwhile, numerous film projects were discussed and debated but came to nothing. By the end of the year, she was back in Britain and announcing that she and Hamilton were to split.

Her American dream was not yet entirely over, though, and she continued a transatlantic lifestyle for a while. But in December 1958, RKO terminated her contract, citing their belief that she 'has become an object of disgrace, obloquy, ill will and ridicule'. With her career in a slump, a divorce in the offing and her finances all over the place, she had started touring an eponymously titled cabaret show around the UK earlier that year. It was during this time that she first met Dawson, an Anglo-American entertainer who was brought in to work on the show's scripts.

The year 1959 got off to a terrible start when Hamilton died at the end of January, aged just 32. Dors was back in the US filming a television show at the time. Although the papers suggested he was suffering from a heart complaint, it was in fact syphilis that killed him. If that were not traumatic enough, Dors was also left to pick up the hefty burden of debt that he – still legally her husband – had left behind.

But it was a case of the Dors show going on. In April she married Dawson in New York and was back in London in May to record a series of *The Diana Dors Show* for television. Although she had a home in Sussex, it was likely the need to be in London for this series that prompted the newly-weds to take their Dolphin Square apartment. At about the same time, Dors fell pregnant with her first child, Mark, who was born the following February. *The Diana Dors Show* ran for two series and helped to pay some bills, but it was not the roaring success she might have hoped – *The Guardian* rather cruelly brandished it 'vapid and amateurish beyond belief'.[6] The ever-game Dors and her husband nonetheless set about raising their joint profile, notching up several appearances together on *Juke Box Jury*. But there was more scandal in the offing.

For one thing, while she was living in the Square, she was also preparing to sue RKO for defamation after her acrimonious split with them. (She sued for over £1 million but in the end agreed on a pay-off somewhere closer to £200,000.) Moreover, she had agreed to write her memoirs and spent a portion of the latter part of the year conducting a tabloid auction for serialisation rights – a battle won by the *News of the World* for a figure rumoured to be £36,000. For that kind of money, Dors was expected to provide something really juicy and she did not disappoint. Her book was published under the title *Swingin' Dors*, with the tagline 'I've been a naughty girl'. The recollections of her life with Hamilton were tawdry, encompassing 'sex parties' (that beloved staple of the Sunday papers at the time), which were said to have included such technical devices as one-way mirrors and microphones in bedrooms to cater for the needs of particularly voyeuristic guests. 'There were no half measures at my parties,' she said. 'Off came the sweaters, bras and panties. In fact, it was a case of off with everything – except the lights … Every night was party night.'[7] It is difficult to imagine that she would have made such admissions were it not for the financial pressures on her. But flashy homes in Sussex and a Dolphin Square pied-à-terre didn't come cheap.

If Dors had hoped that the Square might bring some respite from the chaos and drama of her life, her stint there in 1959 must be considered a failure. Instead, the turmoil only increased, much of it as a result of her own lifestyle. It certainly did not give her the platform to resurrect her Hollywood aspirations (which all but disappeared as the 1960s got into full swing) or to build a solid relationship with her new husband after the disaster of her first marriage (she and Dawson would divorce in 1966). But while Dolphin Square was not able to provide her with peace, she was able to supply it with a peculiarly British type of glitz and glamour.

She was neither the first nor the last to discover that the Square, for all that it can provide anonymity and privacy, cannot make your problems disappear. That it was a place to run to but not necessarily hide was a theme revisited in spectacular style by several of its most notorious residents in the 1960s – a decade in which the Square served as the stage for several era-defining public dramas.

10

'YOU HAVE TO PLAY IT COOL, REAL COOL, MAN'

In June 1960, Wing Commander Sir Norman John Hulbert, the 57-year-old Conservative MP for Stockport North, opted not to contest his wife's divorce petition. The grounds of the petition were that Hulbert had committed adultery with another woman at Dolphin Square.

It was the end of his second marriage. He would wed again in 1962, and that too would be dissolved, although a fourth marriage endured until his death in 1972. His visits to the divorce courts warranted a paragraph or two in the newspapers but it was hardly the stuff of public outrage. Sexual mores were changing and the bed-hopping antics of a middle-ranking MP were not about to cause a rupture in the social fabric.

However, in 1963 Hulbert would find his name hauled once more before the court of public opinion, and this time he would not emerge so unscathed. His crime was to have made a complaint in the House against the BBC's epoch-defining satirical comedy show, *That Was the Week That Was* (*TW3*), which had launched at the end of 1962 with David Frost at the helm.

The item that particularly incensed Hulbert was one in which Winston Churchill's age (he was then 88) was gently mocked, and in which were listed the names of thirteen MPs who had yet to speak in the Commons since the previous general election in 1959. 'I submit,' he told the House, 'that this performance – if one can call it so – was not only an unwarranted attack on the hon. Members I have mentioned, but that certain suggestions which were made were really holding up the House of Commons to ridicule.'[1]

Hulbert had obliviously revealed himself as a man increasingly out of step with his time. The essence of his complaint was that the BBC, in its role as a politically independent public broadcaster, had not shown Parliament the due deference that until very recently had been a given. He had lived in a world in which those with an elevated social position were automatically accorded respect throughout the ranks of society, at least until they had very publicly done something to undermine it. But the expectation that those in positions of power and privilege should be granted unquestioning loyalty and trust was fast diminishing. Where had it got people, after all? A century scarred by two world wars, economic depression, mass unemployment, a new cold war and spy scandals?

When Harold Macmillan came to power in 1957, he told the public that they'd never had it so good. It was true that things were broadly on the up, but it had been a long time coming and was patchy anyway. And if you came from the sort of background Macmillan had, things tended to be pretty good anyway. The same too for Hulbert, who no doubt found a place like Dolphin Square a most agreeable location for a bit of extra-marital hanky-panky. But there was a generation coming up that was not prepared to simply nod through the status quo, entrusting their futures into the hands of the same old people from the same social elites – a ruling class that had led them and their parents through decades of hardship and sacrifice – just because the pendulum was currently on an upswing through the economic cycle.

At least some of Hulbert's parliamentary colleagues had the good sense to treat his rant against *TW3* for what it was worth, chuckling their way through his wrath. The Speaker, too, ruled that the episode in question did not amount to an unacceptable affront. The public, meanwhile, reacted to news of Hulbert's intervention with disdain. Where the 1950s had seen the social contract gradually, almost imperceptibly, reconfiguring, the pace of change accelerated virtually the moment the 1960s arrived. Hulbert belonged to the old Britain and programmes like *TW3* would hold up the ruling class to scrutiny in a way that, as we shall see, had profound consequences for the reputation of Dolphin Square and several of its residents.

Within the Square itself, the transition from old to new guard continued, with the contrast between the two growing ever starker. Among the new 'old faces' to arrive were Ben Lyon and his wife, Bebe Daniels, who took an apartment in Keyes House. The American-born Lyon had been a Hollywood leading man in the 1920s, playing up against legendary female stars including Pola Negri, Gloria Swanson and Jean Harlow. In 1930, he married Daniels, herself a box-office heavyweight, having become Harold Lloyd's 'leading lady' when still a teenager and with mega-hits such as 1929's *Rio Rita* to her name.

Both remained in high demand throughout the 1930s, and in the '40s Lyon branched out to become a successful studio executive, too. His golden touch saw him sign up a young Marilyn Monroe to 20th Century Fox in 1946. But by then, Lyon and Daniels were spending most of their time based in London, establishing themselves as stars of the British wireless, first in *Hi, Gang!* (which also starred Dolphinite Vic Oliver) and then in *Life with the Lyons*, which latterly transferred to television and even inspired a couple of movies.

Sadly, Daniels suffered a stroke in 1963, around the time the couple moved into the Square, and they largely retreated from public life. After a second stroke, she died in their Keyes flat in 1971, with Lyon moving out shortly afterwards. In a sense, they belonged much more with the Bud Flanagans and Vic Olivers who'd arrived in the 1950s – enjoying the twilight years of careers built in the 1920s, '30s and '40s – than with the Basseys and Dors and the other bright young things who'd arrived more recently.

The year 1960 saw another intriguing newcomer to the Square. Sarah Churchill, the actor–daughter of Winston Churchill and the first wife of Dolphinite Vic Oliver, moved into Hawkins House. Sarah and Oliver had married in 1936, reputedly to the unhappiness of her parents who considered him an unlikely prospect to bring her contentment. They may have had a point, as the couple divorced in 1945 – by which time Sarah had established herself as a significant presence on the English stage and was starting to make it in the movies too (a career she built despite having joined the Women's Auxiliary Air Force during the war).

But even as she enjoyed professional success, her private life was deeply troubled. She had always possessed a rebellious streak (her family called her 'Mule' on account of her stubbornness) and she spent much of her life attempting to escape her illustrious origins. In addition, tragedy stalked her. Towards the end of her marriage to Oliver, for instance, she had an ill-starred affair with John Winant, the US ambassador to the UK – at a time, of course, when her father was trying to win a war and the ambassador was meant to be helping him. When the relationship broke down, Winant – who was also struggling with financial problems and setbacks in his career – spiralled into depression and killed himself in 1947.

In 1949, she married the British photographer Antony Beauchamp without the knowledge of her parents and began a new life with him in Los Angeles. Her career went into overdrive, culminating in a starring role as Fred Astaire's love interest in the 1951 movie *Royal Wedding*. But in real life, her marriage was failing and she separated from Beauchamp after just a few years. In August 1957, she was back in London and preparing to see Beauchamp to request a divorce. On the morning that they were to meet, Clementine Churchill rang her daughter to tell her that Beauchamp had killed himself with an overdose of barbiturates.

By 1960, Sarah was at Dolphin Square, as was her cousin, Sarah Spencer-Churchill, who was married to Colin Crewe, the brother of journalist Quentin Crewe. Churchill, though, was now embroiled in another failing relationship – this time with alcohol. Her friends and family were largely in agreement – when she was sober, she was charming and great company. But when she was drunk, it was a different matter. She was still working, but her career was some way from the glory days when she shared top billing with Astaire. In February 1960, for example, she started a run in Gloria Russell's play *The Night Life of a Virile Potato* at Hammersmith's Lyric Theatre. There were money troubles too, and the father whose approval she eternally sought was becoming a shell of whom he had once been.

Sarah had a number of convictions for drunkenness before she ever came to the Square, but run-ins with the local police were an increasingly regular feature of her life in Pimlico. On 6 July 1960 she was charged after being found drunk in Grosvenor Square, Westminster. Less than a week later, on 12 July, she was back in court, this time for being drunk in Ebury Street, Victoria, where she had been found trying to direct traffic in the middle of the night while barefoot. For these two offences, she was fined. She received a similar punishment in June 1961 for being drunk and disorderly in Brighton. The following month, she was picked up once more, again for being drunk and disorderly, this time in Lupus Street, just around the corner from Dolphin Square. At that stage, she was remanded into the custody of Holloway Prison's hospital wing for ten days, during which she was to be the subject of medical reports. She was not an alcoholic, she told the hospital doctors, 'but things had happened that had built my resentment so high – that I could give way to hate – but I didn't. I just drank sometimes instead.'[2]

Whatever help the doctors might have suggested to her, it didn't work. In the August, she was back to her old tricks – charged with being drunk and disorderly in Claverton St, Pimlico. On this occasion, the charge was withdrawn, as she was out on a pass from hospital and it was thought best that she be returned into the hands of her doctors. But it proved only a temporary reprieve. Early in September, an interim injunction was granted in favour of the Dolphin Square landlords to restrain her from 'throwing bottles or leaving broken bottles, or breaking bottles and leaving broken glass in the public parts of Dolphin Square'.[3] The head porter had complained that on 28 and 30 August, she had broken milk and tonic water bottles on her corridor in Hawkins House and left the broken glass on the floor. A week later, Churchill announced that she would be giving up her flat the following month.

A few months later, in April 1962, Churchill wed for the third time. Her groom was Thomas Touchet-Jesson, the 23rd Baron Audley. Her parents were reportedly delighted and Sarah at last seemed to have found the man who could help make her happy. But there was more heartache to come. On 3 July 1963, just fifteen months after their wedding, he died of a heart attack while staying at the Alhambra Palace Hotel in Grenada, Spain. He was just 49 years old.

In the way of Dolphin Square, where interconnectedness seems hardwired into its fabric, Sarah Churchill's eponymous ancestor, the Duchess of Marlborough (1660–1744) was portrayed in the BBC television series *The First Churchills* in 1969 by Susan Hampshire. Hampshire – best known for her starring role in *The Forsyte Saga* in 1967 – had meanwhile spent several of her teenage years living in the Square in Raleigh House. The young aspiring actress was rather less prone to making a spectacle of herself than the second Sarah Churchill, though. As it was later reported, she 'dared not even kiss her boyfriends goodnight outside her front door at Dolphin Square, the block of flats in which she lived with her mother. She kissed them in the lift instead.'[4]

Another member of Churchill's Dolphin Square circle was Julia Lockwood, a fellow actor and the daughter of early Dolphinite Margaret Lockwood. Julia lived in a flat replete with dolls. She was, perhaps, striving to cling on to childhood in the manner of Peter Pan, a character with whom she was self-confessedly obsessed after seeing her mother take the role at London's Scala Theatre in 1949. It was also the play for which Julia would become best known. In 1957, she played Wendy opposite her mother as Peter, and the following year she was Wendy again but this time opposite Sarah Churchill. Then, in 1959, she at last got to play Peter herself, doing so again in 1960, 1963 and 1966.

On 31 October 1960, Lockwood found herself caught up in a story in the *Daily Mirror* that pointed up the emergence of a very different sort of youth culture. The scoop was just a bit of fluff, almost certainly a stunt to garner publicity for the figures involved. It was, however, illustrative of a country where the move from one decade to the next had ushered in a dramatic and not altogether subtle change in the tone of everyday life. A land, certainly, where Sir Norman Hulbert and his ilk no longer felt so comfortable as they once had.

The key figures in the *Mirror's* story were Lockwood, an up-and-coming pop star called Vince Taylor (whom David Bowie years later would claim was the chief inspiration for his Ziggy Stardust character) and his new wife, Perin Lewis. It turned out that Taylor and Lewis (a dancer from the famous Windmill Club in Soho) had secretly married the previous summer. This was particularly surprising given that around the same time he had been publicly declaring his love for Lockwood, even visiting her in hospital as she was recovering from an operation on her tonsils. When questioned as to why he had kept his nuptials secret, he responded in the particular transatlantic slang of the moment: 'The Cats just don't want to know you when you have a wife. So you have to play it cool, real cool, man.'

Lockwood was circumspect about it all, 'Now he won't be able to say he's in love with me anymore. I can't see why he kept his marriage a secret. It seems silly.'[5]

Another Dolphinite, Ken Johnstone, was in his own way another emblem of the profound shifting of the social sands. In 1962, from an office in Beatty House, he advertised himself as the agent and manager of April Ashley, who was just then doing great business in London's theatre land. What made Ashley such a draw was that the glamorous model and actor had been assigned male at birth. After a troubled adolescence and adulthood, which included a stint with the Merchant Navy, Ashley found her way to Paris where she lived as a woman, working in the city's nightclub scene. There, she saved her money and travelled to Morocco in 1960 for pioneering gender-affirming surgery. Returning to Britain and adopting the name April Ashley, she soon found success, including an appearance in *Vogue*. Vic Oliver had met Ashley at several parties before her operation and he and his wife hosted her at Dolphin Square several times afterwards. It was never going to be straightforward for Ashley, though. In Oliver's words, 'We tried to support and protect April against the press and sometimes from her own exuberant follies.'[6] Then, in 1961, she was publicly outed as a trans woman in the *Sunday People*. By that point, she had met Arthur Corbett – who would become the 3rd Baron Rowallan – and they married in 1963. However, it was a short-lived affair and in 1970, the marriage was annulled on the grounds that Ashley was considered legally male, and therefore the marriage was not legally contracted.

Little wonder that her life story drew in the crowds, but this was a show for a modern audience. Ken Johnstone no doubt realised that his client's appeal might not extend to that generation who had been brought up on the more innocent material of the Crazy Gang, Vic Oliver, Ben Lyon and Bebe Daniels. Though from the older generation of Dolphinites, Radclyffe Hall at least might have felt vindicated.

In some respects, though, the world had not changed as much as it might have seemed. Certain age-old tensions persisted. On 6 September 1962, it was announced in several news outlets that explosives experts from the Home Office were studying a home-made bomb that had been found outside the Square. Who was responsible and what was their motivation remained unclear, although the New York-based Jewish Telegraphic Agency suggested that Jews and Israelis living in Dolphin Square may have been the target:

> Efforts had been made to suppress news of the finding of the bomb which occurred several days ago. Officials indicated it appeared the bomb had been placed by British fascists. A resident of the project, the largest block of luxury apartments in Europe, said there had been 'a lot of anti-Jewish feeling' there for some time.[7]

Thankfully, the device did not detonate. But around the same time, a couple of political bombshells were primed to go off, ripping holes through the Establishment and, for a while, putting Dolphin Square front and centre in the national consciousness.

11

BRINGING DOWN THE HOUSE: A DRAMA IN TWO ACTS

Act I

On the evening of 12 September 1962, John Vassall, a civil servant working in the Admiralty building on The Mall, was preparing to go home to his Dolphin Square bachelor flat in Hood House. He left the building by the north-west door and made to cross the road when two men in mackintoshes approached him. They flashed a warrant and then led him to their car, pushing him into the back seat and driving him away for questioning at Scotland Yard. He would not be a free man again until 1972.

Vassall was generally thought of by those who knew him as a decent sort of chap. Personable and always dressed very nattily, he was the sort of fellow whom it was difficult to dislike. He was no alpha male type, never a hint of throwing his weight around or making a scene – at work there were no complaints against his name. He didn't drink, or smoke or rev around the place in fancy cars. In essence, he was the very model of a late-mid-century public servant, and one not seemingly destined to climb much higher up the ranks. As one of his Dolphin Square neighbours, Mrs Norah St Clair Kitchin, a solicitor's wife, put it, 'We seldom saw him out. He was a perfect neighbour … Very quiet, very courteous, very polite.'[1]

But Vassall was an enigma. In certain aspects, he was pretty much exactly as he appeared to be. But he had also been living a secret life since the middle of the previous decade. As he was driven to the Yard, he told the arresting officers, 'I think I know what you are after.'[2] At the station, he was cautioned and then he told them that there were two cameras hidden in his flat, one containing a film, 'I think you will find what you are looking for in it.' He handed over a pair of keys. One of them was for the chest of drawers that stood in his bedroom and contained the cameras. But there was more. Near his wardrobe was a small corner-piece that had a concealed aperture at its base. They would find a rectangular box in the room containing a small bladed tool. They could use it to release a spring catch and remove the shelf. In the concealed aperture, they would discover rolls of film containing secret information copied from Admiralty files as recently as a few days earlier. It was reported that officers retrieved five films altogether, containing some 140 exposures. Vassall, the authorities now knew, had been spying for the Russians for years. Once caught, he made few efforts to hide the fact. It was almost as if exposure had come as a relief.

At the time of his arrest, it felt like Britain was being overrun by spies. Just the previous year, George Blake, an MI6 agent, had been unmasked as a double agent working for Moscow since the early 1950s – a crime for which he was sentenced to forty-two years in prison (he would escape from his jail in 1966 and flee to the Soviet Union). But his was not the only espionage scandal of 1961. The Portland Spy Ring had also been uncovered, further undermining public confidence that the powers that be were on top of the challenges of the Cold War. Vassall played neatly into this narrative. How was it possible that someone so seemingly unremarkable had been able to sell the nation's secrets for so long?

Vassall's flat in the Square, and what it said about his lifestyle, became important aspects of the story. Had no one wondered how a civil service clerk on £700 a year could afford an apartment in a place like Dolphin Square (the rent alone would have swallowed about half of his annual salary)? Let alone deck it out in pricey antiques, stock his wardrobe with several dozen tailored suits, dine out in London's smarter restaurants and take multiple foreign holidays each year? (In fact, those colleagues who gave the question a second thought simply assumed that he had a private income to supplement his salary.)

Vassall and his home had reportedly been under round-the-clock surveillance for weeks. 'Vassall's flat was penetrated,' reported the newspapers. 'The security team knew every detail of its contents. Some of them even played with him at Bridge parties. Vassall was completely unaware of what was happening.'[3] That last statement might have been a stretch. According to Vassall's own later recollections, he'd got an inkling that the game was nearly up several weeks prior to his arrest, when three men dressed in white overalls and carrying a ladder appeared at his front door. They said they were there to check his kitchen because someone in the flat above had spilled acid down the sink. But when Vassall went to double check the story with the Dolphin Square maintenance team, they knew nothing of the incident.

That he might himself have been spied on by bridge partners was not beyond the realms of possibility. Vassall was an enthusiastic and accomplished player, and a regular at the card tables of the exclusive Bath Club – a members' club that the press was quick to point out did not customarily accept middle-of-the-pile civil servants like him. But Vassall would have found the Square itself a good place to play. A club remains active to this day, and when he lived there Victor Mollo was among his neighbours.

In 1917, the 8-year-old Mollo and his wealthy family had escaped the communist revolutionaries in St Petersburg, whose successors Vassall was now spying for. With forged Red Cross papers, the Mollos used their financial clout to buy a train and commandeered it to take the whole family – via Finland, Stockholm and Paris – to London. Mollo taught himself to be one of the best bridge players in the country and wrote extensively on the subject. In fact, in February 1963, he brought a case in the High Court, suing fellow professional Edward Mayer over a review of one of Mollo's books in *The Listener*. The review had, he argued, attributed to him a ludicrous bid on a stated hand that 'brought him into ridicule as a bridge expert'.[4] He lost the case but it left no one in any doubt that bridge was a serious matter.

There was a subtext to the reporting on Vassall: namely, that he was gay. This aspect was manna from heaven for the tabloids, since the British people, or at least its press, were then in the grip of the idea that gay people in public life represented the single biggest security threat to the country. The ramping up of this paranoia can perhaps be dated back to the defections in 1951 of two members of the Cambridge Spy Ring, Guy Burgess and Donald Maclean. Both were widely reported to be gay – although Maclean was likely bisexual – and a link was drawn between gay men of the Establishment and treachery. In 1952, for example, the *Sunday Pictorial* editorialised about 'the unnatural sex vice which is getting a dangerous grip on this country'.[5]

Vassall's story neatly segued into this prevailing view. He had an ostensibly very normal, middle-class upbringing and during the war he joined the RAF volunteer reserve, where he was trained in photography – skills that would come in handy later on. He also saw active service in Europe, after which he returned to London suffering from a dose of wanderlust. In 1954 he was passed by a civil service selection board for a position at the British Embassy in Moscow. He was fascinated by the city, although he felt isolated and somewhat underwhelmed by life in the embassy itself. Before long, he struck up a friendship with a Polish employee called Mikhailsky, who helped him explore the social and cultural opportunities that Moscow offered. Mikhailsky, however, also happened to be working for the Soviet secret service and he was ushering Vassall into a classic honey trap. One night, Vassall found himself in a private dining room in a high-end hotel. As he noted in his autobiography:

> After dinner, everyone seemed to drift away, leaving three of us and the one [nicknamed by Vassall as 'the Skier'] who had brought me to the dinner party. One of them said I did not look well, and it might be better if I lay down on a large divan, which was appropriately placed in a recess. When I got to the bed, I could hardly stand up. I was asked to take off my clothes, including my underwear.
>
> It all seemed to be beyond my control. I did not know where I was or what was going on or why it was happening. I can recall having my underpants in my hands and holding them up at the request of others. Then I was lying on the bed naked, and there were three other men on the bed with me. I cannot remember

exactly what took place. I saw The Skier's friends standing in the room taking photographs.[6]

In due course, as Vassall told it, he was blackmailed by the Russians: provide information or the photos would be sent to his bosses, his social circle, his family. His life as he had known it would effectively be over.

After his two-year posting in Russia came to end in 1956, he returned to England and got a job at the Admiralty in the Office of the Director of Naval Intelligence. Still the Russians pressed him for information, which Vassall felt compelled to provide but which he said he sought to keep relatively low level. Nonetheless, his handlers had now taken to paying him as well as holding the haul of incriminating photographs over him. Vassall would pass on documents at drop-offs reminiscent of the most hackneyed movies. On one occasion, for example, he was told to meet at a nondescript London tube station wearing a green Tyrolean hat (including a brush of feathers) and holding a newspaper. His contact would approach and ask the best way to Belsize Park tube station, to which Vassall was to suggest he take a taxi.

After about a year with Naval Intelligence, Vassall was appointed assistant private secretary to Thomas ('Tam') Galbraith, who had recently come in as Civil Lord of the Admiralty. The pair got on well, developing a cordial relationship about which much would later be suggested. Anyway, Vassall carried on passing documents to the Russians and in autumn 1958 took a flat at Dolphin Square – much to the satisfaction of his handlers, who were keen that he lived in an unshared space. The following year, Galbraith moved on in a Cabinet reshuffle. Vassall was transferred too, this time to the military branch of the Admiralty, where (as far as Moscow was concerned) he had access to his most valuable material yet.

Vassall continued to spy undetected, growing richer as he did so, until sometime around March 1962, when the security services became aware that they had a problem thanks to a recent KGB defector, Anatoli Golitsyn. It was only a matter of time until MI5 got their man. MI5's chief, Roger Hollis, delightedly told Prime Minister Harold Macmillan that the prey had been caught. Macmillan, though, realised the fuller implications. He is quoted as responding presciently:

> No, I'm not at all pleased. When my gamekeeper shoots a fox, he doesn't go and hang it up outside the master of foxhound's drawing room, he buries it out of sight. But you just – you can't just shoot a spy as you did in the war. There will be a great public trial. Then the security services will not be praised for how efficient they are, but blamed for how hopeless they are. There will then be an inquiry. There will then be a terrible row in the press. There will then be a debate in the House of Commons, and the government will probably fall. Why the devil did you catch him?[7]

After Vassall's arrest, matters moved quickly. He faced four charges of espionage at Bow Street on 9 October and his trial at the Old Bailey started a week later. It was front-page news throughout. Much attention was given to his living arrangements and there was plenty of gossip and misinformation. One story held that the Admiralty had given him a reference for the lease on his apartment and, that being the case, questions were asked as to how it was missed that a man of modest income was renting what was, of course, referred to as a 'luxury flat'. (In fact, the Admiralty never provided such a reference, employers only being approached in unusual circumstances where other referees were not available.)

Most crucially, how had he ever been in the position to spy in the first place? Who had vetted him and found him fit to go to Moscow? Why was he later given jobs in sensitive parts of the Admiralty? Did he have a protector there? What the press were really asking was, had no one noticed he was gay and, therefore, a security risk? The newspapers did not hold back. His colleagues, it was reported, had noted a certain effeminacy in Vassall and commonly referred to him as 'Auntie' and 'Vera'. 'The Dandy Clerk Took Up Treachery to Pay for his 30 Suits' blared the *Daily Mirror*, referencing Vassall's collection of tailored clothes.[8] The *Sunday Pictorial* claimed that detectives were drawing up a list of gay people in government positions. A little later on, the *Mirror* even ran an article headed 'How to spot a possible homo'.[9] It was hardly surprising that gay men in Dolphin Square, and the rest of the country, denied their sexuality, and not just because it was illegal.

Descriptions of the Dolphin Square flat were used as evidence. In November 1962, Vassall sold his story to the *Sunday Pictorial* – to pay, he said, his legal fees. Like Diana Dors before him, he gave them what they wanted. He talked about the décor in his flat, the dressing table upon which sat a miniature toy white poodle and other cuddly animals, while a toy cheetah lay on the bed. 'Hardly a night passed without a friend calling to see me,' he revealed. 'Some were men who had a special fondness for me. Few were women.'[10] Readers were left to draw their own conclusions.

At the subsequent independent inquiry into the affair, Norman Lucas, the *Sunday Pictorial*'s crime reporter, gave his impressions. He had visited the Square after Vassall struck his deal with the paper and found a flat that smelled overwhelmingly of perfume, with ten or more bottles in the bathroom. It was, he said in evidence, 'like a woman's flat' and 'with the display of perfumes one felt only the fairy queen was missing'. Moreover, he 'had left behind some cut-out pictures from French newspapers of stocky, hirsute rugby players' and there were 'many letters which … were written in abnormally affectionate terms by a number of men'.[11] (The impact of such revelations were long-lasting. Louis Le Bailly, a celebrated naval officer who became Director General of Intelligence for the defence staff in the 1970s, was years later gravely embarrassed when he found he had been assigned Vassall's former flat when moving into the Square.)

It was an extrapolation from all of this that ensured the political fall-out from the Vassall case was enormous. The rumour mill began to spin that Vassall and Galbraith had enjoyed some sort of illicit relationship. Again, the flat was brought up in supposed evidence. There had been a cache of photographs of the former Civil Lord found there – initially described as studio shots but in fact more along the lines of press photos. There were also fairly innocuous letters from Galbraith but even the forms of address were scrutinised. One letter, dated 16 April 1962, appears to have been in response to an appeal from Vassall for a job either in No. 10 or at the Cabinet Office. It read:

Dear Vassall,

We much enjoyed your visit and it was very nice of you to write. Re
your job, the only person I could speak to at the Admiralty is Mackay
but … he would probably put you on to Elynnott whom you don't
like. Isn't there some sort of Civil Servants appointments board so that
you can make known your preferences? I very much doubt whether,
in fact, you would find either No. 10, or the Cabinet Office or the
Commonwealth Office much better than the Admiralty because
fundamentally I don't think you really like working with paper. I
think you like travel and meeting people and doing odd things suddenly. For this reason I believe being a courier might suit best. Why
don't you try to find out what is involved and if you think I can be a
help let me know. With best wishes.

Yours sincerely.

T. G. D Galbraith[12]

Hardly prose to set the heart of a lover racing, although there is some
pertinent character analysis in there. Yet even the form of address –
'Dear Vassall' – was put to newspaper readers with a nudge and a wink.
Is this really how a boss addresses a colleague? Well, yes, but such logic
was put aside for the time being.

Much was also made of the fact that Vassall had travelled to
Galbraith's Scottish home to deliver official papers on occasion. That
Galbraith's wife was with him and that there was scant evidence that
Vassall even stayed in the home over night was hardly mentioned.
Then a Mrs Murray spoke to journalists. From December 1960
until March 1962, she worked as a cleaner at Vassall's flat on Tuesday
and Thursday mornings, eventually passing the job on to her married
daughter, Mrs Hickey. Mrs Murray and Vassall had been on good, even
affectionate, terms, but perhaps in all the excitement of the case about
her former employer, she had now become rather loose-lipped. She
claimed, among other things, that he liked to entertain and that, judg-
ing from the amount of washing up, there were sometimes gatherings
of twenty to thirty people. Once, she said, she had been there when
Vassall was playing his gramophone and a gentleman arrived. Vassall
took him to his bedroom where the pair spoke for fifteen minutes

or so. When the man left, Vassall is supposed to have told her that it was his 'boss'.

Vassall denied that it was Galbraith. Indeed, Galbraith was not his boss at the time the incident must have taken place. He instead suggested it was one of two other specific individuals, but could not remember which. Galbraith had been to his flat only once, he asserted, in late 1959 about six months after he moved in, for not more than half an hour and in the company of his wife. (However, Galbraith was not a complete stranger to Dolphin Square. His father, T.D. Galbraith, the MP for Glasgow Pollok, had lived in Frobisher and then Nelson House since the war. But when questioned about Vassall's ability to afford such a tenancy, Galbraith Jr told the Minister of Defence in 1962 that he had no idea of how much the rent was, 'My father who has lived there ever since the Blitz has always said it is cheap and rather slummy, but perhaps these are relative terms.')[13]

The truth was that Vassall had been a bit of a social climber, known for his name dropping. He liked to give the impression he was thicker with his political masters than he really was, and that tendency had now returned to haunt him. And while it is admittedly unusual to stockpile images of your boss and random items of correspondence, it is perhaps less so if seen in terms of a man gathering proof of acceptance into a world of which he very much wanted to be part.

With very little basis, a picture had been painted of a dandy Soviet spy protected from above by his lover. The pressure ratcheted up and Galbraith felt he had no choice but to resign from the government. Macmillan was furious that one of his own had been forced to fall on his sword on such flimsy grounds. At the subsequent inquiry, Vassall did not particularly help in laying the matter to rest. When asked about his relationship with Galbraith, he said that there was 'not a physical homosexual attraction', which was an open-ended enough appraisal for those who wanted to read into it. And when asked if there had been 'anyone serving in the Admiralty with whom you had homosexual practices?', he replied, 'No. I don't think so.' A more definite response would have served him, and Galbraith, better.[14]

Nonetheless, when the 'Report of the Tribunal appointed to Inquire into the Vassall Case and Related Matters' was published in April 1963, Galbraith was cleared of any impropriety. Dolphin Square featured several times too, most comprehensively in the following paragraph:

> Vassall's flat has been spoken of in the Press as 'an expensive flat', a 'luxury flat'. We heard several descriptions of it from different viewers, whose descriptions varied a little with their point of approach, and we were furnished with a set of photographs of the interior taken in the autumn of 1962. We have mentioned its accommodation and the rent it commanded. For the rest, it was or in due course became obviously well furnished, with good carpets and curtains and some handsome pieces of furniture and smaller decorations. Judging by the reactions of the witnesses who visited it without any pre-existing cause of suspicion it was not a striking affair.[15]

In essence, the conclusion was true: the fact that Vassall lived in a nice flat in a nice part of town need not have set the alarm bells ringing. After all, it was not like the place had a history with spies ...

Act II

Barely had the dust settled on the Vassall court papers than Macmillan's government was thrust into a new scandal – one that would soon supersede Vassall in terms of the damage done to an Establishment already rocking on its heels. Once more, Dolphin Square was destined to play a significant role. So much has been written about the Profumo affair that there seems little need for more than a brief recap of its key details before exploring how Dolphin Square intruded on the drama.

In 1959, 17-year-old Christine Keeler moved to London and found work as a show girl at Murray's Cabaret Club in Soho. There she met Stephen Ward, an osteopath and artist with extraordinary social connections, and he took her under his wing. Before long, she was living with him in his upstairs flat on Wimpole Mews in Marylebone. He introduced her into a social circle that included aristocrats, politicians, celebrities and spooks. Keeler sometimes slept with some of them, and occasionally she would be given gifts. She smoked and drank and took some drugs, dated people on and off, came and went as she pleased. London was beginning to swing and it was all cool.

Then, on 8 July 1961, Ward took her to a weekend party at Cliveden, Berkshire, the stunning home of the Astor family. Among the other guests was the Secretary of State for War, John Profumo, who was attending with his wife, the glamorous former actor Valerie Hobson. (Dolphin Square makes its first oblique entry into the saga here, since it happened to have been the home of Profumo's mother when he became engaged to Hobson.)

Profumo first knowingly set eyes on Keeler when he spotted her cavorting in the swimming pool at Cliveden (although later on, he would wonder if he hadn't previously encountered her at Murray's Club). Nothing of note happened between them that weekend save for a bit of horseplay among some suits of armour on display in the house. But once back in London, Profumo encouraged Ward to connect them up again and, sure enough, they started sleeping together. Then, on 9 August – only a month after that first meeting at Cliveden – Profumo received a visit from Sir Norman Brook, Secretary to the Cabinet. He wanted a quiet word. The security people were worried about Profumo's association with Ward, who was also at that time friendly with a Soviet naval attaché called Yevgeny Ivanov. There were security implications and he was better off out of it.

Profumo assumed that MI5 had somehow hit upon his affair with Keeler and took Brook's words as a coded warning to set her aside. That evening he wrote her a letter:

> Darling, … Alas something's blown up tomorrow night and I can't therefore make it … I leave the next day for various trips and then a holiday so won't be able to see you again until some time in September. Blast it. Please take great care of yourself and don't run away. Love J.[16]

That, Profumo would argue later down the line, had been that. Their dalliance had been short and sweet and now it was over. Except events span out of his control. For one thing, Keeler had also slept with Ivanov. The newspapers got hold of the story, a potential barnstorming scandal, but held off from running it. Deference was waning but it hadn't entirely gone out of fashion just yet.

In 1962, Keeler found herself embroiled in an unhappy love triangle that also included a Jamaican-born jazz singer called Aloysius 'Lucky' Gordon, whom Keeler's son alleges raped his mother,[17] and an Antiguan dope dealer and jazz promoter, Johnny Edgecombe. It is fair to say that the two men did not get on. While the exact chronology is virtually impossible to pin down, at some point around November or December 1961, Keeler had moved into Dolphin Square after growing tired of Ward's sometimes overbearing ways. She agreed to a flat share with a girlfriend, Mandy Rice-Davies. Rice-Davies was another of Ward's girls (at one point, he even suggested marriage to her) and was the lover of another of his circle, Peter Rachman. Rachman, who had Edgecombe as one of his henchmen, had also been in a sexual relationship with Keeler. He was not only twice successfully prosecuted for brothel keeping, but would become most notorious as a slum landlord who treated his tenants ruthlessly in pursuit of gain. He was some twenty-five years older than Rice-Davies and their relationship was tempestuous. In one of its low points, she had taken a flat in the Square before persuading Keeler to join her. However, she was never happy there and soon returned to Rachman (who died from a heart attack in November 1962). Keeler thus had the flat to herself shortly after moving in. She would later claim that she was pregnant by Profumo at the time and that she had an abortion in January 1962.

From the available accounts, the flat was a base from where she could entertain boyfriends and go out on the town. In truth, the line between 'entertaining boyfriends' and being a sex worker was now very blurry. Her life in this period was reaching a crescendo of chaos. Years later, Gordon would recall: 'One time Chris let me stay and watch her with one of them [her clients]. She told me he was a barrister. I looked through the keyhole while she was whipping some guy with a broomstick while he was on his hands and knees on the floor.' Gordon said she had purposefully messed up the flat before the lawyer's arrival so that he could clean it and that she subsequently called him a 'lazy maid' and threatened to fire him.[18]

John Kennedy, the agent of entertainer Tommy Steele, related another incident after he bumped into her outside the apartments one day:

> She asked me in. I walked into this apartment and I'd not seen anything like it in my life before. Apparently what had happened was this. Christine had an Italian boyfriend who was insanely jealous. He had to go away for ten days and he didn't trust her at all. So he locked her up in her own flat. But he first filled it with things from Fortnums [Fortnum & Mason's, a high-class department store on Piccadilly]. This is what I saw when I first walked in. Cases of champagne stacked halfway to the ceiling, food hampers everywhere. Jars of caviar. Bowls of fruit. It was amazing. Anyway, Christine couldn't stand it longer than two days. She felt she was going mental. So she called from the window and someone found the porter to let her out. I met her as she was coming back from buying some clothes. She looked terrific, black gown, big black hat, jewellery. And after showing me all this food and booze, she said: 'I've got an idea. Let's have a bath together and drink some champagne.'[19]

Then, he reported, she jumped in, fully clothed, arguing that anyone can have a bath naked. Later in the day, the pair were set to visit the nearby River Club. It was an exclusive sort of joint and is indicative of the lifestyle Keeler was then enjoying. Here's how *Tatler* described it in January 1962:

> The only club in London to which you can take your yacht is the River Club in Grosvenor Road, S.W.1. Opposite Dolphin Square on the Embankment is this exclusive haunt of ... princes, presidents and plutocrats, with its own landing stage on the Thames and, now, its own Casino. The River Casino, which is a separate establishment, though you have to be a member of the River Club to play there, is being run by M. Jean Bauchet, the French millionaire who owns

the Moulin Rouge in Paris and three other gambling clubs, together with casinos in Marrakesh and Fedhala in Morocco.[20]

But before they could leave for the club, Gordon arrived at the Square looking for trouble. Kennedy and some friends smuggled Keeler out and when she returned later in the evening, there were three more dates lined up, all expecting to take her out.

Gordon, though, was nothing if not persistent. On another occasion, he arrived at a party Keeler was hosting in the flat, where he spotted a fire axe hanging on the door. He grabbed it, clearing the party of all guests until only Keeler and a single companion remained. He proceeded to hold them hostage for two days, and only when he left to buy some cigarettes was Keeler able to alert the police. This may have been the same time that she described having to run out 'with hardly any clothes on' to get the police to remove him after he had forced her into the flat. Keeler complained that Gordon virtually stalked her during her time in the Square, and that she often felt unsafe.

With Keeler in between them, Gordon and Edgecombe clashed several times in 1962. In one confrontation, Edgecombe slashed Gordon's face with a knife. Fearful that his victim would seek revenge, Edgecombe was intent on handing himself in to the police and approached Keeler for money to hire a lawyer. She, however, refused – possibly in part because she had heard he was seeing another woman. In fact, Keeler threatened to give evidence against him. A furious Edgecombe came looking for Keeler on a winter's afternoon in December 1962, when she was holed up back in Ward's Wimple Mews flat with Rice-Davies for company. When Keeler refused to speak to him, Edgecombe fired several shots at the front door. He had, in effect, just blown the lid off the Profumo scandal.

The police arrived, Edgecombe was arrested and put on trial at the Old Bailey in March 1963. He was acquitted of the attack on Gordon but sentenced to seven years for the firearms offence. Keeler had been expected to give evidence but was nowhere to be seen. The press, meanwhile, stoked the fires of innuendo concerning the relationship between the Minister for War and the absent witness. Over in the Commons, Labour's George Wigg asked for some clarification on the rumours, not (of course) out of a desire to embarrass the minister but because of the potential security issues at stake.

The rest, as they say, is history. Profumo assured his Cabinet colleagues that he knew Keeler but there had been no impropriety. They urged him to say as much in the House, but before long the truth spilled out and Profumo was forced to resign in the June. Coming hot on the heels of the Vassall affair, it was too much for the Conservative Government to weather and Macmillan fell as prime minister before the year was out.

The question remains as to whether Keeler continued her affair with Profumo while she was living in the Square. When Profumo was interrogated by his party's chief whip in February 1963 about the particulars of his association with Keeler, he held that it had 'all taken place between July and December of 1961', and in his statement in the House of Commons on 22 March 1963, he said, 'I last saw Miss Keeler in December 1961, and I have not seen her since.'[21] That would suggest the affair did overlap her tenancy. Although if he ever did visit the flats, perhaps he was simply acting as her partner in a game of bridge with John Vassall ...

There were certainly witnesses who claimed to have seen them together before Keeler left the Square around June or July 1962. One was a man called Hogan, who purported to be her butler. According to *The People* of 4 August 1963:

Hogan, the butler, twice attended her when Profumo was her bed companion. On the first occasion he took them coffee in bed. Afterwards Keeler gave him five pounds. Rachman and Lucky Gordon were other occupants of her bed whom Hogan saw. And almost every morning there was evidence of her previous night's debauch. All around the flat were strewn articles of clothing. Keeler was in the habit of leaving her clothes wherever they happened to fall when she went to bed. Her clothes and appearance, once the paint was off, were less than immaculate. Her finger-nails were chipped and grimy, stained with nicotine. She was often careless about the state of her underwear. Washing it was a chore she tried to avoid. Often, says Hogan, he had to wash it for her. If there was no time for that, she sent him out to buy new sets of underwear. When he began to work for her. Hogan ran her bath each morning. He soon learned his mistake. 'Every other morning, if you don't mind, Hogan,' she told him … In spite of her personal shortcomings. Keeler was making a financial success at her chosen career. She stored notes in a small cardboard box and between the leaves of books. Once she boasted to Hogan that she had saved at least £1,000. But Keeler did not enjoy the fleshpots for long at Dolphin Square.[22]

Lord Denning, who was appointed to look into the scandal, was having none of it, though. He stated in his report:

> It has been said in some quarters that Mr Profumo went on visiting Christine Keeler in 1962 when she was in Dolphin Square. 'Lucky' Gordon gave evidence before me to this effect. So did a man called Hogan. They said they knew it was Mr Profumo by having seen his photographs in the newspapers. I found myself unable to accept their evidence. Mr Hogan had given a story to a newspaper that he was a 'butler' to Christine Keeler and took up coffee on two occasions to Mr Profumo and Christine Keeler in bed. He told me that he had signed a contract for £600 for this story to be split between him and two free-lance reporters. But he was not a butler at all. He was a carpet cleaner.[23]

In his conduct of the inquiry, Denning revealed himself to be a man of the Establishment and it came as little surprise that he did not hang much weight on the words of characters such as Gordon and Hogan. He preferred to believe Profumo, who had already resigned for lying to Parliament, and the judge's dismissal came a little too easily to hand. As Rice-Davies might have put it, 'He would say that, wouldn't he?'

There are other tangential links between the Square and the scandal. In July 1960, Patricia Steele of Keyes House was fined £100 over a licensing offence as proprietor of the Black Sheep Club on Whitehorse Street in Piccadilly. A few months earlier, it was reported that the club's 'boss', 54-year-old 'Hod' Dibben was marrying an 18-year-old dancer called Mariella Capes. He told the press of his plans to transform his bride in the way that Henry Higgins moulds Eliza Doolittle in George Bernard Shaw's *Pygmalion*. And reinvented she was, transfiguring into Mariella Novotný, who was suddenly the supposed niece of Czechoslovak President Antonín Novotný.

The parties of Dibben and Novotný became the stuff of legend but the most famous of all took place at a flat in Hyde Park Square, Mayfair, in December 1961. It became known as the 'Feast of Peacocks' or, after the Denning inquiry, the 'Man in the Mask' party. Named for the roasted peacock that was served at dinner, the guests included famous names from politics and entertainment, as well as Stephen Ward, who was himself a member of the Black Sheep Club. Keeler and Rice-Davies turned up later in the evening. Ward opened the door to them, naked – according to Rice-Davies – except for his socks. There was a similar dress code for the other men present, while the women were 'naked except for wisps of clothing like suspender belts and stockings'.[24] The identity of one guest sporting just a black mask with slits for eyes and a small, lace waitress's apron became a subject of much debate when Denning looked into the matter. Concluding that there was no evidence it was a Cabinet minister, he nonetheless conceded that 'there is a group of people who hold parties in private of a perverted nature'. *Time Magazine* later speculated that the 'man in the mask' was film director Anthony Asquith, the son of former Prime Minister Herbert Asquith, and a half-uncle to former Dolphinite Michael Asquith.[25]

There is also a suggestion that Rice-Davies was back as a tenant in the Square in summer 1963, when the Denning Inquiry was in full swing. In a written history of Granada Television, producer Liz Sutherland told how current affairs programme *World in Action* was filming a profile of the judge. Rice-Davies was due to appear as a witness and had agreed to be recorded by the documentary team. Sutherland recalled:

> Early one morning Tim [her boss on the show, Tim Hewat] sent me to Dolphin Square to make sure she didn't change her mind. She didn't seem particularly surprised when she opened the door to me, wearing a skimpy baby-doll night dress, and retired to bed for a while, leaving me to look at the few books she had – mostly by Georgette Heyer.[26]

In the few short months between Vassall's arrest in September 1962 and Profumo's resignation in June 1963, Dolphin Square was thrust into the limelight in a way that no one could have predicted. No longer merely an address that cropped up sporadically in the newspapers, it had become a location drenched in intrigue, a crucible for scandal that both endangered the nation's security and brought down governments. It was the moment, perhaps, when Dolphin Square stopped being famous and became notorious instead.

12

ALL CHANGE

In February 1969, the death of Lady Gladys Wynne Finch of Rodney House was reported. The daughter of the Earl of Winchilsea and Nottingham, she was the very definition of 'old money'. Her brother, Denys, had been a big game hunter as well as the lover of Baroness Karen Blixen, who immortalised him in her book, *Out of Africa*. Lady Gladys's husband had been killed in action during the First World War. She left an estate of £260,000. But culturally, London no longer belonged to people like her. The capital was not only swinging, it was tripping out, wearing flares and making a peace sign too. In 1965, for example, three women unfettered by traditional social convention decided to go skinny-dipping in the Square's swimming pool, resisting the attempts of both the attendant and a police officer to eject them – a disregard of authority that cost them £2 each 'for using insulting behaviour likely to cause a breach of the peace'. The sexual revolution was at full tilt, too. The academic Elizabeth Wilson reflected in her essay 'Gayness and Liberalism' on the evolution of lesbianism in the 1960s:

> There was one particular group of women who seemed to associate together on the basis of all being very rich and beautiful. They all had affairs with one another – a tiny, incestuous clique. I remember a party of theirs we went to in a Dolphin Square flat where there was no furniture at all except an enormous bed surrounded by mirrors and hundreds of bottles and jars of make-up and scent – just like something out of a movie.[1]

While there was still a place for 'the Man' in Dolphin Square, his position was no longer going unchallenged.

More than ever, the Square was a hinterland where the realities of the outside world regularly crashed up against the domestic lives of its well-to-do and influential residents. Nonetheless, there was still a bubble-like quality to the place, a sense that life here still wasn't quite like in other places. The restaurant increasingly became the focal point of social life, an enclave away from the public eye. In 1964, Frankie Howerd booked the place out to celebrate the first anniversary of his stage debut in the West End hit, *A Funny Thing Happened on the Way to the Forum*. A year later, the celebrated restaurateur Alan de Costa took on the venue – a fillet steak at 15*s* 6*d* was the top-price item on the menu, and the opening was marked by a performance of a water ballet in the attached swimming pool. Class names played there, like Roy Budd, composer of the score for *Get Carter* and an accompanist for the likes of Bob Hope, Tony Bennett and Charles Aznavour. (And for those after a slightly different experience, Villa dei Cesari opened across from the Square in 1965, billed as 'London's Riverside Roman restaurant'. Authentically decorated as a Roman villa, it even had ashtrays simulated to appear like they'd been excavated from Herculaneum. The house band was the Five Bruttos.)[2]

Stories continued to spill out of the Square about star names, some international and others still of the more home-grown variety. Among the latter group was Eric Lander. In June 1965 the newspapers briefly got in a spin about his divorce from fellow actor Barbara Wooley. She was living in Keyes House at the time, and the couple had been separated since 1962. He was the big name though, for his star turn as Detective Sergeant Harry Baxter in the long-running police series *No Hiding Place* and its spin-off, *Echo Four-Two*. But if that was all a bit too unhip and square for your tastes, Mia Farrow and Laurence Harvey brought some A-list Hollywood glamour to Pimlico in 1967 when they filmed scenes for their Cold War thriller *A Dandy in Aspic* on location in the Square. One wonders if either was aware of its grand (and continuing) tradition as a home to many of the spies whose day jobs were based up the road at the Ministry of Defence and with the intelligence services.

In 1964, the nation had ushered a new prime minister into Downing Street, although few realised that he too had once lived in the Square – albeit briefly. Back in 1940, Harold Wilson and his wife became Dolphinites when he was posted to London as a civil servant. Rumour has it that its greatest attraction to him was that it was the only place he knew in London, thanks to its unique district heating system, where you could get a hot bath at four o'clock in the morning. A couple of years after Wilson took office, *Tatler* ran an interview with Lady Denny, wife of the lord mayor, Sir Lionel Denny. She was asked about life at Dolphin Square, where the couple had lived for the past six years. 'There we have everything,' she said, 'shops, a restaurant, even a place to sunbathe; and, of course, we are quite used to some of the people who live there, the oddities.'[3] It seemed a pretty perceptive analysis.

For a while in the early 1960s, the very future of the Square had been in serious doubt. The concern was not that it would disappear altogether, but that it would be changed in character fundamentally. The uncertainty started when the Costains sold their interest in the Square in 1958, and reached a dramatic peak with an Old Bailey trial in 1960. The path to that point was littered with complex financial transactions. Costains had sold to hotelier and property investor Joseph Maxwell for the sum of £2.4 million. He in turn sold it on to Lintang Investments the following year for £3.1 million. It was then that the real trouble began. Herbert Murray, the managing director of the State Building Society, had his eye on a takeover and was looking to spend some £8.5 million to secure the deal. He was assisted in this ambition by a young solicitor of German descent called Friedrich Grunwald. Essentially, the pair were plotting to build a broad portfolio of properties and businesses, and to use £3 million of assets belonging to the State Building Society to prop up their various bids. For a while, Murray had a good eye for a deal and all seemed to be going well. But gradually, he started paying over the odds. When he overestimated the value of a Cardiff brewery, his rapidly assembled empire began to crumble. Suddenly, a hole in the finances to the tune of £200,000 appeared. As the authorities began to probe Murray and Grunwald's operations, it became clear that they had been acquiring assets fraudulently. Found guilty at the Old Bailey, each man was sentenced to five years' imprisonment, with the judge describing

Murray as a 'dishonest rogue' and Grunwald as the one who 'very largely carried out the mechanics of these schemes'.[4]

It had been a very close shave for the residents of Dolphin Square, who could breathe a collective sigh of relief that their potential new landlords had been found out before the sale could go through. After the Square's Tenants Association were frustrated in their own attempts to buy the estate, in 1963 Westminster Council agreed to purchase the apartments for £4½ million. They then sublet them back to the resident-led Dolphin Square Trust. It was a move that brought stability to the Square for over forty years and ensured that a certain quality of life was maintained for tenants, along with a very favourable level of rent.

While Murray and Grunwald were never at risk of the hangman's noose, the question of capital punishment was to become the cause célèbre of one Dolphinite a few years later. In 1966, Charlotte Hurst of Collingwood House headed a campaign seeking to re-establish the death penalty that had been abolished by Parliament the previous year for all but a few offences (including high treason, piracy with violence, arson in the royal dockyards and espionage, along with certain offences guarded by military law). From her flat, Hurst set up and was chair of the Citizens Protection Society, which presented to Parliament a petition in favour of retaining capital punishment that was said to have been signed by 2½ million people.

The level of support she was able to harness was not so surprising. The year 1966 saw the trials of Ian Brady and Myra Hindley for the so-called Moors Murders – the sexual assaults and murders of five children aged between 10 and 17 carried out in Lancashire between 1963 and 1965. (The murders occurred around the parliamentary constituency of a future resident of the Square, Tom Pendry – later Baron Pendry, of Stalybridge in the County of Greater Manchester; he would campaign for both the killers to remain in prison when they appealed their sentences.) Such crimes nudged a swathe of public opinion towards keeping the ultimate punishment on the statute books.

But it was another crime around which Hurst and her supporters particularly built their case: the Shepherd's Bush murders of August 1966. On the twelfth of that month, an unmarked police patrol car was travelling through East Acton, just along from Shepherd's

Bush. The three officers inside – 30-year-old Detective Sergeant Christopher Head, 25-year-old Temporary Detective Constable David Wombwell and 41-year-old Constable Geoffrey Fox – were all in plain clothes. As they turned down a residential road around mid-afternoon, they spotted a parked-up blue van containing three men. The van had no tax disc and was located not far from Wormwood Scrubs Prison. The officers, alert to the possibility that the van might be awaiting escapees from the jail, decided to question the men. Head and Wombwell left their car and soon discovered that Jack Witney, a known criminal, was in the driver's seat. His vehicle insurance, it turned out, had expired earlier in the day. They took down his details as Witney pleaded to be given a break. Then, the passenger in the front, Harry Roberts, whipped out a Luger pistol and shot Wombwell in the head. He did the same to Head as he attempted to run back to his car. The other passenger, John Duddy, then ran over to Fox, who had remained in the car, and shot him dead, too. The three made their escape at speed, hiding the van in a lock-up.

News of the cop killings caused a wave of public outrage and sparked a huge manhunt. (An eagle-eyed member of the public had noted the van registration, having had his suspicions aroused by the speed at which it was travelling.) Witney was arrested at his home just a few hours later and Duddy was seized in Glasgow a few days later. The military-trained Roberts, however, managed to avoid capture for some three months. Ironically, given Hurst's campaign, one of the porters at Dolphin Square reported in October that he had spotted Roberts on the property. Fifteen officers sped their way to the Square in hot pursuit but were unable to find any trace of him. But the sighting followed another a few days earlier, when a woman said she had seen the fugitive in Chelsea, leading the police to suspect he was camping out in the Pimlico-Chelsea area. In the event, he was arrested in Thorley Wood near Bishop's Stortford in Hertfordshire.

In the meantime, Prime Minister Harold Wilson and Leader of the Opposition Ted Heath attended a memorial service at Westminster Abbey for the three slain officers, while thousands of police and civilians lined the route of the funeral procession. In December, a month after the arrest of the third man, the trio faced court in a trial that lasted less than a week. All three were found guilty of the murders ('the most heinous crime to have been committed in this country for a generation or more', according to the judge) and given life with a recommendation of at least thirty years. But for some, it was simply not enough and Charlotte Hurst became a familiar figure in the press and on the airwaves over the next few months as she made the case for the return of capital punishment.

Hurst was one half of a Conservative power couple. Her husband, John, was chair of the Dolphin Conservatives, which went from strength to strength in the late-1960s. By 1968 it boasted a membership of 305. In December of that year, the branch held a social in the Chichester Room, one of the Square's event venues. A hundred members attended along with the guest of honour, John Smith – the MP for the Cities of London and Westminster. Smith was bullish about the party's prospects. He urged that there needed to be less legislation passed and less concern about who was making money, and more consideration given to the fact that money needed to be made. This, he suggested, was the way to restore the 'country's confidence in the world. No one should know that better than the people of Dolphin Square.' If those same people needed reminding of their elevated standing in the social structure, he proclaimed, 'I have always said that Dolphin Square could run the world.'[5] The statement was greeted with laughter and applause, although it was a joke that perhaps carried rather more weight than at your average party branch Christmas do. Efforts had long been made by the Dolphin Square management to maintain broad political neutrality – for every Tory who arrived, there were generally efforts made to ensure that someone from Labour was admitted next as a counterweight. But there was a feeling at this time that the Conservatives were having a moment in the Square.

Spencer Le Marchant, a resident of Frobisher House, typified this sense that the Tories were on the march. A 6ft 6in-tall Old Etonian with a booming voice, he was a member of the London Stock Exchange and had sat on Westminster City Council since 1956. In the 1966 general election he had unsuccessfully challenged the Labour safe seat of Vauxhall, but his time came four years later when, a little before his fortieth birthday, he was elected MP for High Peak in Derbyshire.

In many respects, he fitted the bill of the classic Dolphinite, certainly in terms of social connections and a liking for the high life. In 1955, he'd married Lucinda Gaye Leveson-Gower, whose mother had in 1948 married Ernest Simpson, the husband of Wallis Simpson before she divorced him to marry Edward VIII and spark the 1936 abdication crisis. Le Marchant, meanwhile, had grown quite a reputation for good living so that even Margaret Thatcher would recall him in her memoirs as 'famous for his intake of champagne'.[6] The political journalist Simon Hoggart recalled Le Marchant as the very first MP he met in Parliament – 'a charming man with something of a drink problem'. Hoggart tells how his boss introduced him to the MP in Annie's Bar (a bar within the Palace of Westminster restricted to MPs and journalists only). Spencer asked what he wanted, to which Hoggart indicated a pint. A moment later, he was presented with a large pewter tankard full of claret.[7]

Meanwhile, Michael Brown, himself a Conservative MP from 1979 to 1997, remembered Le Marchant as a kindly whip who 'seemed to know, or be related to, every press baron in Fleet Street and was always able to kill any trouble heading my way'. On one occasion, Le Marchant summoned Brown to his flat after Brown had voted against some piece of government business. Brown expected 'a dressing down over a bottle of champagne' but 'learnt a whole new meaning to this phrase as he [Le Marchant] tried, unsuccessfully, to seduce me. But it was an effective way of ensuring that I voted with the Government thereafter.'[8]

Another Tory, Peter Blaker, was on his way out of Dolphin Square just around the time that John Smith was making his speech to the local party faithful in 1968. Sally Tooth, the tenant who took over his tenancy, had good reason to remember him. At that time, it was possible for tenants to find their own replacements and 'hand on' the flat for an agreed price if the new tenant was willing. Blaker had wanted £400 for his flat complete with all its furnishings. Tooth, however, balked at the price as she was not keen on the furniture on offer. Instead, she agreed to pay £100 for the flat unfurnished, save for the white goods in the kitchen. Blaker agreed to move out the rest of his belongings but in the event did not do so.

Tooth was able to get rid of most of it herself but Blaker had left two boxes full of Hansards that he said he'd arrange to have collected.

After a while, she decided to call him on one of two numbers he had provided – this one with a Chelsea area code. A woman answered and Tooth asked to speak to Blaker. The woman said he wasn't there and then asked if she could help. Tooth said it was about the Dolphin Square flat. 'About the WHAT?' came the reply. The Hansards were removed the next day. Tooth was left with the distinct impression that the recipient of her call had been Blaker's wife and that she had no idea about his Dolphin Square bolt hole. 'He never had any post,' Tooth mused. 'I got post for the previous tenants. He was here, but I don't think anybody knew he was here!'[9]

Regardless of his domestic arrangements, Blaker enjoyed a successful political career, serving as MP for Blackpool South between 1964 and 1992, and holding ministerial offices in the Ministry of Defence and the Foreign Office. He was knighted in 1983 and given a peerage in 1994. However, in the 1990s he became embroiled in an unseemly wrangle with Owen Oyston, the very successful businessman, and staunch Labour-supporting chairman of Blackpool Football Club. In 1996, Oyston faced three trials on charges of sexual assault and rape. After two acquittals, the third trial saw him convicted of those offences against a 16-year-old girl. He was sentenced to six years in prison. But Oyston protested that he was the victim of a large-scale conspiracy involving business rivals and political figures including Blaker and Robert Atkins, an ex-Minister for Sport and the MP for South Ribble in Lancashire – and also a Dolphin Square resident. He said that they had waged a vicious campaign against him for over a decade.

Oyston claimed to be in possession of tape recordings of Blaker, Atkins and a Blackpool businessman called William Harrison that he said proved they 'were running a conspiracy against me and members of the North West Labour Party'. Four years earlier, Granada TV had run a documentary alleging Blaker had paid a private detective £5,000 to look into alleged links between Oyston, a modelling agency and a prostitution racket. Blaker confessed to having paid the money but denied he was politically motivated. At the time, the MP had interests in various cable television businesses that were frequently in competition with Oyston for licences. Oyston was on the brink of bringing an action against Blaker, among others, for conspiracy to defame when he was arrested for rape. The Dolphinite Lord Tom Pendry recalls listening to the tapes at Oyston's mansion prior to his conviction. 'I was on the platform on the terrace,' Pendry recalls, 'listening to tapes from those two MPs in which they're actually saying what they're going to do to Oyston. It's all on tape.'[10] It was not enough, though, to overturn Oyston's conviction, nor to bring a successful legal action against Blaker, who died in 2009. It is a story, however, replete with hints of political intrigue.

And while Blaker's brush with criminality via the Oyston saga came long after his exit from Pimlico, the 1960s saw a surge in serious crime within and related to Dolphin Square itself.

13

CRIMES AND MISDEMEANOURS

While crime, as we have seen, was always a feature of life in the Square, the ante was upped in the 1960s – both in terms of violence and organisation. On 22 September 1963, for example, *The People* reported that the offices of Metro Minicab in 'plush' Dolphin Square had been targeted by mobsters because the company's owner had refused to give in to the demands of gangsters running a protection racket. The unlucky businessman had his premises ransacked, furniture broken and the radio system crucial to his operations smashed. The assailants threatened the staff and drivers with violence, too. It would not be long before the switchboard operator, a man called Del Norton, was lured from his post and badly beaten up. It all bore little relation to the sort of petty theft that had been commonplace in previous decades but had the hallmarks of a new sort of gang violence that sought to intimidate and control. Dolphin Square had been a prime battleground in the war between London's traditional black cabs and a wave of new private minicab firms. In 1961, Square resident Tom Sylvester had launched his squadron of twenty-five black-and-white-liveried Fiat 600 Multiplas, catering for those keen for a cheaper alternative to the black cab to get around the capital. Such new businesses relied on a legal loophole that allowed them to sidestep many of the regulatory requirements faced by black cabs on the basis that these private hires did not 'ply for hire' on the streets but took telephone bookings instead. 'My chaps are instructed not to wait at cab ranks and not to draw in when signalled,' Sylvester insisted.

The identity of the criminal group responsible for the 1963 attack on Metro Minicab was not known (at least, not in public) but echoed the modus operandi of gangs like those of the Richardsons and the Krays, who in this period were coming into their prime, seizing control of the capital's underworld from their respective bases in south and east London.

There were more tough-man antics in May 1966, when the Square's branch of Lloyds Bank was the scene of a terrifying armed robbery by bandits equipped with guns and ammonia. The raiders arrived wearing white hoods and fired a shot at one of the staff, although fortunately no one was hurt in the incident, in which the robbers escaped in a waiting car with £5,000.

Not long afterwards, in August 1966 the Square found its way into the story of the Krays. The pivotal figures in the saga were three brothers – Alfie, Bobby and David Teale, each in their twenties – who over time had become integrated into the twins' milieu. Their association would end in the dock of the Old Bailey in 1969, with the Teale brothers giving evidence against the Krays in the trial that would culminate in the brothers' imprisonment for decades to come.

The Teales' decision to testify led some in the underworld to consider them *personae non gratae*, traitors to the unwritten criminal code: thou shall not rat on thy partners in crime. But the Teales would in due course claim that they had been atrociously ill-treated by the gangsters. Two of the brothers, David and Bobby, have said that they were raped by Ronnie Kray, and David alleged that his wife was also raped by the twins' brother, Charlie Kray.

The brothers' road to Dolphin Square had begun in June or July 1966. The twins' firm was arguably in its pomp around this time. The police and the press had given them a wide berth since 1964, scared off after Lord Boothby had claimed a huge payout from the *Sunday Mirror* over essentially true assertions that he had an unsuitable association with the Krays. Then, in 1965, they got off on charges of demanding money with menaces from a West End club owner. All the while, their empire was expanding and they seemed equipped to bat away any legal challenge to their operations.

But all was not well behind the scenes. Ronnie's mental health was deteriorating and his behaviour was increasingly unpredictable.

In March 1966 there had been a ferocious fight between some of the Kray gang and their rivals, the Richardsons, at a venue in Catford. One of the Krays' associates was killed. The following day, George Cornell – a man with ties to the Richardsons but not present at the previous night's brawl – was drinking in the Blind Beggar pub in Whitechapel, which the Krays considered to be their territory. Cornell and Ronnie had history as well. Ronnie saw an opportunity for revenge, so corralled a member of his Firm to drive him to the pub, where he shot Cornell through the head. Relying on fear silencing the several bystanders who had witnessed the execution, Ronnie now went into hiding – at David Teale's house. As Teale tells it, he and his wife and young children were essentially held hostage in their own home as Ronnie laid low for several days. Bobby Teale was there too and he was particularly concerned for the well-being of his younger brother, who was also present, fearing that Ronnie was taking a sexual interest in him.

When Bobby was allowed out of the house to buy some provisions, he went to a phone box to call the police and inform them of Ronnie's whereabouts. He expected a quick raid and that Kray would be marched off in handcuffs. He was literally risking his life on that assumption. But no such raid happened. The police were nervous as to how Ronnie might react – whether he would endanger the young family holed up with him. Moreover, the police knew they lacked the evidence for a successful prosecution. Instead, as Bobby Teale tells it, he found himself signed up by the police as a secret informant, expected to feed back intelligence on Kray for weeks, months, perhaps even longer. He knew the consequences if he was ever discovered, and kept his activities secret even from his own brothers.

There was another problem. As he fed information to the police, just as quickly there seemed to be leaks back to the twins. Bobby is convinced that there were Met Police officers on the Kray's payroll and the twins not only realised they had a mole in their midst, but they also knew it was him. He says that on one occasion, Reggie drove him to Epping Forest and attempted to shoot him. Bobby Teale was spooked and now appealed to his police handlers to somehow get him out of a hole. Leave it to them, they told him.

Sometime in the June or July, Bobby says, he was out one night in the West End when a stranger struck up a conversation with him. He was a man in his late forties, who called himself Wallace, although it was unclear whether this was his first name or a surname. They had a drink together. Wallace had a flat in Dolphin Square. Bobby considered him 'clearly homosexual' but that did not prevent them striking up a friendship over the next few weeks. Bobby says he sometimes took refuge at Wallace's flat when he suspected the Krays were after him.

At one point, Bobby was driving Wallace's car, a Triumph TR3 that he says Wallace loaned him, when it was stopped by the police. His passengers all ran off but as Bobby tried to escape, he ended up in an altercation with an officer and was charged with obstructing the police and assault. But his friendship with Wallace carried on regardless.

According to David Teale, he and his two brothers were drinking in the Rugby Tavern in Holborn on 8 August 1966. They were discussing buying a market stall in Chapel Street Market, Islington, for which they needed £900. Bobby then suggested that his new mate, Wallace, might be worth approaching to see if he'd put up some capital. He had a pad in Dolphin Square and wasn't short of a bob or two. (According to Bobby's account of events, he had also had a conversation with Wallace about the possibility of bringing his brothers to a party at the Square.)

Wallace came to meet them that same evening and they drank in several pubs and bars before all returning to Dolphin Square. David says they got to his flat by going up in a lift and then down a long corridor. The flat itself, he says, was small but well-kept and kitted out stylishly and expensively. Then, the Teales say, Wallace offered Bobby a loan for the market stall, for which Bobby offered to write out a receipt with repayment details. By the time this had all been agreed, it was 1 a.m. and so it was decided the brothers would stay the night, each finding a space in the living room while Wallace slept in his bed.

At half past seven the following morning, the doorbell rang. It was at this stage that the brothers realised Wallace was no longer in the flat. They opened the front door and were greeted by six plain-clothes police officers, accompanied by their host of the previous night.

Wallace was now telling the police that he had been held hostage by the Teales, who were demanding money from him. He had been forced to escape, he claimed, via the rubbish hatch – that architectural feature of the Square that has so often seen usage never intended by the original designers. The Teales were duly arrested and taken to the nearby Rochester Row Police Station, where they were charged with demanding money with menaces (the same charge as the Krays had successfully fought off a year earlier). The Teales were placed on remand at Brixton. Bobby was sure this was all part of a police scheme to get him and his brothers to safety in light of his informing. A sentence of, say, six to nine months would take them off the scene and diffuse the twins' suspicions that he was 'the rat'.

Except, their trial was scheduled for Court No. 1 at the Old Bailey. In other words, the authorities were not treading lightly. The brothers were faced with a judge, Alan King-Hamilton, who also seemed hostile to them. He opened their trial by reporting that he had heard allegations of attempted jury nobbling and asked the twelve jurors if any of them had been subjected to an illicit approach. No one said they had but, as the Teales tell it, their integrity had already been fundamentally undermined in the eyes of those charged with deciding their fate. When Wallace appeared as 'Mr X' in the witness stand, the outcome was all but decided. They were each found guilty and sentenced to three years.

Whether this was a police co-ordinated attempt to bring in the brothers for their own protection that got out of hand, or something else entirely, will likely never be known. But Dolphin Square proved the backdrop for a drama that took out three individuals who would, in the not too distant future, play a crucial role in taking down arguably the most notorious gangsters that the country has ever produced. The true identity of the mysterious Wallace, and his reasons for being in the Square, has meanwhile never been established.[1]

If the Krays and their ilk posed a threat from the outside, there were unscrupulous figures within the Square, too. In 1960, for example, Frederick Harvey, employed as the assistant manager of the butchers in the Square, pleaded guilty at Bow Street Magistrates to stealing the contents of the shop's safe – a total of £134 – and never returning to the business again. 'I had a lot to drink,' he told the court, 'and went back to the shop later, and emptied the safe.'[2] Seven years later, Peter Frederick Worley, a 31-year-old resident of Hawkins House, was fined by the Inner London Sessions and also had his 'E' type Jaguar confiscated by the customs authorities after he pleaded guilty to knowingly carrying 241 smuggled and fake watches. Public records show that a Peter F. Worley was born in Shoreditch in April 1935, a birth date that tallies with the Hawkins House scamster. It also tallies with that of the 83-year-old Peter Worley, a resident of Ashford,[3] who was reported in 2018 as having been convicted of fourteen historical sexual offences, including two rapes. His crimes were committed during the 1980s (by which time he had moved away from the Square) against two girls, one of whom was only 4 when his attacks started. He was sentenced to twelve years in prison.

One of the most extraordinary crimes linked to the Square occurred in June 1966, when a Grenville House resident – the appropriately named Peter Dolphin – was the victim of kidnap. Dolphin was a 25-year-old disc jockey with Radio City, a British pirate radio station that broadcast from an abandoned Second World War Maunsell Fort in the Thames Estuary.

The previous autumn, Radio City – which had been founded in 1963 as Sutch Radio by David Sutch (better known as aspiring pop star and political renegade, Screaming Lord Sutch) and his manager, Reginald Calvert – discussed a merger with one of its larger pirate rivals, Radio Caroline. A new transmitter was delivered to Radio City's fortress base but then the merger collapsed. Ownership of the transmitter now became a source of contention. In the early hours of 20 June 1966, a retired army major called Oliver Smedley, who believed ownership of the transmitter was his, dispatched a team of men to seize control of the fortress. On the evening of the following day, Calvert went to Smedley's home to demand the removal of the men and the return of transmitter parts. What happened at the property is the subject of conjecture but there is little doubt that a fight broke out. Smedley would suggest that he feared Calvert wanted to kill him and he was also worried for the safety of his housekeeper. Whatever the exact circumstances, Calvert was shot dead by Smedley.

Peter Dolphin had been present when the fort was overrun and had taken flash-lit photographs of the assailants on a camera that he then gave to a station engineer for safe keeping. About a week after the invasion and Calvert's death, Dolphin said two men arrived at his flat claiming to be from Scotland Yard. They questioned him about the station and undertook a search of his flat, before telling him to go with them 'or it will be the worse for you'. They were, he said, 'with-it' types and he soon doubted that they were police at all.

They took him to a blue Ford and then, he claimed, drove him to a flat in Mile End, where he was held in a basement room with barred windows. His fear was that they had discovered his camera with the images of the fort raiders. He was, he said, held from Friday until the afternoon of the following Monday, always with a guard present. He was repeatedly questioned and, before being freed, warned not to go to the police since his captors knew where he lived. With that, his ordeal was over.[4]

Smedley faced trial in the October for the manslaughter of Calvert but was acquitted after his self-defence argument was accepted. Dolphin, meanwhile, went off to take up an acting role in *Crossroads* (he had previously had a part in *Danger Man*, but one suspects he might have had his fill of crime-based thrills) and never returned to Radio City. He did crop up in the newspapers again in 1968, though. On that occasion, it was because someone had sent him an unwanted gift of a 7ft boa constrictor called Sarah to his flat in Dolphin Square. He told journalists that he planned to give it away but not before he had posed for photos with it around his neck.[5]

Dolphin Square also found its name associated with the crimes of a serial killer during the decade. In 1964 and 1965, a swathe of west London was terrorised by a series of six murders. All the victims were women who worked in the sex industry. The crimes came to be known by the press, unable to resist a catchy nickname, as either the Hammersmith murders or the Jack the Stripper murders (each of the victims was found in a state of undress in or around the River Thames). Their shared profession was deemed another reason to draw parallels with Jack the Ripper, the still unidentified murderer who killed at least five victims in the East End of London in the 1880s (although modern research has helped to debunk the idea that the Ripper's victims were, in fact, all prostitutes).[6]

Among the 1960s victims was 30-year-old Hannah Tailsford, originally from the north-west of England. She was discovered on 2 February 1964 on the shore of the Thames a short way west of Hammersmith Bridge. She had been strangled, was missing several teeth and her underwear had been stuffed inside her mouth. Her killer would never be caught and his identity has been the source of much speculation over the decades. Several researchers who have written on the subject have suggested that Tailsford was a visitor to Dolphin Square in the weeks before her murder.

David Seabrook, in his 2007 book *Jack of Jumps*, reported rumours that Hannah had attended sex parties hosted by a man called Andre, believed to have been employed at the French Embassy (but never traced).[7] However, Dick Kirby, in his 2016 book *Laid Bare*, suggests that this host led Tailsford to believe he was French but was in fact called Andrej and associated with the Czech Embassy. When Detective Inspector David Woodland went to speak to him, he could find no trace of him either in the Square or at his embassy. 'My only thought at the time,' Woodland told Kirby, 'was that his immediate superiors may have felt he could be vulnerable to an approach by our security services and, as a precaution, he was returned home.'[8] There is no firm proof that Tailsford's death was related to events in the Square, but the connection has nonetheless inspired a slew of conspiracy theories that she 'knew too much' about the activities of influential people and had to be silenced. In particular, she was known to have appeared in pornographic photoshoots, so the question has been raised as to whether she might have been in possession of compromising photos that she could use for blackmail purposes. The more likely – and more mundane – truth is that she was killed by a psychopath whose path she was unfortunate enough to cross. But her association with the Square is further evidence that the place had a growing propensity to find its name mixed up in shady goings-on.

Less grisly but highly emblematic of the period was the trial in July 1969 of Muzzafar Mustapha Khan, a 21-year-old student who was then living in Howard House. He was charged with conspiring to import 67lb of cannabis resin, with a street value of about £20,000. The operation was, in truth, all a bit 'Fred Karno'. The trial and its reporting, meanwhile, played into a narrative of racial stereotypes that suggested that any hippy-ish vision of a multicultural nirvana was yet to impinge on the Old Bailey or Fleet Street.

The principals in the drama were Pakistani national Khan, Anil Johar (described by the *Daily Mirror* as the 'dashing ... son of an Indian film star') and 18-year-old Jane Whitworth, the privately educated daughter of a retired Jersey businessman. Virtually all reporting of Whitworth included the clarification that she was 'attractive'.

The crime ring made two attempts to smuggle drugs. In the first instance, Whitworth flew out with two companions to Paris to meet Johar, who was bringing in a consignment of cannabis from Bombay. However, with police officers seemingly on to the scheme, he abandoned his suspect suitcase before the handover could be made and flew back to India. Whitworth then flew out to meet him in Bombay (then a hotspot on the Hippy Trail) and agreed to carry a suitcase back to London herself, containing 31lb of drugs. But the plan soon dissolved into farce. Her airline managed to lose her luggage, a loss that she reported back in London. Her bags were soon recovered but customs agents then discovered the cannabis. They extracted the contraband and replaced it with stones of the same weight. The luggage was then reunited with its owner at a hotel in London, and a few minutes later officials arrived to question her. She confirmed that the cases were hers, thus incriminating herself, and more cannabis was later found in a false compartment of her vanity case.

At trial, Johar was depicted as the villain of the piece. Whitworth was portrayed as an innocent who had met him in London a year earlier and within months he had moved into her flat. According to her defence counsel:

> She did what she did because of her infatuation for Johar. She was grievously sinned against by him. He completely dominated her. He was prepared to corrupt this young girl's life, to try to get her to smoke pot, involve her in its importation, and he then proceeded to skulk away in India, leaving her to stand here and have

the responsibility put on her shoulders while this Indian Don Juan remains in Bombay.[9]

The subtext was clear. Nice girls from Jersey don't do this sort of thing, at least not unless they've been got at by some fiend from the old Empire. The jury was not so sure, though. Whitworth was found guilty and given a six-month sentence, suspended for two years. Khan, Dolphin Square's own wannabe drug runner, was given eighteen months. So ended an everyday 1960s story of sex, drugs and casual racism.

14

CARRY ON UP THE DOLPHIN

If Peter Finch and Vivien Leigh in the 1950s had brought an 'RSC/ Hollywood' sense of class to their Dolphin Square shenanigans, Sid James and Barbara Windsor did their own *Carry On* version of the grande passion in the 1970s. For a while, the Square seemed to have turned into the set of a British sex comedy and while there were a lot of cast members, Sid and Babs were top of the bill.

Although both had appeared separately in previous movies in the *Carry On* franchise, it was 1967's *Carry On Doctor* that saw them paired up for the first time. Windsor was by then three years into a marriage to Ronnie Knight, an underworld figure who had links to the Krays (as did she, having slept with two of the three brothers, Reggie and Charlie). Sid, too, was married but as they worked on further films – not least *Carry On Camping*, in which Windsor's bra infamously popped off to the gleeful sniggering of James – he, already in his late fifties and some twenty-four years her senior, fostered a growing infatuation. According to her own account, Windsor became convinced that a one-night stand would cure him of his obsession,[1] but it most certainly did not. So, in 1973 the pair embarked on a lusty affair that lasted until his death three years later.

Windsor's first brush with the Square had come a few years earlier, in 1968, when she had considered leaving Knight and moving in with another paramour. She was shown a flat she adored but, in the end, did not take it because of the Square's 'no pets' rule, which would have meant a split from her beloved poodle, Freddie. But equally, she came to the conclusion that she was not yet ready to ditch her marriage to Knight either.

By March 1974, Windsor and James were locked into their destructive relationship. She was intent on keeping their romance secret, while his growing jealousy made it virtually impossible to do so. They were also spending a lot of time together professionally, which brought additional strain. By then, the pair were several months into the run of the stage show *Carry On London* at the Victoria Palace Theatre, which not so many years before had been the spiritual home of the Crazy Gang. In the same month, shooting started on *Carry On Dick*, in which James stars as highwayman Dick Turpin, who adopts the personage of a mild-mannered vicar as a disguise. This character of the outwardly respectable society figure with a secret other life might well have chimed with some of those who lived in the Square.

James's marriage to his wife, Val, was showing signs of stress and she was spending long periods over in France while James worked in England. He seized upon her absence and came up with a plan to entice Windsor still closer to him. He told Val that an old back injury, caused by a collapsing stage curtain, made it too difficult for him to drive back to the family home in Buckinghamshire each night. He would instead get a place to crash in town not too far from the theatre. Dolphin Square fitted the bill perfectly. He and Windsor could now continue their affair much more at their leisure. 'It was the perfect love nest,' she would recall, 'and I'd often stay the night there with Sid after dinner.'[2] (Sadly, the pair were just a few years too early to enjoy the Greek dinner and dances at the Square's restaurant on Monday nights: £6.50 including a cabaret from Aphrodite who 'makes merry and suggestively with the guests between deliciously sung songs', before each table was given plates to 'smash maniacally and cathartically'.[3])

But the move was not an entirely successful one. James's possessiveness started to grate ever more. He repeatedly tried to persuade Windsor to break things off with Knight but he was also making life difficult at work. Unable to contend with other men giving her attention, he would sweep in at the merest hint of competition and on one notorious occasion tore a strip off fellow *Carry On* regular Bernard Breslaw simply because he had helped Windsor get off stage one night.

As autumn 1974 approached, *Carry On London* was due to finish, which would end James's excuse for renting a flat in the Square. Then, on 4 September, James and Windsor were having dinner one night when she found out that a man named Alfredo Zomparelli had been shot dead in Soho. Zomparelli had only recently been released from prison for stabbing to death Ronnie Knight's brother. Now Ronnie was prime suspect for his murder. Windsor's life was thrown into immediate turmoil. Knight would eventually be acquitted of the killing in 1980, although he later admitted to hiring a hitman before then denying it again. But all these circumstances ensured that James and Windsor could not simply carry on as before. The affair limped on but the idea that Windsor might ditch Knight for James was never really on the cards. *Carry On Dick* was James's last appearance in the series and within two years he was dead from a heart attack while on stage at the Sunderland Empire in, of all things, a farce called *The Mating Season*.

Even before 'The Sid and Babs Show', there were overtones of *Carry On* in an exposé by *The People* on 17 January 1971. The subject of its article was Sybil Benson, the tenant of a three-bedroom flat on the third floor of Duncan House. She ran it as a brothel – an establishment, the newspaper excitedly revealed, that catered particularly for 'clients with perverted sexual tastes'.[4]

The Square, it said, was 'the pride of Westminster City Council ... probably the most luxurious block of council flats in Britain'. But Benson billed her flat as 'a Torture House', for which she paid £13 7s 6d per week while the weekly revenues it generated averaged a spectacular £1,260. The good folk at *The People* felt duty bound to investigate the business, and were sure that the 'respectable tenants of Duncan House' would 'be shocked to learn of the brothel in their midst'. The paper began its infiltration by putting in a phone call to the flat, the reporter posing as a Kuwaiti visitor seeking female companionship. 'Come along,' Benson was reported to have urged him.

The reporter then related how he was greeted at the flat by Benson, who offered him whisky and sherry 'of good quality'. She apologised that the girl she had assigned to the visitor was running late and chatted candidly about the nature of her business. She usually had at least two girls working, she revealed. Clients were charged a base rate of

£25 for the introduction to the girl, plus a further £10 for use of the flat. But depending on the client's particular requirements, the girl's fee might rise to as high as £100. Benson retained 25 per cent of earnings as her commission.

It seemed that Benson could not stop herself sharing details of her business with the undercover journalist. He described her as being 'not only frank but boastful'. In one room he spied various gadgets that Benson referred to as 'instruments of chastisement'. She was also quick to emphasise that her disorderly house was actually quite orderly – not least in restricting the number of clients to six a day (opening hours extended from 12 p.m. until 6 p.m. every day except Sundays). Her clientele, which she said included politicians, actors and members of the aristocracy, did not take kindly to being rushed. Moreover, she had the neighbours to think about – not least a senior figure at the Czech Embassy who lived next door to her.

On a second trip, the 'Kuwaiti' reporter arrived with another journalist and a photographer – presented as a business associate and his company photographer. The ever-amenable Benson agreed that they could take some photos of the girls – Rene, who 'worked for the British Export Council modelling fashions', and Vicki, who 'formerly worked as a secretary for a West End firm'. Both girls, the newspaper reported, 'undressed down to fancy pants and bras and made it plain that they were prepared to indulge in any kind of sexual sport'. Armed with their photographs, the reporters made their excuses and left. They promptly presented their evidence to Westminster City Council, who proclaimed it 'astonishing' and suggested there was a clear breach of the morality clause in the tenancy agreement. Almost as soon as the story broke, Benson surrendered her lease. (She did not live in the flat anyway, commuting instead from a property in Brighton.) And *The People* was satisfied that it had done its bit to maintain the tone in Dolphin Square and uphold the nation's morals.

Not all the businesses operating in the Square were quite so risqué. There were for a time numerous talent agencies. Paul Dainty, for example, had been running Atlantic Artistes Managements from Hawkins House since 1968. He notably worked with Roy Orbison (someone who had stayed in the Square, prior to a UK tour earlier in the decade, with his wife and one son before they were tragically killed) on several international tours, which paved the way for him to launch the Paul Dainty Corporation that counted ABBA, the Rolling Stones, Diana Ross and the Bee Gees among its clients. A little later on, another impresario called Danny O'Donovan came to the Square, from where he too worked with Diana Ross, along with the likes of the Jackson Five, Stevie Wonder, Lionel Richie, The Who and Pink Floyd. He also pulled off a coup by enticing Henry Fonda to the West End to stage his one-man play *Darrow*, about the celebrated American lawyer Clarence Darrow.

Then there were the Askews, two sisters who set up a ground-breaking modelling agency in the 1960s that achieved international success with branch offices in Milan, the US and Japan. Valerie and Gloria Askew founded the Askew Team modelling agency in a basement on Bruton Street, Mayfair, in 1966, just below the studio of designer Jean Muir. While they admitted to learning their trade on the job, success came quickly. There was, for instance, a reception at the Hatchett's nightclub in Piccadilly, complete with London's first illuminated dance floor, the Beatles on the guest list and Billy Connolly providing the entertainment.

It was always a family affair, though, with the sisters' parents assisting with childcare as they got the business up and running. It was through their mother that the association with Dolphin Square began. She moved there in the late 1960s after she was widowed and stayed for some thirty years, reaching her 100th birthday. In fact, when her telegram from the queen was delayed, Valerie rang the Palace with the result that the missive and a large tin of biscuits were apologetically hand-delivered to the Square by a footman.

The Askew sisters were regular visitors to the Square with their families, and in the 1980s Valerie moved in to be close to her mother. Gloria followed in the 1990s, while her daughter also took a flat with her husband. The agency was still going strong then, not least because they had talented-spotted a youthful Naomi Campbell in the mid-1980s. For over half a century, then the Square played an important part in the family and business lives of the Askews, who helped mould the fashion modelling landscape in that period.[5]

Another of the Square's notable agencies was that run by Bunny Lewis, a decorated war hero, and his French-born wife, Janique Joelle. Lewis previously had some success as a lyricist, writing for Vera Lynn and Elvis Presley among others, while Joelle had a starring role in Alfred Hitchcock's 1944 short French-language propaganda film, *Bon Voyage*. But it was as agents that they truly had the golden touch. Their roster of talent would include Terry Thomas, Katie Boyle and singer Craig Douglas (the latter two both themselves Dolphinites). But arguably Lewis's real power came through the group of disc jockeys he represented.

In March 1967, the *Sunday Mirror* had felt compelled to ask: 'Should the Monopolies Commission look into pop? ... About 12,000,000 people seem to have their pop diet dictated by four men.' This gang was identified as Alan Freeman, Pete Murray, Simon Dee and Jimmy Savile. In particular, the newspaper criticised their dominance as presenters of *Top of the Pops* and panellists on *Juke Box Jury*. 'Nearly all the top DJs have the same agent,' the article continued, 'Mr Bunny Lewis. He says: "I do not agree that public taste is formed by the big four. Influenced yes, but the public is not brainwashed by them." Even so, is the present state of affairs desirable?'[6] (Lewis, incidentally, was himself a regular on *Juke Box Jury*.)

Craig Douglas, born as Terrence Perkins on the Isle of Wight in 1941, was for a while billed as 'The Singing Milkman' (a nod to his earlier professional life) and in 1959 achieved his sole Number One hit, 'Only Sixteen'. He lived in Hawkins House for some twenty-seven years from the early 1960s, although he was often touring during that time. He does recall, however, meeting Jimmy Savile in Bunny's basement office on numerous occasions, particularly during the 1980s. Although Savile's history of serial sexual abuse only came to light after his death in 2011, and Douglas had no reason to suspect him of any wrongdoing, there were, in retrospect, warning signs. Lewis, for instance, told Douglas that Savile used to visit morgues to look at cadavers. Douglas also asserts that there were meetings of the Entertainment Agents' Association, which is based in Dolphin Square, at which aspects of Savile's disconcerting behaviour were discussed.[7]

DOLPHIN SQUARE.   GARDENS, LOOKING WEST

When it was built in the 1930s, Dolphin Square was unlike any development previously seen in London in terms of extent and design. It remains a style icon to this day. (Chronicle/Alamy)

Oswald Mosley, leader of the British Union of Fascists, was an early resident. It was on returning to his apartment from a jaunt in the country that he was arrested in 1940 and interned for three years. (PA Images/Alamy)

John Vassall, a mid-level civil servant, was unmasked as a Soviet agent in 1962. Spy cameras and secret documents were discovered at his Dolphin Square flat. How a man of his rank could afford such an apartment became a focal point of the subsequent public inquiry. (Keystone Press/Alamy)

Sid James was one of the best-known faces in entertainment. While starring in the West End in the 1970s, James rented a flat which served as the base for his affair with *Carry On* co-star Barbara Windsor. (AF archive/Alamy)

In January 1971, *The People* ran an exposé of a brothel run from a flat in Duncan House by Sybil Benson. She claimed her clientele included politicians, aristocrats and entertainers. (Mirrorpix/ Getty)

Nicholas Fairbairn was a flamboyant and outspoken Conservative MP who lived in the Square. He was also subject to a series of allegations of sexual impropriety, including child sex abuse, both before and after his death in 1995. (Independent/Alamy)

An on-site bar/restaurant has long been a distinctive feature of the Dolphin Square offering. Artist Glynn Boyd Harte oversaw this redesign after Nicholas Crawley took over the Dolphin Brasserie in the mid-1980s. (Nicholas Crawley)

The swimming pool, a place of exercise and, sometimes, a place to see and be seen, too. Culture Club even referenced it in one of their videos. (Nicholas Crawley)

Understatement has not always been the watchword when it comes to Dolphin Square's nightlife. Nigella Lawson once called the Dolphin Brasserie 'one of the vulgarest restaurants in town'! (Nicholas Crawley)

"Must you play the National Anthem so loudly every time they come in?"

Dolphin Square found itself in the media glare when Princess Anne took up residence in Drake House, along with her then new second husband, Commander Timothy Laurence. (*Evening Standard*)

Whatever her true feelings about the place, Princess Anne retained sufficient warmth towards it to return as guest of honour at one of the Square's famed summer fetes. (Christine Forrest)

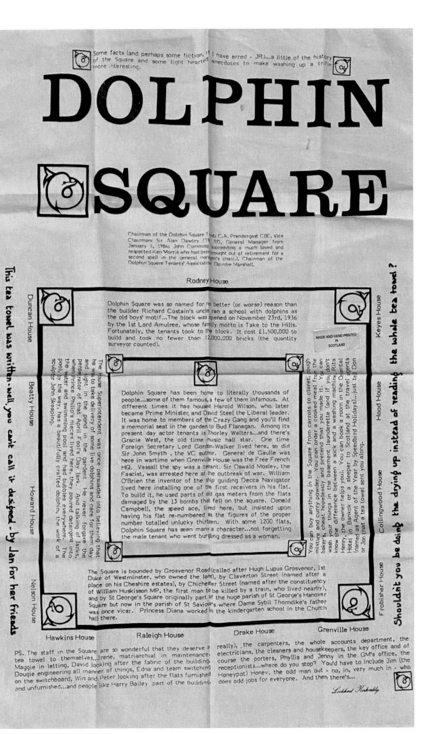

A tea towel designed by long-term resident Jan Prebble, displaying an array of the truths and untruths that have been written or uttered about the famous address.

Clockwise from above: David Ingle was just 15 years old when a neighbour in Lincolnshire, Gordon Dawson, began to sexually abuse him and to take him for weekends at Dolphin Square where he was introduced to other men. (David Ingle)

Aware of the mounting allegations against him, Dawson was found dead in the grounds of his Lincolnshire home in 2007. He had suffered a gunshot wound to the head. His passing and subsequent police enquiries left many unanswered questions. (David Ingle)

Carl Beech, also known as 'Nick', claimed that a VIP paedophile ring had been in operation at Dolphin Square and was responsible for the murder of a number of children. Beech's account was found to be false and he is currently serving an eighteen-year prison sentence for his crimes. (Julia Reinhart/Getty)

There is no indication that Lewis had any sense of the extent or nature of Savile's abuse either. A joint report by the Metropolitan Police and the NSPCC released in 2013 connected Savile to over 200 criminal offences, including over thirty rapes. Among the allegations made against him was that he had admitted committing necrophilia in the mortuary of Leeds Royal Infirmary. Yet Lewis was apparently naïve to such crimes. In an interview he gave in 1998, he said of Savile:

He's got a couple of caravans down Bournemouth way that he puts poor or ill people into for a week in the summer. He's also got a room at the hospital and another room at Broadmoor. He goes down to the hospital and he's there all day, and sometimes I say 'Would you like to come down the road and have a drink?' and he says 'I can't.' 'Why?' 'I've promised this fellow who normally sits in with the corpses that he can have the night off.'[8]

There is no reason to think that Savile ever practised his abuse in Dolphin Square but he was nonetheless a familiar face in Pimlico during the period of his offending.

If Savile at this time was generally considered as an unfathomable eccentric – and nothing much more sinister – he had some rivals in the Square. The decade was something of a golden era for eccentrics, even by Dolphinite standards. There was that very particular social mix, as rich as at any time in its history, that saw political heavyweights, lowbrow entertainers, madams, Nobel Prize-winners and many others beside, all somehow managing to rub along within the Square's walls.

So it was that four years after the Sybil Benson revelations, Dolphin Square was back in the papers but this time in relation to the death of Lord Patrick Blackett, who had spent the last few years living there. Born in 1897, Blackett was one of the greatest physicists of his generation, notably in the fields of cloud chambers, cosmic rays and paleomagnetism. During the Second World War he had been an advisor to the government on military strategy and research – in which role, he concluded that the UK was incapable of developing an atomic bomb on its own but should instead co-operate with the Americans, ultimately leading to the attacks on Hiroshima and Nagasaki. In 1948, he received his Nobel Prize 'for his development of the Wilson cloud chamber method, and his discoveries therewith in the fields of nuclear physics and cosmic radiation'[9] and in 1965 he was made president of the Royal Society. By that stage, he was also a senior advisor to the Wilson Government – he was by inclination a left-winger – and was instrumental in the establishment of the Ministry of Technology. If he wished to maintain the sense of being at the heart of things in his dotage in the Square, he could hardly have picked a better address. (The Square, incidentally, was also the sometime home of Sir William Cook who, as deputy chief of the Weapons Group of the United Kingdom Atomic Energy Authority, was a pivotal figure in the development of the hydrogen bomb. Under Harold Wilson, he also advised the French on their own hydrogen bomb programme, in part with a view to winning the support of French president, Charles de Gaulle, for the UK's application to join the European Economic Community – support that in the event was not forthcoming.)

In the same year as Blackett died, a Labour MP called Raymond Fletcher moved into Frobisher House. He had been the representative for Ilkestone in Derbyshire since 1964 and three years later had been appointed parliamentary private secretary to Roy Mason, the Minister for Defence Equipment. He had also acted as a historical advisor on Joan Littlewood's *Oh! What a Lovely War* in 1963. By that point, though, Fletcher was engaged in another enterprise not unfamiliar to a good many other Dolphinites over the years – espionage. At least, that was the claim of Vasili Mitrokhin, a senior KGB operative who defected to the UK in 1992, a year after Fletcher's death. Mitrokhin brought with him a vast haul of intelligence papers that became known as the Mitrokhin Archive. Among its many revelations was that Fletcher had been recruited as a Russian agent in 1962, when he was working as a journalist, and had been given the codename PETER. Not long afterwards, Fletcher had published an aggressive repudiation of the Conservative Government's defence policy, including its nuclear deterrent, and also suggested that 'classification is more a device for concealing incompetence than for concealing information from a potential enemy'. Mitrokhin's haul further suggested that the KGB was aware of Fletcher's contacts with the Czech secret service, the StB.[10] Before his death, Fletcher admitted that he did indeed have dealings with figures at the Czech Embassy but said he always notified the Foreign Office of who they were. Meanwhile, he believed MI5 had long kept him under surveillance and said that they had 'nearly broke my spirit'. When word of his alleged dealings with foreign intelligence agents came out, Fletcher's wife was adamant that the claims were not true and that he had, in fact, been working for MI6.[11]

Another of the Square's traditions – that of notable thespians in residence – was continued by, among others, Ian Bannen. Nominated in 1965 for an Oscar for his turn in *The Flight of the Phoenix*, he gained a reputation for prowling the basement, learning his lines and on one occasion terrifying two old ladies as he cried, 'Murder, Murder!' Meanwhile, over in Beatty House lived Michael Wild, an actor and cabaret performer, playwright and composer. Here was a man of many talents whose career too often seemed cursed by bad luck. He wrote a series of musicals that played well in the regions but never quite managed to fire in the West End. At one stage there was talk of Rex Harrison taking his musical *Little Lord Fauntleroy* to Broadway, with Disney interested in the film rights, but in the end it came to nothing. Nonetheless, the 1970s were moderately kind to him.

In 1976 he appeared as a straight actor on the West End stage for the first time in *Mr Laurel and Mr Hardy*. The following year saw him achieve an elusive West End hit with his musical version of J.M. Barrie's play *What Every Woman Knows* at the Shaftesbury Theatre (although the first night was almost ruined when Dame Anna Neagle's microphone started picking up the intercom messages of a nearby taxi firm). Anna Sharkey won an Olivier Award for her performance in the show, delivering an acceptance speech that consisted of just four words: 'I can't say anything.' In 1999, Wild was briefly involved in a legal wrangle with Andrew Lloyd Webber and Tim Rice. Wild asserted that the song 'Superstar' from *Jesus Christ Superstar* bore an uncanny resemblance to his own song, 'Gloria', written some ten years before 'Superstar' debuted in 1970. However, Wild's case did not last long once heavyweight lawyers became involved. Wild seems to have reconciled himself to his 'close but no cigar' career, however, and shortly before his death in 2018 he published an autobiography entitled *Composer, Known Only to God and Anna Neagle.*

Another resident of similar vintage who also did not enjoy the riches he surely deserved was Michael Ash. In April 1976 he faced the bankruptcy court, blaming his financial problems on his desire to back small businesses with big ideas – a strategy he believed was in the national interest. Ash was, after all, a man who himself had big ideas, several of which came to spectacularly successful fruition.

Born in Calcutta in 1927, Ash read maths at Trinity College, Cambridge, and, for several years he was the managing director of Crookes Laboratories, where he notably oversaw the purchase of the licence for an anti-depressant that became the most widely used in the country. He was also a founding governor of Templeton College within Oxford University, focussing on business and management studies. But it was for his work as a researcher and developer with the Guinness brewing company that he is best known. The Square already had a historical association with Guinness through the presence of Diana Mosley, who had previously been married to a member of the brewing family. But Ash's contribution to the business was truly unique.

He headed a team who perfected a blend of nitrogen and carbon dioxide that allowed an untrained bartender to pour a perfect draught pint of the black stuff. The 'high and low' taps traditionally used in pubs were to give way to Ash's 'easy serve system'. He designed a bespoke keg that was divided into two parts – one for the beer and the other for a pressurised cocktail of the two gasses. It was first distributed to pubs in 1959 and sparked controversy among purists, who nicknamed it 'Daft Guinness'. But over time, it gained acceptance and changed the way the drink was served around the world. At last, it became possible to pour a pint in a matter of seconds. The ideal head, Ash worked out through complete guesswork, was ⅜ of an inch in a standard half-pint glass. Some may ask whether any Dolphinite has made a more significant contribution to national life. If only he had earned a royalty on each pint pulled using his system.

Yet for all Ash's brilliance, perhaps the outstanding local legend of the period was a man named Leonard Plugge (pronounced Plooje), who was the type of figure one might have expected to encounter in a *Carry On* movie. Among his many achievements, he established quite the property empire in the Square, leasing three flats and a suite of basement rooms between 1950 and the early '70s.

Plugge was born in 1889 and made his name as a pioneer of wireless broadcasting. He travelled extensively across Europe in the 1920s – one well-publicised trip involved him and a friend travelling in separate cars and staying in touch via radios installed in the vehicles. On one of his trips, he hit upon a scheme to buy airtime from owners of transmitters on the Continent to broadcast English-language commercial content. He was particularly successful with his broadcasts from Normandy in France, and in 1931 launched the International Broadcasting Company (IBC). Investing in technical innovations, the reach of Radio Normandy quickly extended so that the IBC came to be regarded as a serious rival to the BBC. Especially on a Sunday, when Plugge kept up a supply of pleasing light music while the BBC was dedicated largely to religious programming – in the south of England on a Sunday evening, his station consistently boasted higher listening figures than the national broadcaster.

In 1935, Plugge was elected the Conservative MP for Chatham in Kent, defeating the future Labour leader, Hugh Gaitskell. Plugge then shamelessly spent a large part of his ten-year parliamentary career promoting the interests of commercial radio in the House. But by the time he left the Commons in 1945, his radio empire was in serious difficulty. Although he managed to keep broadcasting in the early days of the war, many of the locations where he had based himself fell under Nazi occupation. The Normandy transmitter itself was sabotaged by French troops with the intention that it should not fall into German hands.

In his heyday, Plugge made an absolute fortune from his broadcasting ventures. He also gave career breaks to several notable broadcasters, including future Dolphin Square resident Roy Plomley. Plugge continued to innovate after the war, continuing offshore operations and using the IBC's London headquarters as lucrative music production studios. He lived extravagantly, socialising with royals and celebrities (among them fellow Dolphinites Sarah Churchill and April Ashley) but in reality his funds were seriously depleting.

By 1970 things were beginning to fall apart. The Plugges had leases in Beatty and Hood House in the names of Leonard, his wife Gertrude (from whom he had split in the 1950s) and his son Frank, while another son, Greville, was living in Frank's apartment. Leonard's flat was a sight to behold. The taps were gilt dolphins and the toilet resided under a green velvet throne. There was a four-poster bed, too, which Plugge claimed had once belonged to Marie Antoinette, and the ceiling was adorned with a spectacular mural of Rubenesque naked women.

But in March 1970, there was a serious fire in one of the Plugge apartments caused by a candle that had been lit because the electricity had been turned off. There were also bailiffs calling, seeking repayment of a debt of £475. In April 1970, Plugge decided his best bet was to get out of town. He made first for Mexico and then to California, yet he remained determined to keep his hand in at Dolphin Square. As the family's various leases came up for renewal, he fought to retain them even as the management committee undertook legal proceedings to evict them. It took the committee until 1973 to do so.[12]

By then, tragedy had twice befallen the family. Firstly, in 1972 Plugge's daughter, Gale Benson – by then married to senior Black Power activist Hakim Jamal – was living on a commune in Trinidad and Tobago linked to the prominent Black Power activist Michael X when she was murdered by two of his followers. Then the following year, Greville Plugge was killed in a car crash in Morocco. Plugge himself lived out the rest of his life in Los Angeles, dying of a heart attack in 1981.

Another of the great characters of this period was Frederick William John Augustus Hervey, better known as John Jermyn or, after inheriting the title in the 1980s, the 7th Marquess of Bristol. Born in 1954, there was something of the Lord Byrons about him – he was a man 'mad, bad and dangerous to know'. In the 1970s, he came into several million pounds of inheritance and embarked on an extreme form of hedonistic living. Educated at Harrow and the University of Neuchâtel, he modelled himself in part on Oscar Wilde, pursuing sexual relationships with both men and women and taking on an extraordinary volume of drugs and alcohol. While he could be charming and generous to those he liked, he could also be rude, abusive and hard to handle.

Some who knew him put his personal problems down to a dysfunctional relationship with his father, Victor. Hervey Snr was a firebrand himself and, in his youth, had served a three-year prison sentence for jewellery robberies in Mayfair. The demons seemed to pass from one generation to another. After John had fled Britain for tax reasons and relocated first to Monaco and then to Paris and New York, in 1983 he was suspected of smuggling heroin into the US, and in 1988 he served prison time for cocaine transportation. In 1991 he was deported from Australia and he was again imprisoned for drug possession back in the UK. Amid various claims that he had slept with as many as 2,000 rent boys, that he was suffering from Aids and that he had burned through a fortune estimated at £35 million, he died in 1999 at the age of 44. A decade later, the *Daily Mail* would call him 'the Satanic Marquess' and wonder whether he was 'Britain's most amoral aristocrat ever'.[13]

But in Dolphin Square in the 1970s, he was merely a rich young man going wild. He was already mired in the hard-partying lifestyle, with its dangerous quantities of sex and drugs and booze. There were also warning signs that his high jinks were getting out of hand. In January 1975, for example, he was fined £20 for the theft of some 'no waiting' cones that he had stolen, which he intended to use to prevent illegal parking outside his own car showroom.[14] Meanwhile, an intimate of Hervey's recalls his habit of flying his helicopter from over the river in Battersea to the family estate at Ickworth in Suffolk. He would often be drunk or high at the controls. 'They were crazy times,' the confidante confides. 'As long as he was awake, I wasn't too worried about it. It was when he was nodding off that was the worst.'[15] With the marquess, there was always that sense that it might be fun while it lasted but it couldn't go on forever. But for a while at least, he made sure it was going on in Dolphin Square.

And, of course, there was always *something* going on, even when it felt like there wasn't. The Square's swimming pool was briefly a bone of contention when Westminster Council's plans to build a new public pool were put on hold in 1973. As one correspondent to the local newspaper highlighted, a great many people within the borough did not know that the council owned the Square's pool so were perhaps less aggrieved than they ought to have been that an entrance fee of 55p put it beyond the budgets of many less well-off families. Dolphinite David Steel – at the time the Liberal chief whip and a future leader of both the Liberals and the Liberal Democrats – was all for promoting greater usage of the pool. In 1970 it was reported that he had invited several of his parliamentary colleagues for a daily constitutional swim, noting that it was very congenial 'apart from being frequented by an occasional Tory MP'. Among those he invited, and who took up the offer, was the Liberal leader, Jeremy Thorpe, who we now know was, at the time, designing all sorts of elaborate plots to dispense with the problem of a former lover, Norman Scott, who had become convinced that Thorpe had ruined his life and was willing to go public with the fact. The affair would end in a bungled attempt on Scott's life in 1975, leading to Thorpe standing trial in 1979 accused of conspiracy for murder – charges of which he was ultimately acquitted despite significant evidence of his involvement.

At the time, the Square was home to a counter-culture figure who may have seemed rather out of place amid the prevailing impression of well-to-do tastefulness. John Krivine was the son of a prominent Jewish family who, in 1974, had opened a clothing stall called Acme Attractions on the King's Road in Chelsea. He and his business partner, Steph Raynor, were heavily influenced by Malcolm McLaren and Vivienne Westwood's boutique, SEX, whose fashions helped mould the punk aesthetic. Acme soon evolved into Boy London, with Don Letts employed as manager. He did not stay long, though, describing the rebranded store as 'the bastard child of Acme, created to capitalise on the tabloid punk'. Instead, he went off to manage punk band the Slits and became a creative partner of the Clash and many others.

There were also increasingly loud rumours of dark goings-on in the Square. Rumours of sexual abandon and legal impropriety were nothing new, but suggestions of targeted abuse were. Such claims would swirl around the place for decades to come, but the first serious seeds of concern were sown in the 1970s. Take, for example, the recollections in 2017 of Toyah Wilcox, who back in the late 1970s was newly arrived in London and building a career as an actor and musician. In 1978 she was offered a role in Derek Jarman's cult classic, *Jubilee*, which depicted a decaying Britain in which Elizabeth II had been killed in a random mugging. She recalled:

> One of the cast members lived in Dolphin Square and we were all hearing stories of the abuse of male prostitutes there. I think he [Jarman] was commenting on a society that allowed that kind of abuse to take place, which was justified because of their Etonian backgrounds. I think he did everything he could to make the gay world safer, to bring it into the light.[16]

But for all the light that he and others shined, there was an overwhelming feeling that aspects of life in Dolphin Square were merely getting darker.

15

MURDER COMES TO THE SQUARE

Carry On Dick was the last of the *Carry Ons* that Sid James made and the series itself wound down over the decade. It's end-of-the-pier-cheekiness still spoke of a certain mindset in the nation but it somehow seemed a less good fit than in its 1960s heyday. Dolphin Square's own bed-hopping antics and its cast of brilliant eccentrics and oddball misfits also reflected only one aspect of life in the Pimlico haven. There was an uneasiness to 1970s Britain that Jarman was picking up on – a sense of discontent and bubbling violence gradually displacing the idealistic if frustrated hopes of the previous decade. Harold Wilson's early 1960s aspirations for a prosperous nation 'forged in the white heat' of the 'scientific revolution' ultimately gave way to a country beset by unemployment and raging inflation, by strikes, energy shortages and three-day weeks, by the Irish 'Troubles' and violence on the football terraces, by growing public panic at the perceived explosion of 'vice' on the streets and the bent coppers who facilitated it. This was no longer the age of *Dixon of Dock Green* but *The Sweeney* instead. And, in its usual way, Dolphin Square reflected the nation, albeit in a 'House of Mirrors' kind of way.

In 1970, the death of resident Sarah Bissolotti was in no way suspicious but did serve as a sad reminder of how easy it has been to be 'unseen' in the Square. Bissolotti, who was 61 and lived alone following the death of her banker husband, was suffering from tuberculosis when she passed away in her bath. The coroner would deliver an 'open verdict' on her death, which was put down to alcohol and barbiturate poisoning. She had lain undiscovered for a month.[1]

She was just the latest victim to fall down that yawning chasm so long a feature of Dolphinite life. It had always been possible to exist happily and independently in the Square, socialising merrily if one desired, or else retreating into the privacy of home. It is a place of community, but only for those who want it. If you prefer to be left alone, the right to solitude is both accepted and observed. But that is why, perhaps, it has been possible for a string of residents to have lain dead in their baths for extended periods over the years. And also why other tragedies and travesties have been able to occur inside this urban village.

On 7 March 1973, Tommy Foster was working in the Square's underground car park as normal. At some stage, a foreman approached him about one of the cars parked down there. It was a Ford Cortina and it was taking up one of the residents' bays – there were also metred spaces for members of the public. The foreman told him that the car could not stay where it was. So, Foster jacked up the vehicle and manhandled it some 70yd out of the way. Little did he realise that he had just shifted a live bomb that the next day would form part of a murderous IRA attack in the capital – the first time the capital had been bombed by overseas attackers since the Blitz.[2]

The terror plot was an intricate scheme headed by a 22-year-old student teacher called Dolours Price. Working out of Belfast, she had assembled an eleven-person active service unit (ASU) that included her sister, Marian, and which had identified a number of targets in London – including the Old Bailey, the Ministry of Agriculture, an army recruitment office near Whitehall and New Scotland Yard. The plan was to plant a car bomb at each venue. It was to be the IRA's first major attack in London since the Troubles had taken hold in the late 1960s.

In preparation, four vehicles – a Hillman Hunter, Ford Cortina, Ford Corsair and Vauxhall Viva – were stolen in Northern Ireland in the weeks leading up to the attack. Each was given a new number plate and a respray, while the suspension was strengthened to cope with the weight of explosives. They were then shipped to the mainland via ferry from Dublin to Liverpool. The Royal Ulster Constabulary warned their British counterparts that an ASU was on the move, but were not able to provide intelligence of exactly what was planned. Meanwhile, an opportunity to halt the bombings was missed. One of the cars was stopped as it came off the ferry in Liverpool because it had no tax disc, but a search of the vehicle that might have revealed its explosives was not undertaken.

The four cars were now driven down to London. One of the drivers even collected some Green Shield stamps when they stopped for petrol – an oversight that would provide crucial evidence of the conspirators' actions in court. Their rendezvous point in London was designated as Dolphin Square's underground car park and by the end of the day, all the vehicles were in place. The gang then spread out, taking rooms in five different hotels in the local area. They even had ideas for an evening out – ticket stubs were recovered for a performance of *Freedom of the City* at the Royal Court Theatre – a show written by Irish playwright Brian Friel about a group of protesters at a Civil Rights meeting in Derry in 1970.

At six o'clock on the morning of 8 March, the four vehicles were removed from Dolphin Square, driven to their assigned destinations and their explosives primed. The idea was that they would each explode at three in the afternoon, by which time the ASU members would all be well on their way back to Ireland. However, all did not go according to plan. The car planted outside Scotland Yard was spotted by an eagle-eyed police officer, who noticed something off about its licence plate. The bomb inside the car was eventually defused. Another of the cars parked near the BBC's armed forces radio studio in Dean Stanley Street was also identified and disarmed.

However, the Metropolitan and City of London Police struggled to co-ordinate their efforts as the day progressed. A little after two in the afternoon, the Met passed word to its City colleagues to look for a green Ford Cortina in the vicinity of the Old Bailey. It was found over half an hour later. At 2.49 p.m., while the area was still being cleared, the car exploded. Shortly afterwards, another of the car bombs, this time in Whitehall near the Ministry of Agriculture and an army recruitment centre, also detonated. Over 200 people were injured in the attacks and one man, 60-year-old Frederick Milton, died of a heart attack brought on by the events.

The bombing crew, meanwhile, made it only as far as Heathrow before they were picked up. One of their number, an 18-year-old typist called Roisin McNearney, provided the police with details of the operation ahead of a high-profile, ten-week trial at Winchester in autumn 1973. She was subsequently acquitted of all charges and given a new identity. Another of the gang pleaded guilty and the rest were all convicted, receiving sentences of between fifteen years and life. (By curious coincidence, in 1974 former Dolphinite Clementine Freeman-Mitford and her husband, Sir Alfred Beit, were victims of a robbery at their stately home in Ireland, during which a number of valuable paintings were seized. The robbers were led by an English heiress-turned-IRA supporter, Rose Dugdale, and the works – which were valued at £8 million and included pieces by Vermeer, Goya, Gainsborough and Rubens – were offered in exchange for a ransom and the transfer of the Price sisters from British to Irish prisons.)

The attack sparked a surge in attacks on the mainland. Two people died in a separate attack at London Bridge before the year was out, and there were also bombs at Euston and King's Cross stations. The following year, the Birmingham pub bombings would claim a further twenty-one lives, the Guildford pub bombs five, while another twelve died in the M62 coach bombing and dozens more perished on the mainland at the hands of the IRA's so-called Balcombe Street Gang. In 2012, Dolours Price noted of the assaults that she had spearheaded (and to which Dolphin Square was pivotal), 'I was convinced that a short, sharp shock, an incursion into the heart of the empire, would be more effective than 20 car bombs in any part of the North of Ireland.'[3] General Sir Peter Hunt, who had a flat in Howard House and was Chief of the General Staff from 1973 until his retirement in 1976, was among those on the British side who were faced with formulating a response to these escalating tensions.

Tommy Foster, meanwhile, recalls how police officers came to question him about the events in the Square's car park a few days after the explosions. They were particularly interested as to whether he could identify the owners of the vehicles. They drove him to Scotland Yard, where he spent several hours studying pages and pages of mugshots, but all to no avail. At the end of the fruitless day, he was told that he could leave. Would they be able to drive him back to the Square, he asked. Having failed to provide them with the information that they were in search of, he was informed that he would, in fact, be walking.[4]

While terrorism thankfully remained a relatively rare occurrence in relation to the Square, there were other sources of peril for many as they went about their everyday lives. For example, there was an evident trend of the Square becoming significantly more dangerous for men on their own in the 1970s. In 1970 itself, for example, Arthur Skeffington – an MP, parliamentary private secretary to the Minister for Housing and Local Government, and chairman of the Labour Party's National Executive Committee – was walking alone through the gardens. He had reportedly just finished having dinner with some friends when he was attacked by two young men who attempted to run off with his suitcase containing correspondence and clothes. In the event, another man chased down the thieves and retrieved Skeffington's property. The two attackers were apprehended and one was subsequently convicted of the attempted robbery and sentenced to nine months.

The following year, Donald Milner, a 53-year-old company director, was badly beaten and his flat ransacked in what a judge described as a 'completely vicious and unprovoked assault'. Milner suffered fractures to his nose and cheek and needed twenty-five stitches for cuts to his face. According to the evidence heard in court, he had met a 21-year-old man, James Watson, at a West End club the previous night, and Watson had then turned up at Milner's apartment at two in the morning in the company of another man, Peter McLean. The assault began as soon as Milner opened the door, with McLean beating him 'simply for the sake of it'. Milner's hands and feet were bound with ties and he was punched repeatedly in the face as he lay on his bed, while Watson made his way around the flat and took some £200 worth of property. Twice Milner made a break for freedom but was caught by the assailants and beaten again until he was covered in blood. 'The man got naughty and I thumped him a few times,' McLean would tell the court. McLean was sentenced to two-and-a-half years for the crime, and Watson to fifteen months.[5] But it would not, tragically, be the last attack of its kind. On 24 June 1975, the *Daily Mirror* ran a truly disturbing story. 'A solicitor was found murdered yesterday,' it read, 'with his head battered and throat cut.'[6]

The victim was a 39-year-old solicitor called Michael Shepley – seemingly the first recorded victim of murder at Dolphin Square in the estate's history. He had been born in Johannesburg, South Africa, and was schooled in England before studying at the University of Witswatersrand in Johannesburg and then at the University of Oxford. He was, according to his family, a kind, funny and highly intelligent man, who was very fond of the theatre, music and the arts in general. At the time of his death, he was working as a solicitor for the Greater London Council, where he was well regarded and highly valued for his professionalism. To the world at large, he seemed to be doing extremely well for himself, earning enough to support a rich and rewarding metropolitan lifestyle. But Michael Shepley had an unspoken secret: he was gay.

Homosexuality in England and Wales had been decriminalised back in 1967, yet by the time of Shepley's death almost a decade later, he was one of the many who still felt compelled to keep that vital component of their identity secret. Whatever the law now said, coming out of the closet posed myriad risks – professional, social and personal. Openly gay men routinely found their career aspirations curtailed, they were subject to abuse from strangers on the street and risked rejection even by their nearest and dearest. They might even be murdered and there would be the suggestion that their sexuality was to blame, that they had somehow brought it upon themselves. Decriminalisation had been a historic landmark but being gay in London in the 1970s was barely any easier than it ever had been.

After his death, it was soon apparent that Shepley had never felt able to broach the subject with his family, whose shock at the brutal nature of his death was compounded by the revelation of his sexuality. A close family member, for example, referred to his homosexuality as 'the other police story of his life' – as if it had been invented by the authorities to cover up some other 'real' reason for his death. 'He must have read all about Oscar Wilde,' the relative wrote, 'and realised that that life can only end in tragedy – for oneself and one's family.' The travesty of his death was immersed in the further tragedy of a loved one who would rather accept a conspiracy theory than the truth about his sexual orientation.[7]

Shepley's death was utterly needless, the result of an explosion of violence during what was, in reality, a run-of-the-mill robbery – albeit of a type that single gay men were at much elevated risk of suffering. In common with many gay men – and several Dolphinites – Shepley was in the habit of visiting Piccadilly Circus to pay for sex. Piccadilly had long been a notorious focal point for 'rent boys' (known locally as 'Dilly Boys'), who, since at least Oscar Wilde's time, had congregated along the railings in the Circus until the area came to be called 'the Meat Rack'. A great many local lads and newcomers to the city found their way to the Rack, either with an eye to making a quick buck or via the coercion and trickery of others. As of the mid-1970s, it was a grim place, the prostitution mixed up with serious organised crime and sexual abuse.

Shepley was enough of a regular in Piccadilly that the police were aware of him and had even spoken to him about the danger he was putting himself in. They had warned him to be wary as there had been a spate of recent attacks on gay men by assailants working in pairs. While one would accompany the victim to their home, the other would secure entry into the property and then they would assault the victim as they robbed him. The risk-reward calculation was simple: the attack was typically two against one and the victim would likely not wish to involve the police given their unwillingness to have to explain the surrounding circumstances of the attack.

A young officer called Ian Graham – only eleven weeks into his training – was one of the two initial responders to the Shepley attack. The scene that greeted him and his colleague was traumatising and while he would not encounter another quite like it, he did become used to reports of assaults on gay men in the Square. Numerous victims received severe beatings, he reports, but more often than not refused to formalise complaints for fear of the repercussions in revealing their sexual orientations publicly.

Around Friday, 20 or Saturday, 21 June, the police discovered, Shepley had visited Piccadilly Circus and picked up an 18-year-old called William Whiteley. The pair then returned to Shepley's flat in Duncan

House. At some point, they were joined by Whiteley's accomplice, 24-year-old George Chapman, a kitchen porter of no fixed address. The level of violence used against Shepley soon escalated, although it is not clear why this should have been as there were no obvious signs of a struggle. But the end result was, according to the post-mortem, that Shepley succumbed to a stab wound to the heart. There were also bruises around his throat. (Those early suggestions that his throat had been cut do not seem to have been accurate.) His body lay undiscovered until it was found by a porter on the Monday morning, at least thirty-six hours after the solicitor had died.

Initially, the police feared they had a serial killer on the loose. The murder was linked to two other recent local deaths, including that of accountant Thomas Wilson, who was found dead in his bed two streets away and nine weeks earlier, having been hit around the head with a sharp object. The *Daily Express* went so far as to talk of a 'maniac killer' at large.[8] Shepley's mother, meanwhile, clung to alternative theories. She understood that her son's flat had previously housed a plain-clothes army intelligence officer who had served several tours of duty in Northern Ireland. She had apparently even said to her son that she hoped the IRA would not come after him by accident, in response to which Michael had laughed. But now she was seriously considering the possibility. The IRA had bombed those two pubs in Guildford the previous October, one of which Shepley had apparently sometimes visited and which the police knew about. Had he, she wondered, been used to gather intelligence for the police about the bombings and had his cover been blown? After all, the ties between Dolphin Square and the paramilitaries had only just recently been headline news. It was all highly unlikely but it was perhaps more palatable for a grieving mother than the alternative suggestions.[9]

Another resident of the time, who worked as a chauffeur, recalls his own distressing experience a short while after Shepley's death. He was, he says, in the habit of going to some of the bars in King's Road at the time and was there one evening when he got chatting to two or three people who said that they too lived in Dolphin Square. Then, some evenings later, he got a knock at the door and there was this same man asking whether he and a friend could pay to be driven to the airport.

But before he could respond, the pair had pushed past the chauffeur into his flat, knocking him to the ground. They punched him, he recalls, and then tied him up, before taking his wallet and other valuables from the flat, while also demanding the keys to both the company car he drove and his own personal vehicle.

After they left, the victim immediately called the police and the assailants were in custody within twelve hours. The police were particularly interested in the fact that initial contact had been made between the victim and one of the attackers in a bar. They voiced suspicions that these two might have also been responsible for the attack on Michael Shepley. From the victim's account, it seems likely that the threat of being connected to that murderous attack was enough to convince his attackers to plead guilty to the less serious assault on him – for which they both received three years in jail.[10]

As for Shepley's killers, they too were in court by the following summer. There was no mention of links to Ireland or terrorist plots. Whiteley, who during the trial was said to earn some £100 a week on the Meat Rack, was acquitted of murder but found guilty of conspiracy to steal and sentenced to a period of borstal training. His co-defendant, Chapman, was convicted on the murder charge and received a life sentence. After the initial, sensationalist reporting of the discovery of Michael Shepley's body, the case hardly garnered a mention in the press, save for a few short reports on the verdicts and sentencing that ran in the *Daily Telegraph*.[11] Scarcely a fair reflection of Shepley, a man of accomplishment and culture whose only real 'crime' was to be gay in an era when to be so automatically rendered him a target.

16

POLITICAL BLUES

On 28 March 1979, the Labour Prime Minister Jim Callaghan faced a vote of no confidence in the Commons. It had been brought by the Conservative leader of the opposition, Margaret Thatcher, and the count could not have been closer. For a while, it seemed like Callaghan might just defeat the motion, although at significant personal cost. Dolphinite Spencer Le Marchant was one of the Conservative tellers that day and it fell to him to announce the result: 'The Ayes to the right, 311. The Noes to the left, 310.' Callaghan had, in fact, lost by the narrowest of margins. The Tory ranks erupted into jubilant celebration before Le Marchant even managed to get his words out. The path was cleared for a general election in May, which would give the Conservatives a parliamentary majority and thrust Thatcher into Downing Street. The political landscape instantly shifted and Thatcher's eleven-year reign was about to re-sculpt the nation.

For much of her tenure, the Conservatives seemed virtually untouchable. What troubles they faced stemmed mostly from breakdowns in their own party unity. Europe and the ill-conceived poll tax would ultimately do for her, but that was all a long way off as Le Marchant made his pronouncement. For a large part of the 1980s, the Iron Lady commanded respect on the international stage, while at home she divided the nation between those who adored her and many others who reviled her. That part of her that would forever be the grocer's daughter from Grantham set about running the country like a business, convinced that the market and the then dominant cult of monetarism would bring affluence across the social classes.

But the promised riches of drip-down economic growth faltered. A few earned unimaginable fortunes, but the nation's wealth increasingly centred on the financial institutions in London. Elsewhere there was decline as old industries fell away and nothing was brought in to replace them. The division grew between the haves and have-nots and those falling behind in the wealth race felt abandoned by a system too often devoid of compassion. In an interview with *Woman's Own* in 1987, Thatcher gave voice to the idea that the government was not in the business of saving you if you were falling. 'And, you know, there's no such thing as society,' she said. 'There are individual men and women and there are families. And no government can do anything except through people, and people must look after themselves first. It is our duty to look after ourselves and then, also, to look after our neighbours.'

But for much of Dolphin Square, the question of how to keep one's head above water or how best to eke out your DHSS money until the next payment arrived was not generally a major problem. Instead, for many of its residents the arrival of Thatcher was an indicator that the good times were about to roll. There was perhaps no greater symbol of this era of affluence than the Dolphin Square restaurant, which came under new ownership in 1986 as Thatcher approached arguably the peak of her powers.

In 1978, the restaurant had for the first time come under the management of a woman, Pat Faris. The *Marylebone Mercury* congratulated her on 'the delightful ambience she has created',[1] but by 1981 she'd had enough and sold on to Alain Lhermitte, who since 1972 had been the proprietor of the much-loved Mon Plaisir in Covent Garden. Although the Square's restaurant has often been well regarded through its many permutations over the years, he joined the long list of those who could not quite work out how to make it pay. In 1986, the challenge fell to Nicholas Crawley, then in his early thirties and with a soaring reputation for restoring old houses and opening them up as hotels. He raised enough capital to buy the restaurant, going into business with Shaun Wilson, an old friend with whom he'd trained at the Savoy. They asked celebrated Rochdale artist Glynn Boyd Harte to overhaul the interiors for what was to become the Dolphin Square Brasserie. Harte was given free rein on everything from styling the bar to designing the crockery and dictating the look of the menu. Artist Jessica Ridley, daughter of Nicholas Ridley who was at the time Secretary of State for Transport, assisted in designing a few features, too. The over-arching theme was that of a decadent, art deco cruise liner; a promising French chef was installed in the kitchen.

The Brasserie's grand reopening was covered by the press and prompted a slew of (mostly positive) reviews. Harte was not only an artist but also a talented musician and part of the cabaret duo, Les Frères Perverts, who specialised in French *chanson*. Les Frères played at the restaurant and Harte even followed in the tradition of Edward Halliday – responsible for the original restaurant design – by composing a waltz especially for the venue. Nigella Lawson, the daughter of the Chancellor of the Exchequer, called it 'one of the vulgarest restaurants in town', although she didn't mean it in an entirely negative way (though she did think that the 'sitting pretty' motif on the loo roll holders in the ladies' toilets a step too far).[2] Meanwhile, Meredith Etherington-Smith wrote a feature on Nicholas Crawley in which she teasingly noted of the Square, 'I hadn't been there since I ended up at a sinister party in Frobisher House in the late sixties, given by someone called Raymond, who may or may not have been an MP.'[3]

The Brasserie was for a while a real London destination for those with some money to spend. It was not the only place in town, though. Patrick Gwynn-Jones, himself a Dolphinite, was the patron of Pomegranates, on the corner of Grosvenor Road adjacent to Dolphin Square. Since opening in the 1970s, Pomegranates had grown an enthusiastic clientele that included Frank Sinatra, Britt Ekland, Diana Ross, Peter Sellers, Sammy Davis Jnr, Princess Margaret, Anthony Armstrong-Jones, Laurence Olivier, Michael Caine and David Frost. But the Brasserie was now in a position to compete with the Pomegranate magic. It hosted a party for David Hockney and another for Paul McCartney, for example. John Davis, the chairman of the Rank Organisation, had his 80th birthday there not long after it had opened. The guest list that night included Princess Alexandra and the Hon. Angus Ogilvy, Sir Geoffrey and Lady Howe, Lord Arnold Goodman, Lord and Lady

Birkett, Lord and Lady McAlpine of Moffat and, for good measure, Mr and Mrs Donald Sinden, too. There was even a synchronised dance performance in the swimming pool. (The pool, it should be noted, was subject of the ultimate cultural accolade of the early 1980s. When Culture Club, those leaders of the New Romantic movement, made their video for 'Do You Want to Hurt Me?' in 1982, they included a scene set at 'Dolphin Square Health Club, 1957' – although the footage was actually shot off-site.) In the end, the Brasserie found it as hard to make money as its predecessors but for a while in the mid- to late-eighties, it felt like the centre of the world.

The notion that the Square was a Tory stronghold in this period was given further weight when in November 1986, the *News of the World* ran a piece on 'How to Pick Up an MP'. There were a number of assumptions in the article, not least that MPs were by default male, and that there was a large female market eager to seek them out and hook up with them. Whether or not that was true, the newspaper stated that the place to snare a Conservative was the Dolphin Brasserie.[4]

Naturally, even though the party was in the ascendency, Conservative MPs still faced myriad challenges thrown up by life in politics. But in 1988, Hector Munro of Keyes House, the long-time MP for Dumfriesshire, faced a peculiarly awful situation. Four days before Christmas, Pan Am Flight 103 was downed by a Libyan-backed terrorist bomb over Lockerbie, in his constituency. In total, 270 people lost their lives, including everyone on board and eleven people on the ground. For a while the incident put more mundane political considerations into perspective, and Munro rose to the occasion, prompting his fellow MP, Brian Wilson, to describe him as 'a man who is truly a part of the community that he represents'.

For those MPs of other political persuasions living in the Square (and there were many), the 1980s was a time for introspection as they considered how to overcome the dominance of their rivals. An opposition politician with a particularly memorable CV from days gone by was Denis Howell, a Birmingham MP from 1955 until 1992, with the exception of 1959–61 when he was out of Parliament. He was Minister for Sport during the tenures of Harold Wilson and Jim Callaghan, most memorably taking in the 1966 World Cup. On 28 October 1974, a year or so after the trial of the car bombers who'd used the Dolphin Square car park, Howell's car was blown up by an IRA bomb while his wife reversed it out of the driveway of their constituency home in Birmingham. Their son was also in the car at the time. It is thought that the boy and his mother were only saved from serious injury because the bomb fortuitously dropped off the exhaust pipe as the vehicle moved. Howell was down in London at the time. 'I haven't the faintest idea why I was picked on,' he would later comment.[5] A couple of years later, his ministerial portfolio was expanded to include responsibility for responding to the drought that hit in the summer of 1976. It was said that No. 10 had even suggested he try a rain dance. But in the event, it was not necessary and a few days after his appointment, the heavens opened. The Minister for Drought was quickly renamed by the newspapers as the Minister for Floods. Having been identified as 'the weather man', he was then appointed Minister of Snow during the particularly harsh winter of 1978–79.

After its disappointing if predictable defeat of 1979, Labour lurched to a far more damaging turnover in 1983 under the leadership of the old-school left-winger Michael Foot. For a while, the country was without a reliably functioning opposition as Labour became engrossed in a battle between its moderates and its left-wing militants – a bout of narcissistic navel-gazing that left many voters doubtful whether the party might ever be electable again. Indeed, it was not just the voters who harboured such concerns, but key figures within the party itself.

A few had seen the problem coming for a while. In March 1981, four prominent Labour politicians (known as the Gang of Four) left the party to form a new one, the Social Democratic Party. The SDP was pitched firmly in the political left of centre and there was genuine hope that, in light of Labour's troubles, it might fill a political vacuum. The four consisted of two sitting MPs, David Owen and Bill Rodgers, plus Shirley Williams (who had lost her seat in 1979 but had once been considered a potential future Labour leader) and Roy Jenkins (the former Chancellor, Home Secretary and deputy Labour leader, and at the time president of the European Commission).

In total, twenty-eight Labour MPs and one Conservative would defect to the new party. Among them was Square resident Dick

Crawshaw, a lawyer who had been the Labour MP for Liverpool Toxteth since 1964 and had served as the Commons' Deputy Speaker from 1979–81. He resigned the Labour whip in February 1981 and joined the new party on its foundation a couple of weeks later. Another inaugural member was Crawshaw's flatmate when Parliament was sitting, James Dunn, the MP for Liverpool Kirkdale. He joined the SDP in October 1981. A former junior minister, he'd gained some notoriety the previous year when he was found guilty of shoplifting a map (worth 60p) and assorted other goods valued just short of £15 from the Victoria branch of the Army & Navy Stores. He was, the court heard, under the influence of prescribed anti-depressants at the time.

Both Dunn and Crawshaw found their constituencies were abolished by boundary changes ahead of the 1983 election, and neither was returned to Parliament. Both died relatively young too – Dunn in 1985 aged 59, and Crawshaw the following year. He was 69 and his death shocked colleagues who were expecting him to take part in a parliamentary rowing regatta the following day.

The SDP started amid great optimism and in June 1981 forged an alliance with the Liberal Party, then under the leadership of another Dolphinite, David Steel of Beatty House. He had succeeded Dolphin Square swimmer and accused murder conspiracist, Jeremy Thorpe, in the role. (The pool, incidentally, hosted a Commons vs Lords swimming gala during the decade, adding to its air of exclusivity.) Steel had welcomed the arrival of a new political force, but not everyone in his party was so enthusiastic – notably, the Liberal 'big beast' Cyril Smith, who concluded that the SDP should be 'strangled at birth'.[6] But the SDP–Liberal Alliance was an instant hit, leading the poll ratings for a while in the year of its creation. 'Go back to your constituencies, and prepare for government!' Steel had told delegates at the Liberal conference that year.[7]

Yet, by the time of the next general election in 1983, Thatcher's Conservatives were riding a wave of post-Falklands popularity. The Alliance polled a respectable 25 per cent of the vote but came in a distant third and boasted just twenty-three MPs. Shirley Williams was among those without a Commons seat. It was a grave disappointment and essentially sounded the death knell for the Alliance as a significant electoral force at the national level.

If Steel's public life was tumultuous in this period, his private life (much of it played out in Dolphin Square during his prime years) was hardly much calmer. In December 1984 his 20-year-old adopted son, Billy, was taken into police custody after failing to appear before London magistrates on a charge of disorderly behaviour. He was alleged to have been involved in a fist fight at Victoria railway station. Steel Snr issued a statement that his son had not understood he had been due in court in the morning. Billy Steel subsequently received a £50 fine at Horseferry Magistrates, where the judge told him, 'You're getting yourself quite a little record … if this goes on you will find yourself in more serious trouble'.[8]

The incident marked the beginning of a series of run-ins with the law by the Steel sons. In 1985, the Liberal leader's then 19-year-old son, Graeme, was given seventy-five hours of community service for his involvement in a shop raid, during which cigarettes, lager and groceries were stolen. Then, in 1987, he was fined £50 for assaulting a police officer outside a Galashiels nightclub, and in 1995 he was jailed for nine months for cultivating cannabis at his home in the Scottish Borders. Steel's lawyer stated, 'He was worried that any reports he was buying cannabis on the street would get out and reflect badly on his father.'

Meanwhile, in 1991 Billy was banned from driving for three years and fined £200 when he refused to take a breath test at a police station after his car was involved in an accident near Edinburgh. More recently, in 2018 a woman in her forties, Claire MacCabe, died after falling ill in a hot tub at a party at Graeme Steel's home, having consumed significant quantities of alcohol and drugs. While no blame attached itself to Graeme, it was nonetheless another difficult episode in the family's history.

A year later, it was David's turn in the spotlight. After ending his career as a party leader in 1988, Steel had served as an MP until 1997 and then went up to the Lords. He was also the first Presiding Officer of the Scottish Parliament, where he sat between 1999 and 2003. However, in evidence provided to the Independent Inquiry into Child Sex Abuse

(IICSA) in 2019, Steel admitted that he'd had discussions with Cyril Smith in 1979 (when Steel was Smith's boss as leader of the Liberals), from which he'd concluded that Smith had previously sexually abused children.[9] However, he failed to act on the information (and allegations against Smith carried by *Private Eye* magazine around the same time) or to investigate whether Smith still posed a risk. Following Smith's death in 2010, it emerged that he had been a serial abuser of young boys for many decades in his Rochdale constituency and beyond. Moreover, he had consistently used his influence to evade capture, even in the face of numerous police investigations. Despite his admitted concerns, Steel even supported his knighthood in 1988. As a result of his revelations in 2019, Steel was suspended from the Liberal Democrats (the successor party to the SDP–Liberal Alliance, and a party Steel briefly led in 1988) but was soon readmitted until resigning from both the party and the House of Lords in 2020. Shortly beforehand, IICSA had characterised Steel's handling of the Smith affair as an 'abdication of responsibility'.[10]

Having seen off Labour and tamed the SDP threat before the 1980s were very old at all, the Conservatives seemed well and truly to have the upper hand. Margaret Thatcher's press secretary when she was in opposition in the 1970s and her political secretary from 1981 until 1983 was Derek Howe, who was another politico to have an apartment in the Square. Among the many duties he carried out for her was to inform her in March 1979 that Airey Neave, her shadow secretary of state for Northern Ireland, had been killed by an IRA bomb planted under his car at the House of Commons. In 1985, though, Howe was intent on suing *The Times* after it had described him as having his 'hand in the till' while running a north London housing association.[11] The court found in his favour and awarded him damages. It seemed as if the Conservatives could not lose.

And then suddenly, Dolphin Square found itself a prime battleground for an internecine conflict that threatened one of the greatest political scandals of the Thatcher years. It all started in 1986 as a local matter in Westminster after Labour had run the Conservatives closer than expected in local elections. The leader of Westminster Council since 1983 was Shirley Porter, the daughter and heiress of Tesco founder Sir Jack Cohen. She was a politician in the Thatcherite mould

– no nonsense and convinced that politics was really a case of firm management of people and resources. Her often brusque style was not to everyone's taste, neither among the opposition nor her own ranks.

Moreover, after the Tories had comfortably held control of the council in 1982, the 1986 vote had shaken her badly. Labour were only 106 votes off securing the Cavendish ward that would have given them control of the council. Instead, the Conservative majority was reduced from twenty to four seats. Porter's response was to devise the 'Building Stable Communities' scheme. It was, in truth, a vast gerry-mandering scheme with a view to moving likely Labour voters out of marginal wards and replacing them with likely Conservative voters. Eight key wards were identified and a process begun whereby council homes were sold to owner-occupiers or to third parties (the assumption being that those taking advantage of the Thatcher-driven 'right to buy' scheme would be more natural Conservative voters). Properties in these wards were renovated to attract buyers and money diverted for infrastructural improvements with a similar political motivation. Meanwhile, there were concerted efforts to remove typically 'non-Conservative' constituents, including the homeless, those who resided in hostels and temporary accommodation, as well as groups perceived as sympathetic to the opposition, like students and nurses. Some were moved to safe Conservative wards within Westminster or were encouraged to leave the area altogether.

Porter's deputy at the council was a long-term resident of Dolphin Square called David Weeks. Weeks had arrived at the Square in 1970 – initially living in Hood House, although he and his wife Heather later had flats in Frobisher and Beatty – and built a career in advertising and marketing. He joined the council in 1974 as a fresh-faced 28-year-old, was chair of the Chelsea Young Conservatives (in which role he wined and dined the likes of Jeffrey Archer and Enoch Powell in the Dolphin Square restaurant) and unsuccessfully stood for Parliament in 1983.

Porter and Weeks oversaw a highly effective gerrymandering campaign for a while, which required the co-operation of assorted council officers. But it was not long before disquiet started to grow at some of what was being demanded. The leader of the Labour group in the council was Paul Dimoldenberg, and he began to receive brown envelopes full of incriminating paperwork as to what was going on. His sources included not only those in opposition but dissenting voices from within the Conservatives themselves. However, when Dimoldenberg started to demand to know exactly what was going on, he was met most often by a wall of official silence.

While Dolphin Square was in one of the safe Tory wards and thus not subject to the 'Building Stable Communities' plan, it nonetheless prompted concerns in its own right. In particular, this vast complex seemed to make precious little contribution to alleviating the council's housing problems by taking any of those close to the top of the housing list. Once more, Dimoldenberg asked questions but was again stonewalled. In his own words:

> The more and more I asked, the less and less I got answers, and it became clear that this was like a closed housing association. It didn't operate by the rules of other housing associations, which basically had to take nominees from the council as part of the deal. No, Dolphin Square never took any nominees from anybody, it operated its own waiting list and its own allocation policy. I suppose it was that they allocated homes to people who they wanted to allocate homes to … They had no rules other than the ones they made up, so the only conclusion you could come to was that it basically allocated flats to people like them.[12]

About the same time as the gerrymandering intrigue was getting into full swing, Porter was responsible for another highly controversial bit of council business. At the start of 1987, Westminster sold three cemeteries, a crematorium, several residential properties and over 12 acres of land in a deal worth 85p. The rationale was that it would relieve the council of costs of some £400,000 per year for upkeep of the graveyards. The buyer almost immediately sold on the land to developers for a seven-figure profit, while a flaw in the original contracts meant that no one now had responsibility for upkeep of the graveyards, which soon fell into disrepair. Amid public protests, the council was ordered to buy them back, with the original sale declared illegal (although by that time Westminster could not claw back the prime land sold to developers). After years of legal wrangling, in 1992 Westminster, then under the leadership of Weeks, resumed ownership of the cemeteries at a cost to taxpayers running into the millions. Labour councillor and future MP Peter Bradley was moved to observe, 'Shirley Porter will go down in history as the woman who sold three Council cemeteries for five pence each and David Weeks will go down in history as the man who bought them for £4.25 million.'[13]

But that loss would pale against the total cost of the 'Building Stronger Communities' scheme. And it was two of Weeks' fellow Conservative Dolphinites who played a vital part in exposing the scheme. They were Tony and Simone Prendergast, an old-school Conservative husband and wife. She was a cousin of Neville Laski, who had sued Dolphinite Henry Newnham back in the 1940s, and was the granddaughter of Michael Marks, the co-founder of Marks & Spencer. Once a chair of the London Conservatives, she was a personal friend of Margaret Thatcher, sometimes even allowing the PM to use her flat for party political broadcasts. Simone was awarded an OBE in 1981 and a damehood five years later. Tony Prendergast, meanwhile, had been Westminster's youngest ever lord mayor in 1968. Although his parliamentary career had never taken off, the Prendergasts were important party political figures and significant players on the scene. (They had also been caught up in the Brighton IRA bombing when attending the 1984 party conference.)

Tony Prendergast represented something of the old patrician Westminster Council and Porter was by no means his ideal for the job of leader. But what might have begun as misgivings turned into something more substantial as details of the gerrymandering scandal emerged. In 1988, he broke ranks to give an interview to the *London Programme*, criticising the Porter regime in light of the cemetery sales. The incident caused bad blood between Porter and the Prendergasts, with Porter summoning Simone to a post-interview showdown at which both sides stood their ground. But the walls were starting to close in on Porter.

Sources on the Conservative side continued to feed information to both Labour and the press about the council's illicit dealings. Then, in 1989, the BBC's investigative *Panorama* team broadcast a programme on the scandal. By now, the affair was stirring questions in Parliament and the policy of 'Building Stronger Communities' was put on hold while it was referred to the District Auditor. But it was still not the end for Porter, who retained her position as leader of the council in 1990. Ironically, it was the poll tax, which so damaged Thatcher, that came to Porter's aid: the Westminster rates were so low by national standards that the tax was a positive vote-winner in the borough. However, by 1992 she had left her position as council leader, with Weeks coming in to succeed her. The Prendergasts, meanwhile, continued to stand up to Porter. On one occasion, Simone clashed with her in public, speaking up for what she referred to as 'the people who hand out leaflets and make chocolate fudge for jolly fund-raising events ... the people who want to be good Conservatives and help the Conservative government'.[14]

The auditor's investigation and subsequent legal appeals against it would take many years to complete and came at a steep price. In early 1994, Dr Michael Dutt, who was one of several councillors facing a surcharge in relation to the policy, killed himself with a shotgun at his home in St Albans. Papers relating to the saga were found scattered around his body. He was 43 years old. The auditor would ultimately conclude, 'My view is that the Council was engaged in gerrymandering, which I have found is a disgraceful and improper purpose, and not a purpose for which a local authority may act.'[15] His conclusion was that the scheme had cost the public purse £36.1 million, for which he declared Porter, Weeks and four other officials liable. The High Court upheld his view in 1997, although assigning liability only to Porter and Weeks. That judgement was overturned by the Court of Appeal in 1999 but reinstated by the House of Lords in 2001. Lord Bingham of Cornhill condemned Porter and Weeks as guilty of 'deliberate, blatant and dishonest misuse of public power ... not for the purpose of financial gain but for that of electoral advantage. In that sense it was corrupt.'[16]

Although Porter continued to maintain her innocence from her new home in Israel, a financial agreement was finally reached in 2004 in which she paid back £12.3 million and David Weeks £44,000. In 2009, Colin Barrow, then the leader of Westminster Council, said, 'What she

[Porter] did was wrong, illegal, and we are unreservedly sorry. I personally want to make it absolutely clear I believe Shirley Porter and her policies did significant damage and it is a legacy I want to bury once and for all.'[17] But Weeks remains defiant, saying in 2021 that Porter 'was much maligned and hard done by'.[18] The Audit Commission's district auditor, he insisted, had an over-exuberant solicitor and they over-reached themselves. Wherever truth might lie on that, Dolphin Square had provided key members of the cast in one of the grimmest scandals of the Thatcher age.

17

THE END OF THE PARTY

Despite its promising beginnings, the Dolphin Square Brasserie struggled financially, just like its predecessors. It had arrived on the scene with a bold vision and there had been plenty of memories made in its brief life, but its stylish design and glitzy patrons were not enough in the end to sustain it. By 1989, it went up for sale and was purchased by the Parasol Corporation, part of the giant Allied Breweries. It somehow seemed a fitting metaphor for the age.

As the business changed hands, so too were the Thatcher years approaching their end. After the debacle of the 'Homes for Votes' scandal, a few more Dolphin Square residents were to play a part in her downfall. Among them was Alick Buchanan-Smith, who had been MP first for the Scottish constituency of North Angus and Mearns and then for Kincardine and Deeside since 1964. He had served as Parliamentary Under Secretary of State for Scotland under Ted Heath from 1970 until 1974, before becoming Minister of State for Agriculture, Fisheries and Food (1979–83) and Minister of State for Energy (1983–87) under Thatcher – despite rumours when Thatcher took over the party leadership in 1975 that he might refuse to serve under her.[1]

There were enduring tensions between Buchanan-Smith and the party leader. He was made shadow secretary of state for Scotland when the Conservatives went into opposition in 1974 but resigned the post two years later when Thatcher opted to oppose calls for the devolution of Scottish power. Her stance on Scotland still rankled with him thirteen years later, when in June 1989 he launched a public attack on her leadership. With Scotland at the time being used as the testing ground for the poll tax (officially called the Community Charge), he warned that she needed 'to listen, not to impose' if she were not to put the Union at risk. He went on to say that 'arrogance in anyone, in public life or in private life, is something to be deplored'.[2] His fellow Scottish Tory MP and Dolphinite Nicholas Fairbairn argued in response, 'He is talking nonsense, joining and encouraging the dreadful Scottish political habit of whingeing.'[3]

But Buchanan-Smith was one of a growing number of Conservatives increasingly disquieted by Thatcher's tone and policies. In 1989, another Dolphinite, Sir Anthony Meyer, the Conservative MP for North West Clwyd, took on what he believed to be the role of stalking horse in a challenge to her leadership. In many ways, Meyer represented everything that Thatcher was trying to move away from. He was an Eton-and-Oxford man who came from a wealthy background in which he'd developed a philosophy of liberal Conservatism and a profound belief that the UK ought to be an integral part of the wider European community. He was, in his own words, 'an old-fashioned sloppy wet' of the sort that his party leader found unacceptable.[4]

By the end of the decade, Thatcher's increasingly autocratic style of government was making her more and more enemies on her own side. The economy was jittery and her long-term Chancellor, Nigel Lawson, had just resigned in protest at her reliance on particular advisors. The poll tax crisis loomed on the horizon and many of her colleagues found her anti-European stance insupportable. The mood was ripe for a change at the top and Meyer hoped that by throwing his name into the ring, he would entice others with a greater chance of overthrowing Thatcher to follow. None did, however. 'The Wets were wet indeed,' he would comment ruefully as he privately cast himself not as 'stalking horse' but as 'burnt offering'.[5] Lacking a groundswell of support from the parliamentary party, Meyer nonetheless conducted a competent and sometimes rather stirring challenge.

But when the votes were counted, it was not good news for the Meyer camp. He won just thirty-three votes to Thatcher's 314, with three abstentions and twenty-four spoiled ballot papers. A poorly

Buchanan-Smith was among those who lent his support to Meyer, although illness meant he voted by proxy. Meyer said of the result: 'I was quite surprised to get so many votes, I thought I'd be beaten by the abstentions. The total result I think is rather better than I'd expected and not quite as good as some of my friends were hoping for.'[6] Having managed to distance herself from the 'Homes for Votes' scandal played out in part between Dolphinites, Thatcher had now survived a direct challenge to her authority from another of the Square's occupants. But it was a shot across the bow and set in motion a series of events that would culminate in her tearful exit from Downing Street the following year.

Dolphin Square was not all about the politics in the 1980s, even if it often seemed that way. There was plenty else going on away from council rooms and debating chambers. In July 1981, for example, Sir John Millar, the Crown Equerry (responsible for overseeing the queen's vehicular transport), caused a ruckus when he crashed a horse-drawn carriage into a car outside Dolphin Square as he was returning from a croquet championships at the private Hurlingham Club in Fulham. The Red Datsun that he hit belonged to one of the Square's tenants and was utterly demolished.[7]

A rather more successful transport-related event had occurred a few months earlier, on 13 October 1980, when National Car Parks, who ran the Square's underground car park, hosted a champagne reception to mark British Leyland's launch of the Austin Mini Metro. The Deputy Speaker, Bernard Weatherill, was the guest of honour that day but it was a young woman working nearby who in the end did much more to promote the new car.

Just across from Dolphin Square, in St George's Square, was the Young England Kindergarten where a 19-year-old Diana Spencer worked as a teaching assistant. The launch of the Metro was a big deal for the British motor industry, with Prince Charles doing his bit by taking one of the vehicles for a test drive from British Leyland's flagship Longbridge factory. Clearly impressed by its handling, a short while later he purchased one of the cars – in red – for £3,495 and gave it to Diana. Not long afterwards, in February 1981, he proposed to her, marking the end of Diana's time at the kindergarten. In the two years or so that she had worked there, she had become a familiar face in the Square as she visited its branch of Lloyds Bank to pay in monies from the nursery. While she is reputed to have been much in love with her red Metro, it would not be long before she swapped that too for rather grander models.

From the ultra-famous to the hardly known, in 1988 there was the little-commented upon death, at his own hand, of a one-time Dolphinite by the name of Frank Wolfe – a man deserving of a footnote in history. Born in Bavaria and of Jewish descent, Wolfe had been something of a playboy in the 1930s before settling down in 1937 into the first of his five marriages. As the Nazis' grip on his native country intensified, he and his new wife moved to England, where he learned the language fluently and forged a successful career in business. But his greatest moment came when he served as chief translator from German to English at the Nuremberg Trials in 1945 and 1946. He became a well-known figure around the German courtrooms, not least for his habit of bringing his pet Great Dane, named Tiny, along with him. It was Wolfe who had the job of indicating to Hitler's right-hand man, Hermann Göring, and the former German Foreign Minister, Joachim von Ribbentrop, the death sentences passed on them. 'I am proudly aware of my minor claim to fame as the Voice of Doom which Göring et al heard,' he would later note in his memoirs.

Another resident to die by their own hand was the actress Jill Bennett, who overdosed in her Howard House flat in October 1990 at the age of 58. She was suffering from depression but Bennett had been a popular figure in the Square in the 1980s, when she could be seen most days taking a dip in the swimming pool. A highly accomplished actress on stage and screen since the 1950s, her recent output had included an appearance in the 1981 James Bond movie, *For Your Eyes Only*, and playing opposite Helena Bonham-Carter in 1986's *Lady Jane*.

Bennett had also been the fourth wife of playwright John Osborne from 1968–77, a union that quickly turned toxic. It was characterised by mutual dislike and distrust that frequently played out in abusive behaviour. She was known for publicly goading him as impotent and gay, while he seems to have at least partly blamed her for the downturn in his career during that period. Nonetheless, his absence of compassion, affection or even regret at her death was breathtaking. Writing of her in his autobiography in 1991, he said:

> Everything about her life had been a pernicious confection, a sham. I have only one regret now in this matter. … It is simply that I was unable to look down upon her open coffin and, like that bird in the Book of Tobit, drop a good, large mess in her eye.[8]

Meanwhile, the Square maintained its knack of integrating figures from the highest of high society and the lowest depths of the underworld. In the 1980s, the Liverpool-based gangster Tommy 'Tacker' Comerford sometimes used the Square as a base for his international drugs- and arms-smuggling operations. It is said that Comerford was sufficiently ferocious that he once persuaded the Krays to give up on their ideas of expanding their own criminal empire into Liverpool after he went to Lime Street Station to meet them off the train and convince them of their miscalculation. Yet for all that he bestrode that city's underworld, he also spent a great many years in prison. When he was on trial in 1985 for his smuggling activities that stretched across continents, the *Liverpool Echo* claimed that drugs and guns were delivered to the Square, where he stayed in apartments at 'cheap rates'.[9] He was sentenced to fourteen years in prison, so securing a long-term let at an even cheaper rate at her majesty's pleasure.

Crime and sleaze, however, were not the preserve of the underclass. Take the flamboyant Nicholas Fairbairn – the man who had taken Buchanan-Smith to task for his 'whingeing' – who managed to present a public face of respectability amid suggestions of the most disreputable and appalling misconduct in private. A resident of Hawkins House, he was seldom far from some scandal or another. A QC, he had become MP for Kinross and West Perthshire in 1974, when he was in his early forties, and quickly became known for his outspoken line in libertarianism, as well as the extraordinary kilts, trousers and cravats that he wore and which he often designed himself. Nor did he make any secret of his prodigious sexual appetite, proclaiming: 'Let us say I have spent all night screwing a mongoose, and next morning I have to appear in the House or in court. The vital thing is: does it show? If a sexually frustrated fellow, or woman, does not let their indulgence affect their professional performance, then bollocks, it doesn't matter.'[10]

In 1979, he was appointed Solicitor General for Scotland and his star seemed in the ascendant. But it was not long before his career started to derail. In late 1981, the married Fairbairn's secret lover, Pamela Milne – a former House of Commons secretary – made a suicide bid at his apartment (although Milne denied claims that Fairbairn's teenage daughter had needed to cut her down from a lamp post). Another resident of the Square, MP Michael Mates, was dragged into the scandal when it was suggested he had been telling tales on his friend Fairbairn to the parliamentary whips – claims that Fairbairn and Milne themselves denied.

While Fairbairn just about survived that particular infidelity and its fallout, he could not parry the criticism that surrounded his decision the following year not to prosecute a gang of men suspected of the multiple rape and assault of a Glaswegian woman working in the sex industry. Fairbairn broke accepted protocol to explain to a journalist that he believed the victim was too traumatised to be considered credible in the witness stand. The victim subsequently undertook a private prosecution of her attackers, all of whom were convicted, and Fairbairn was forced to stand down as Solicitor General.

He would never hold high office again but he was knighted in 1988. However, the honour prompted a new complaint against him. On 13 June 1988, an individual – whose identity has been withheld in the public record – wrote to Margaret Thatcher in response to the news of the knighthood:

On the evening of Saturday 13th September 1986 at 6.50 p.m. my daughter [NAME REDACTED] was returning home. Mr Fairbairn approached [NAME REDACTED], shouted and repeatedly swore at her and struck her across the face and chest. The police were called, and they interviewed six witnesses who confirmed [NAME REDACTED] story. The Police Sergeant from Dalgety Bay Station would not go to Mr Fairbairn's home on the Saturday evening. He said he preferred to wait until the Sunday when Mr Fairbairn would have sobered up. The Police Sergeant said he did not want to remain a 'tea boy' for the rest of his working life. The Police returned on the Sunday and informed us that all the details would be forwarded to the Procurator Fiscal in Dunfermline, but since this incident we have been unable to find out what is happening. My family and myself are extremely concerned about this situation, and we are now wondering if there is one law for MPs and another law for members of the public.[11]

Downing Street responded that the prime minister was not in the practice of commenting on names included in the Honours List and that the allegations made in the letter were not matters for No. 10 but for the police instead.

Fairbairn died in 1995, but claims of impropriety continued to stalk him even in death. In 2009, for example, journalist Dame Ann Leslie was interviewed by fellow journalist Carole Cadwalladr and told her that the first time she had appeared on the political panel show *Any Questions?*, she had been sat next to Fairbairn who started 'determinedly groping my crotch'.[12] Back in 2000, an individual known as Julie X made claims to police that she too had been sexually assaulted by Fairbairn when she was a child. However, when details of her story began to leak into the public domain, the complainant decided not to pursue further action. Then, in 2014, she waived her right to anonymity to go public with her accusations. She was Susie Henderson, the daughter of Robert Henderson QC, a friend of Fairbairn. She said that both men had abused her, and that it had started when she was 4 years old and that Fairbairn had raped her when she was 4 or 5.[13] She suggested the pair were part of a wider circle of paedophiles in the Scotland legal profession at that time. Her father and Fairbairn were both dead by 2014, but another of the men she accused – the QC, John Watt – was extradited from the US in 2020 to face charges of abuse related to Henderson and three other complainants, and was remanded into custody at Livingston Sheriff Court in November 2020 to await trial.[14]

Nor was Fairbairn the only Dolphinite to be the subject of serious abuse allegations from this period. London-based criminal defence solicitor Jeffrey Gordon, who qualified in 1956 and was still practising sixty-four years later, claims that in the early 1980s he visited the Square to interview and take instructions from a fellow solicitor (whose identity cannot be revealed for legal reasons), who at the time was seeking to appeal his conviction for sexually abusing a minor. The victim, according to Gordon, was the child of the landlady of a property where the solicitor sometimes stayed when he was working at a branch office of his firm in the north of England.[15] There could be no doubting that the rumours of serious wrongdoing within the Square were growing.

18

DAVID INGLE

David Ingle is a man who says that he was abused at Dolphin Square when he was a teenager in the early 1980s. He brought his claims to the attention of the police almost a decade before the suggestion of a Westminster paedophile ring, before the testimony of 'Nick' (see chapter 22) threw the spotlight on Dolphin Square. David's allegations are yet to be tested in a court of law, although not out of his choice.

In 1982, David was 15 years old. He seemed to have it all going for him. Bright, articulate, handsome, he came from a good family who had recently relocated to the pretty village of Skendleby in the Lincolnshire countryside. Rural life was perfect for him – he was an outdoorsy type of teen, into cycling and horse riding, fishing and hunting.

One day that year, the Ingles received a house call from a near neighbour, Gordon Dawson. Dawson was a local farmer with a large estate that included Dalby Hall and the smaller Dalby House, where Dawson and his family – his wife, son and daughter – lived most of the time. David's father had previously done some business with him but Dawson had come around on this occasion to say sorry for a small accident during which his uncle had clipped Mrs Ingle's wing mirror. It was the start of a lasting friendship between Dawson – a large, intelligent man with an avuncular quality – and the Ingles. A friendship that turned David's life upside down, and one he is still in the process of setting back on its axis.

Dawson was a prominent figure in the local area. He was an important member of the Church community in the county, a member of the

Synod for Lincolnshire diocese, a man with connections. Everyone in Skendleby and around knew who Gordon Dawson was. In his leisure time he was also a keen shooter, possessing an array of weapons. He was eager to share his knowledge and would sometimes take groups of local lads on shooting expeditions. Before long, he offered to take David out on his own. The unworldly teen was at first delighted by the invitation and the pair would go rabbit hunting together in the early summer. Sometimes they would go at night, shooting from Dawson's car.

Dawson would hold David as he lined up a shot. But David was soon aware that he kept hold of him even after the shot had been fired. Gradually, the physicality became more invasive. Dawson would put his hand on the boy's leg, then his groin, then inside his underwear. David was frozen with fear, uncertain as to how he should react. Dawson raped him. And he would do so on repeated occasions. Then he would drop David at home and be charming to the Ingles. It was a classic pattern of behaviour by such a perpetrator. His victim did not dare to tell his parents what was going on and so Dawson came to be regarded as an even dearer friend, welcome in the family home at any time.

After a nightmarish summer of abuse, David decided he had to get away from his abuser. His method was to tell his parents that he was miserable at his new school in Lincolnshire and so wanted to return to his old school in Cambridgeshire. He would stay with old friends close to school during the week, a good two hours' driving distance from his tormentor. David was banking on taking himself out of harm's way. In fact, he was unknowingly providing Dawson with a new form of access to him.

Dawson started offering to pick David up on a Friday evening and drive him back to Lincolnshire. Dawson was often out and about on business, including in London, so it would be no problem for him. David now found himself regularly trapped in a car with his abuser for prolonged periods of time. Customarily, the journey back to Lincolnshire would be punctuated by a stop on a quiet country road and a new sexual assault. Then, a short while into the autumn term of 1982, Dawson had a new suggestion for the Ingles: how would David like to come to London with him for the weekend and they could take in a show? How about *42nd Street*? David's parents were delighted.

How kind of this local grandee to take an interest in their son and show him the capital's sights. It was to be the first of many trips that Dawson and David made to London. David's mother is sure there were at least ten. But it would be decades before David told her what actually happened to him once Dawson's car was beyond sight of the Ingle family home.

Dawson had them make a beeline for Pimlico. Sometimes the 15-year-old David was encouraged to drive. When they arrived in Dolphin Square, they would park in the underground car park then walk up some stairs to the arcade of shops, then up some more flights to a flat. David was struck by the grandness of the place. He thought it was a hotel. Indeed, Rodney House, with its short-term lets, operates very much like a hotel, offering short-term serviced apartments. Years later, David described the interior of the flat Dawson used to journalist Patrick Strudwick, 'Very bijoux, cottage-y, magnolia walls, but the curtains were quite pretty – yellows, blues, and greens – and that theme ran throughout.' David was unable to identify the exact location of the flat when he reported his abuse to the police in 2007 but he has been told by a family friend that it was owned (which would, of course, have meant leased) by Dawson and two friends. David recalls that the general atmosphere at the Square was 'jolly' and that Dawson was clearly known there and would chat to other residents he met in the corridors.

David frequently went shopping on these London visits. Dawson also regularly took him to Church House, the nearby headquarters of the Church of England, because he had diocesan business there. He was taken out to dinner, too – he has particular memories of going to Motcombs, something of a Belgravia institution, although there were other restaurants. Dawson would take him and they would be joined by several guests at the table. A couple of times, there was another teenage boy in attendance but David was never sat with him. He did not know who the other men were but listened in to their conversations. Some spoke of what they had been up to in the Commons that day. Others he understood to be Church figures and some he understood to be in the army and navy. David says Dawson was, he remembered, deferential, as though he considered them men of significance. But when

David asked him who they were, he would tell him not to ask questions, just to accept that these were important people and he was to feel privileged to be in their company and not tell anyone else about the evenings.

At Motcombs, Dawson would give David red wine to drink. He recalls on one occasion particular excitement among his fellow guests at the arrival of a Beaujolais Nouveau. Then things would start to get hazy. He struggles to remember getting back to Dolphin Square. But he does have memories of waking up in the flat the next morning, sometimes hearing the voices of men milling about the apartment. He frequently experienced pain in his body that he knew did not correspond to the physical effects of the rapes that Dawson had perpetrated. In other words, he was assaulted by some person or persons other than (or in addition to) Dawson on these weekends. Unable to recall the specifics of the attacks, he would feel ashamed, stripping the bed of soiled sheets, removing the very evidence of his abuse in his anxiousness that no one should know what had been done to him. He might then take a bath, where Dawson sometimes insisted on joining him. David cannot say for certain, but the 'black-out' nature of his memory suggests his wine was likely spiked.

They might stay in the flat for breakfast and sometimes lunch, too. There may be a shopping expedition or a trip to Church House, where David recalls uninterestedly watching meetings from a balcony. Then it would be time to go back to Lincolnshire. Dawson would remind his teenage passenger, 'No one's going to believe about Dolphin Square.'

According to David, he suffered abuse in three locales: in Lincolnshire, at Dolphin Square and in guesthouses close to the spectacular Blickling Estate in Norfolk. All the while, David's life away from Dawson was unravelling. He became withdrawn and his previously high performance at school dipped steeply. His only real peace came in the company of the horses he loved to ride. After two years of abuse, when he was 17, he began to build the strength to get away from Dawson, but it took time. He used a variety of strategies to ensure he avoided Dawson's company but his confidence was low and his feelings of shame about the abuse all took their toll.

In his twenties, David worked as a racehorse trainer but his experiences at the hands of Dawson and his companions continued to mould his life. Feeling unable to address the subject with his family, in 1996 he told an old family friend (who told him that she had been expecting such an approach), who in turn persuaded him to talk to his doctor. This he did, although he requested that their conversations should remain completely confidential. He took some solace from an abuse survivors' group he attended, but the burning sense of injustice, of a wrong not righted, eventually persuaded him that he should tell the police what had happened to him.

The year was 2007. Years before Savile. Years before Dolphin Square filled the front pages as the location of an alleged Westminster paedophile ring. A time when if someone knew about Dolphin Square at all, it was because they were a resident, a Westminster aficionado or perhaps remembered something to do with that spy who lived there in the 1960s. So, David approached Lincolnshire Police and a detective sergeant, Geoff Harrison, took a statement from him.

It so happened that David was not the first to make a complaint against Dawson. Lincolnshire Police's 2017 summary of their investigations provided to David confirms that there were 'several' complainants,[1] and David is aware that these included members of Dawson's own family. Moreover, Harrison's evidence at the coroner's inquiry reveals that he had conducted interviews with at least five other complainants prior to speaking to David. It was because of these other complaints that Dawson was initially arrested in December 2006. Not surprisingly, Dawson had denied any wrongdoing. David says that when he asked Harrison if he was the only victim, the officer had almost had to stifle a laugh as he told him that he was not, that Dawson had been under investigation for years and the case would likely be the largest of its type the country had ever seen. David and his family, the officer suggested, should prepare for a media storm. With David's new testimony, the police seemed spurred to move against Dawson once again.

With a re-arrest in the offing, David says he suggested to the police that they remove Dawson's arsenal of weapons from his property. But, he says, Harrison would inform him that the request to do so was denied. David went ahead and signed his statement. Then, in the late afternoon of 23 March 2007, Harrison rang Dawson to warn him he was to be arrested and questioned again. A date was set for the following week when Dawson would turn himself in at the station. Harrison had done similar at the time of the first arrest, so as to be 'considerate to [Dawson's] needs'.[2] This was clearly a matter of judgement, and not an unproblematic one.

David says Harrison then rang him and revealed that he had disclosed to Dawson that David was the complainant. Dawson did not, it is alleged, 'react well' but 'did not give me any indication for any cause for concern of his welfare or safety'. At 6 o'clock that same evening, David's phone rang again. It was a friend. Had he heard? Dawson was dead. They'd found him in some woodland on his estate, shot in the head.

And that, to all intents and purposes, was that. With their chief suspect dead, Lincolnshire Police stopped investigating. Despite the suggestion of multiple offenders, nor was the case referred either to the Metropolitan Police or the Norfolk Constabulary in order to look into the allegations related to their jurisdictions. The Independent Police Complaints Commission declined David's request to investigate the handling of the case, so Lincolnshire Police's professional standards department was left to review the actions of its own colleagues.

The inquest into Dawson's death was held in May 2007 and returned an open verdict. In other words, the coroner could not be certain if Dawson had died at his own hand or not. After the inquest, David says he was approached by Chief Inspector Tom Bell, who had conducted the review of the case. Bell, David holds, told him that he could find no evidence that Harrison ever requested the removal of Dawson's firearms. But David would never receive a copy of Bell's full report. When he made a Freedom of Information request to see it, it was refused. Then, using data protection legislation, it was revealed to him that the report had been destroyed at an unspecified time 'under Management of Police Information rules'.

Fast forward to 2015, when the now debunked allegations of 'Nick' had brought Dolphin Square into the public eye. The Metropolitan

Police established Operation Fairbank to investigate allegations of historical abuse involving public figures, so David decided to make contact with officers. He had little reason to suspect that he was about to walk into the eye of a storm, one that would mingle together in the public conscience wildly different allegations from sources who had no previous connection to or knowledge of each other. All the excitement (for want of a better word) was around the notion of a high-level 'ring' of people involving household names guilty of unimaginable cruelty and, indeed, murder. But David's allegations, first made to the police eight years earlier, did not fit that template.

The questions he wanted answered were stark and had serious implications but were not, in his words, 'sexy'. Why had the Met not been passed the files on his case years before? Why had no one sought to find out who leased the flat in Dolphin Square, or who the guests at those meals out might have been? Why was Dawson told of his forthcoming arrest? Especially when it was known he had access to firearms? Why did Dawson's death signal the end of the investigation when other living people were potentially implicated? And why was David never allowed to see Lincolnshire's own review of its handling of the case?

His initial interview with Met officers gave a cause for optimism, but not for long. Within a few days, he received an email to say that his case did not fall within the remit of the operation. David fired back a response: 'I was systematically abused and raped as a child by men at Dolphin Square. All I want is some credible answers.' On 25 March 2015, David received a response from Detective Sergeant James Townly of Operation Fairbank. Because David could not name any of the men at the dinners, the police were unable to investigate his allegations, according to Townly. [3] Similarly, various other names he did provide – witnesses who might have information and also the names of the men he believed leased the flat – were not already known to the police, so they would not investigate further. It felt to David as if he would only be listened to if he could come up with the name of a 'big-hitter' to investigate, or else he would need to produce a signed confession from one of his abusers, or perhaps a videotape.

'What frustrates me as a survivor,' he says, 'and wanting to find out the truth, is that if I had somebody bright and shiny and attractive as part of this story – a well-known person – people would want to know far more about it and be all over it. But to me, I just want to know the truth about what really happened, no matter how dull it might be to other people. The fact is, it goes on because it's normally conducted by people who do go under the radar, or who you don't think could possibly be part of something so heinous.'

David's leads, it seemed, were not worthy of following up, and the door was slammed shut on any further investigation.

If all this of itself were not frustrating enough, there are other disturbing aspects to the case. Not least the inquest into Gordon Dawson's death. There are several contradictions and queries that arise from a comparison of the post-mortem report and the statement given by the dead man's wife, Beth Dawson, who found his body. There may be simple explanations, but they surely deserve scrutiny given the circumstances. Why, for instance, did Mrs Dawson say that the time was 'approaching 1800' when she discovered the body, but the post-mortem gives a time of 1900? Given that he had a gunshot wound 2cm above his right ear, was it not surprising that when Mrs Dawson found him, he 'appeared to still have his glasses on'? She also mentioned that he left the house at approximately 16.20, twenty minutes before he spoke to Detective Sergeant Harrison (who had left a message on his mobile, having failed to make contact on the landline). What happened to that phone? Was it recovered, and its contents examined? Were statements taken from the paramedics who were presumably in attendance? Or other officers on the scene?

There were several perplexing findings from the medical examination, too. The evidence suggested a .22 calibre rifle was fired at a right angle against his skull above the right ear. Such a rifle is naturally long and it seems a highly inconvenient way to dispatch oneself, especially given that, as Mrs Dawson confirmed, Dawson suffered from sciatica that restricted his mobility. It is also stated that two discharged cartridges were discovered at the scene, and that Dawson's skull revealed an entry point but no exit wound. Yet no bullet was recovered from the brain.

What happened to the bullet? There were also several other injuries detected on the body including bruises to the face, knee and hands. Could these have been suggestive of a struggle? Nor is it clear whether there was evidence of gunpowder residue anywhere on the body other than the head. The coroner's office declared there were no suspicious circumstances and there was no evidence of third-party involvement. Yet the verdict was 'open' – some other mode of death other than suicide could not be entirely ruled out. Which leads back to a question: did Dawson have secrets to hide, or secrets to tell?[4]

After his experiences with the Met in 2015, David returned to Lincolnshire Police to request the paperwork in relation to the case. This prompted a renewed investigation of his original allegations, but with the same result: in June 2018 he received a letter notifying him that 'we have progressed these matters as far as we are feasibly able to take them'. 'We have,' he was assured, 'carried out further enquiries with other victims who have not managed to provide us with any further details.' It was also stated that further investigations at Dolphin Square had 'failed to identify a particular flat, or indeed the owner of such a flat, where the abuse you suffered took place'.[5]

David was also presented with several pages summarising the investigative actions taken by Lincolnshire since his initial complaint in 2007. They included an interview in early 2017 with a woman who David said he and Gordon would often visit for a cup of tea on trips back home from Dolphin Square. It is stated that she told the interviewing officers that Dawson often travelled between Lincolnshire and London, both for his work with the Synod and the National Farmers Union. When asked explicitly if she knew whether he had a flat in Dolphin Square, she said she did not think he did. But then the report states, 'She said at that time Dolphin Sq. was a hive of Paedophiles.' Where this must have seemed a line of questioning ripe for pursuing, the report indicates that the conversation moved on to other subjects. The subject of the Square is raised again a few paragraphs later. The witness revealed that she had in fact lived in Dolphin Square prior to her marriage in 1959 but that the flat then changed hands – to whom, she did not know, although she did state that 'it was not kept in the family'. The interviewee was then asked what the address was, which she gave reluctantly.

This association with Dolphin Square could be purely coincidental, but certainly warranted further investigation. The leaseholder of the named flat as of 2017 was identified but the police were unable to establish who had resided there previously. Certainly, the Square's own filing systems could be haphazard. When a new tenancy began, it was not unusual for the old paperwork simply to be thrown away. Yet, given the potential value of the information, it is surprising that the police could find no means to establish the identity of previous leaseholders.[6]

This is particularly so as David has subsequently learned that the interviewee was in fact the sister of one of the men he had previously been told leased a flat with Dawson and who had been present at the dinners at Motcombs and other restaurants. This was something of a revelation to David, who had known both siblings independently without ever being aware of their familial relationship. David does not have reason to believe that the brother was one of his abusers but when the brother was interviewed separately, he did confirm that he would sometimes stay as a guest in Dolphin Square although he asserted that he did not have a tenancy, nor knew anyone who did. According to David, he made the police aware of the sibling relationship as soon as he learned of it but was frustrated that they ostensibly made so little of it. It would seem to have been an important piece of new evidence, surely worthy of thorough investigation. What is clear beyond doubt is that Dawson had friends with connections to Dolphin Square.

Today, David is sceptical that he will ever find justice. So, what is left? The accused – a man suspected of years of abuse against multiple victims – long dead, his life ended in woodland at the end of a gun. Multiple police forces convinced they have run out of leads or lacking the impetus to progress them. A narrative that keeps leading back to Dolphin Square. And questions. Many unanswered questions. But David is not prepared to give up. As he puts it:

Some people have said to me, 'Why can't you just forget about it?' Well, you know, this is my cancer. You can't just say, 'Why can't you just forget about that tumour and pretend it's not there?', because it's going to kill you, and that's what happens with survivors of abuse. It eats you up, you cannot turn your back on it. It doesn't work like that.[7]

19

CANED

Less than a year after serving as the Dolphinite 'burnt offering' on the altar of Margaret Thatcher's premiership, Anthony Meyer found himself back on the front pages. This time, it was as the headline act in a classic tabloid sex scandal exposé. The *Sunday Mirror* of 23 September 1990 ran a front-page proclaiming: 'World Exclusive: I bathed my spanking MP in Champagne'.

The story warranted a double-page spread under the headline: 'Sex and spanking with kinkiest MP'. There then followed revelations from 'sultry model' Simone Washington, who claimed she had enjoyed a twenty-four-year affair with Meyer, a married father of four. Washington, described as a 'Martinique-born bit-part actress' and 'leggy former blues singer', was apparently fed up that she had not garnered a mention in Meyer's memoirs and she now wanted to set the record straight. Meyer, she said, had first seen her at a catwalk show in 1964 and had then sent her a bouquet of flowers, along with his phone number.

The details that followed were lurid. Meyer, according to the article, was a fan of sadomasochism, and especially caning. Washington would give him 'six of the best' (and on one occasion at least, twelve of the best), sometimes cooling the resulting welts with freshly poured champagne. 'I thought every public schoolboy liked it,' Washington said. 'I assumed it was part of growing up to become important in British society.'

There were other revelations, too. Meyer claimed that in the 1950s, he had been subject to an attempted KGB honey trap using a woman named Olga. Washington told the newspaper that Meyer had later 'taken revenge' by sleeping with a prostitute with the same name. Another time, he met with a prostitute in Soho but managed to leave his diary at the scene. It included various sensitive details, including appointments with the prime minister, so Washington was sent to retrieve it. She, meanwhile, was presented with various gifts and cheques from her lover, sometimes for as much as £500 a time.[1]

By the time the story broke, Meyer's Clwyd North West constituency party had already deselected him, largely in response to his leadership challenge, which some regarded as a betrayal. Although cast out of Parliament, he nonetheless remained in politics, pushing a pro-European line and eventually joining the Liberal Democrats, for whom he unsuccessfully contested a seat in the European Parliament. But when he died in 2004, it was for his challenge to the Iron Lady and his submission to Simone Washington that Meyer would be best remembered.

About the time Meyer was being deselected, in January 1990, Labour MP Ron Brown was in court facing charges of theft and criminal damage in relation to an event the previous April at the apartment of his former lover, Nonna Longden. Brown had a reputation as a fiery backbencher, suspended from the Commons on several occasions. In 1981, for example, he received a five-day ban for calling Nicholas Fairbairn a 'liar' and in 1988 he was suspended for twenty days for damaging the Commons mace in a debate on the poll tax. There were also rumours about several meetings he had with the Soviet agent Oleg Gordievsky, although the precise nature of their association remains a mystery to this day. But at the hearing at Lewes Crown Court at the start of 1990, he swapped political theatre for drama of a far more domestic kind.

Brown was married but had maintained a long affair with Longden before she eventually left him for another man. Neither lived in Dolphin Square but according to the evidence given at court, Brown had arrived at Longden's flat and begged her to come back to him and to 'start a new life' with him in the Square. When she refused and left the premises, he proceeded to smash several glass objects and was subsequently arrested at the local railway station, where he was found to be in possession of artefacts including a photo of Longden as a child, various jewellery and two pairs of his former lover's knickers. She, meanwhile, was accused by Brown's defence counsel of having stolen politically sensitive tape recordings from him to use as a bargaining chip in ongoing financial negotiations. In the end, he was found guilty of criminal damage and fined £1,000 but was acquitted on the theft charge. More importantly, the incident helped seal the Square's reputation as the place where misbehaving MPs expected, or at least hoped, to find sanctuary.

In 1997, the Square lost its on-site divorce specialist – a figure one imagines might have been in quite high demand there. Eulalie Evan Spicer lived in Frobisher House and was a trailblazer from the time she qualified as a solicitor in 1938 – one of the few women working in the legal field then. When war came and took many male practitioners into active service, she and the 163 other women holding licences to practise at the time suddenly found themselves more valued than ever before. In 1942, she was appointed supervisor of the Law Society's services divorce department – a section that was consistently overstretched as the conflict put strain on marriages. After the war, Spicer – who preferred to go by Miss Spicer or else just 'EES' – was a key figure in establishing the Legal Aid system and served as secretary for the 'No. 1 (London)' area, the country's largest Legal Aid division. When she retired in 1966, the area was dealing with some 25,000 applications every year. With her trademark Eton crop, a penchant for travelling by motor scooter and a love of shooting revolvers, she was another of the Square's eccentrics who helped to fundamentally change the national landscape in an understated way.

While Spicer was departing the scene, other notable eccentrics were continuing to arrive. Among those who made their home in the Square in the 1990s was explorer Colonel John Blashford-Snell, who lived in Keyes House with his wife Judith – although Blashford-Snell was often to be found somewhere other than home.[2] Born in Hereford in 1936, he always had a spirit of adventure. As a young child, he would ride on the family's 11 stone St Bernard dog, who was kitted out with a specially fitted saddle. He later joined the army, which allowed him to intersperse tours of duty with adventures in foreign climes. His explorations have taken him literally all over the world – from searching for Almas (a creature akin to the Yeti) in Mongolia to driving from Alaska to Patagonia, sailing across the Atlantic as Thor Heyerdahl had once done, protecting bears in Peru, examining Loch Ness for evidence of its reputed monster and delivering a grand piano to a remote tribe in Guyana.

Often, his expeditions have allowed for vital conservation work or infrastructure projects. Arguably his two most spectacular trips were his 1968 expedition down the Blue Nile (during which he and his companions developed the techniques that now underpin the sport of white-water rafting) and his 1974 navigation of the Zaire River, which followed in the footsteps of Henry Stanley 100 years earlier as Blashford-Snell and his team sought to better understand the causes of river blindness.

A tall, imposing man inclined to tweeds when not in military garb or explorers' khakis, Blashford-Snell at once thrust exploration into the modern era even as he retained a foot in the past of *Boy's Own* adventures. In 1969, he founded the Scientific Exploration Society and in 1984 he brought Operation Raleigh (now Raleigh International) into being – an initiative that has since sent over 40,000 young people on expeditions around the world. He has picked up much wisdom along the way, not least on how best to deal with a rampaging bull elephant – 'I always say, if an elephant charges you, make sure your wife is in the front. Like some butter with that?'[3] An undoubted one-off – fellow explorer Sir Ranulph Fiennes insists, 'Join Blashers and you will age slowly …'[4] – he explored the world and for a while chose Dolphin Square as home.

Nor, of course, was he alone in being drawn to this Pimlico enclave. Whatever its problems over the years, the Square continued to demonstrate its pulling power for big-hitters. Before the decade was out, the dethroned Margaret Thatcher was among those to make an appearance, albeit a brief one. In November 1999, she attended an 80th birthday party in the Square's Chichester Room for Gordon Tooth, a friend of her husband, Denis.[5] Tooth's wife, Sally, recalls that on the Tuesday before the Sunday of the party, she took a phone call from Denis's office. 'I was waiting for "Very sorry but he won't be able to come",' she remembers, 'but in fact they said "Do you think Margaret would be able to come as well?".'

While Thatcher's visit was short, others were in for a rather longer haul. In 1993, arguably the Square's single most famous tenant moved in – Princess Anne. Although her main residence remained Gatcombe Park in Gloucestershire and she had an apartment at Buckingham Palace too, she and her then new second husband, Commander Timothy Laurence (they'd wed at Balmoral the previous December), decided to begin their married life together in the Square's Drake House.

Many struggled to understand why the couple would swap royal luxury for what was, by comparison, the slightly faded and more utilitarian comforts of Dolphin Square. The answer seems to have been that Laurence – a naval man and a former equerry to the queen – pushed for it, both to be near to his place of work, the Ministry of Defence, and also to show that he could support his wife. As a result, Anne was said to be the first member of the core royal family to live in a private apartment in the capital.

The flat itself was, in fact, two flats knocked through and included facilities to cater for a permanent police presence. Laurence took out the lease in his own name and the annual rent was somewhere in the region of £15,000. There was a brief outcry when it was revealed that the couple would pay less community charge (the successor tax to the poll tax) on their central London pad than some agricultural workers were paying for much humbler abodes on aristocratic estates in the country. It was also reported that the flat's previous lease-holder, Richard de Meath, had received an eighteen-month sentence for his part in a financial dispute related to another property he rented elsewhere.

Whether Anne or her husband enjoyed living in the Square is a somewhat moot point. Certainly, life was different to what she, at least, was used to. She was apparently warned, for instance, that one of her neighbours opposite had a telescope that could be trained on the newly-weds' bedroom.[6] On 16 April 1993 the *Daily Mirror* reported, 'Princess Anne has given the thumbs-down to her new flat.' A 'pal' of the princess was quoted as saying, 'I believe she may have spent only one night there since they took possession seven weeks ago. Honestly, I think she finds the place pretty naff.'[7]

But residents from the time are less sure that she was so unimpressed. She certainly returned for a summer fete one year, where she was by all accounts charming and sociable. And those who encountered the royal couple when they were in residence remember a down-to-earth pair who shopped in the arcade and frequented the greengrocers. Another says Anne told her that she 'loved living in Dolphin Square' and commented on the large numbers of residents that she encountered when she had to leave for work early in the morning who crept around with dogs they were not meant to have according to their leases.[8] On one memorable occasion, the queen and Prince Philip were also spotted visiting, so Anne cannot have been too ashamed of her address. But it was only a temporary move. She was often to be found at Buckingham Palace rather than Dolphin Square and Laurence gave up his lease in 1996.

It is not known whether Anne ever bumped into the 37-year-old Texan-born John Bryan, who at the time was known to play squash at the Square's sports club. If she did, it would surely have been an awkward encounter. On 20 August 1992 Bryan had been the focus of a splash in the *Daily Mirror*, which published pictures of his 'holiday romp' with Sarah, Duchess of York – then still the wife of Anne's brother, Prince Andrew. Bryan was described as the duchess's financial advisor and the pair had been pictured sunbathing in St Tropez, with Bryan apparently sucking his topless companion's toe – a gesture widely considered to be a breach of royal etiquette.[9]

Anne's arrival also gave journalists a chance to ruminate on what sort of place the Square was. The novelist Sebastian Faulks was among them, writing in *The Guardian* on 6 February 1993:

> In the intervening 50 years, Dolphin Square has moved via the raffish to the edge of seediness. The radios installed in each sitting room no longer work; the Bakelite control on the wall, that once switched to Home, Light or Third, is reminiscent of an NHS hospital in need of a refit; the silent speaker above the door has a look of Orwellian intrusion. The long corridors of Hood House in powder blue paint with a dolphin-swirled patterned carpet have a whiff of the institutional ... Its sophisticated inhabitants are of the type who need never be told to 'forget' having seen something. It is a place for which the term 'off the record' might have been invented.[10]

If that was hardly the most flattering appraisal, it was by no means the most damaging. Over its relatively short lifespan, a publication called *Scallywag* had an impact that far outweighed its circulation. Operating between 1991 and 1995, it was the brainchild of editor Simon Regan and his half-brother, Angus James, and originally billed itself as 'Camden's only alternative community magazine'. Its aim was to venture into territory where other investigative and satirical publications (most notably *Private Eye*) feared to tread. But too often, *Scallywag* overstepped the mark or got things demonstrably wrong. It was ultimately undone because Prime Minister John Major successfully sued it in 1993 for suggesting he'd had an affair with a Downing Street caterer. It never financially recovered and closed in 1995, but not before running an incendiary article on Dolphin Square in 1994. It alleged that Conservative politicians had been involved in sexual abuse there for years, naming several individuals as either themselves abusers or close to others who were. 'We often have underage boys wandering around, totally lost, asking for a particular flat,' one source was quoted as saying. However, at least one of those named was later shown to be the subject of mistaken identity, as admitted by one of his accusers. To some, *Scallywag* was the ultimate in fearless, campaigning journalism, but to others it was too reckless for its own good, making it virtually impossible to discern where truth ended and falsehood (perhaps inadvertent) began. It played its part, though, in fermenting the Square's reputation as a place where bad things could happen.

In 1999, the Square was implicated in further serious, though very different, criminal endeavours at the wide-ranging Flood Tribunal. The tribunal, chaired first by Judge Fergus Flood, was set up in 1997 to look into allegations that politicians in Ireland had received illegal payments in return for political favours, particularly in the area of planning. What was meant to have been a fairly brief investigation turned into a Leviathan that cost hundreds of millions and stretched into the 2010s. One of the key claims that sparked the inquiry was that Joseph Murphy Snr, the boss of Joseph Murphy Structural Engineers (JMSE) and a man involved in major building and development schemes in Ireland and the UK since the 1940s, had made a payment of £30,000 to a former Irish Government Minister, Ray Burke. Burke was in return expected to ensure that areas of Dublin were re-zoned in the company's favour.

Then, in a sworn affidavit to the tribunal, the Murphy Group's former CEO, Liam Conroy, alleged that Murphy had both evaded tax and breached currency control laws. Conroy stated, 'He had ... evaded Guernsey tax [Murphy lived on Guernsey] by having bank accounts in Ireland in his name and UK accommodation addresses such as Goulton Road and Dolphin Square in London. He failed to declare his income from these sources.'[11]

Murphy denied the various claims against him, pleading complete ignorance of the payment to Burke and dismissing Conroy as 'totally bananas' and 'a professional conman'.[12] He died at his home on Guernsey in August 2000 at the age of 83 – a full twelve years before the final report of the Flood Tribunal (by then known as the Mahon Tribunal, after its last chairman) was published. By that time, the Taoiseach Bertie Ahern, who had commissioned the inquiry in the first place, had resigned amid its fallout. Mahon would conclude that corruption in public life 'continued because nobody was prepared to do enough to stop it. This is perhaps inevitable when corruption ceases to become an isolated event and becomes so entrenched that it is transformed into an acknowledged way of doing business. Specifically, because corruption affected every level of Irish political life, those with the power to stop it were frequently implicated in it.'[13]

While Dolphin Square may have been a somewhat tangential player in this long, drawn-out examination of the Irish political scene, it continued its tradition of acting as a barometer for the UK's broader political climate. After the Tory decade of the 1980s, the political sands shifted again in the 1990s. But in 1991, before those changes had started to take real effect, it was time for Labour to wave off one of its old-school left-wingers, the Dolphinite Eric Heffer. Born in Hertfordshire in 1922 into a working-class background, he was turned on to politics when a Dolphinite of an earlier vintage, Ellen Wilkinson, had led the Jarrow March through Hertford back in 1936. Profoundly moved by the experience, he joined the Labour Party three years later, and then moved over to the Communist Party of Great Britain when the Nazis invaded the USSR in 1941.

Having later returned to the Labour fold, he became MP for Liverpool Walton in 1964 and was briefly Minister of State for Trade in the mid-1970s under Wilson. He was also party chairman from 1983–84, a period in which he attempted to navigate a path between the militant wing of the Labour Party, then at the peak of its powers in the city he represented, and the party leadership who wanted to expel them. (Heffer had stood against Kinnock for the leadership in 1983 as the candidate of the Left, but secured less than 7 per cent of the vote compared to Kinnock's more than 70 per cent.) In 1984, Heffer left the opposition front bench, never to return, and a year later walked off the stage at party conference when Kinnock gave a speech that implicitly condemned the actions of Liverpool Council.

Heffer retained his seat at the 1987 election but was increasingly out of kilter with the direction of his party under Kinnock. In 1988, he unsuccessfully stood for the deputy leadership and a year later, by which time he was suffering from terminal cancer, he announced that he would not contest the next election. In March 1991 he was awarded the freedom of Liverpool and when he died at his flat in the Square a couple of months later, the news was greeted with dismay from friends and political foes alike. While he would doubtless have struggled to find a home in the New Labour that was soon to come, few ever doubted the strength of his political convictions even if they disagreed with them.

Margaret Thatcher – who was somewhere around polar opposite him on the political spectrum – sent a letter of condolence to his widow and attended his memorial service. Having been ousted from Downing Street just the previous November, she no doubt had time to reflect on those among her supporters and opponents whom she actually rated, regardless of ideological differences. Meanwhile, her successor John Major defied pollsters to win the general election in 1992 – a victory that prompted Neil Kinnock to step down as Labour leader, to be replaced by John Smith, who would shockingly die of a heart attack within two years. His successor, Tony Blair, then famously reconfigured the party and led the rebranded New Labour to electoral success in 1997.

In this long chain of cause and effect, that electoral defeat prompted Major to give up his stewardship of the Conservatives, paving the way for a Dolphinite to take over the reins. Thirty-six-year-old William Hague – an MP since 1989 for Richmond in North Yorkshire and Secretary of State for Wales since 1995 – won the party's leadership election in June 1997, defeating Tory 'big beast' Kenneth Clarke in a final ballot. He joined a line of leaders of major parties who have lived in the Square that includes Harold Wilson and David Steel.

But, in truth, Hague might never have been leader were it not for a midnight flit to the Square by his old friend from their days at Oxford, Brooks Newmark. Recently engaged to Ffion Jenkins, his private secretary when he was at the Welsh Office, Hague was not ide-ally placed to take on the leadership in 1997. Former Home Secretary Michael Howard, on the other hand, was set well for a run at the top job and invited Hague to join him on the ticket. Deputy leader of the Conservatives would have itself been quite an achievement for a politician still in the early part of his parliamentary career. Hague was tempted to shake on the deal, and Howard was quietly confident that he would. But others in the party were keener that Hague have a tilt at the very top job.

Among them was fellow MP Alan Duncan, who was up north when news reached him of the potential Howard deal. He immediately rang his and Hague's mutual friend Newmark (who himself would sit in the Commons from 2005–15) with orders to get round to Hague's Dolphin Square flat and talk him out of playing second fiddle to Howard. Newmark was initially unable to dredge up Hague's exact address but used his mobile phone to guide him, arriving sometime around midnight. He then sat up with Hague – who in the meantime was receiving calls from other supporters and well-wishers – and attempted to persuade him that he should seize the moment. At seven the next morning, Hague informed Howard that he would now not be running with him, but against him instead.[14]

To cap a memorable year, Hague and Jenkins married in the Palace of Westminster in December. The couple then lived together as hus-band and wife in the Square. Hague would eventually serve as Foreign Secretary from 2010–14 in the government of David Cameron, but his aspirations to be prime minister were snuffed out when Blair secured a second term in 2001.

Hague's chief of staff while leader of the opposition was the former middle-distance Olympic champion Sebastian Coe. Coe was instrumental in persuading Hague to take up judo, a move that some observers suggested was behind a surge in Hague's self-confidence and willingness to politically attack. On one occasion, Coe is said to have passed out after his boss got him in a neck-lock, while Hague fractured the rib of another opponent. But Hague's newly minted love for the martial art most famously brought Dolphin Square to the fore again when reports emerged of he and Coe grappling topless with each other in the health club.

The health club was also a setting for one of the more curious episodes in the Square in the 1990s – the prosecution of resident Bernice Weston, the founder of WeightWatchers. The millionaire appeared in Southwark Crown Court in 1997 charged with having stolen £150 worth of beauty products from the health club back in late 1995. From early on, the proceedings were farcical. The chief prosecution witness was a therapist, Helen Bailey, who was honeymooning in New Zealand and had refused several requests to return to give evidence. Without her testimony, there was no real case and the judge threw it out of court, observing that it was 'so flimsy as to be virtually non-existent'. Weston, meanwhile, explained to journalists that the products she was supposed to have taken had actually been part of a display she was organising.[15]

If it was all going on at the health club, the restaurant remained something of an enigma. Eagle-eyed television viewers of the time could have spotted it as a backdrop in popular dramas like *Poirot* and *The Camomile Lawn*. Away from the cameras, Gary Rhodes was the next big name to take on the challenge of making it a commercial success, opening Rhodes in the Square in 1997. With a celebrity profile, a distinctive look and a role at the head of the modern British culinary revolution, he brought Michelin-star quality to the set-up (along with first-rate sous chefs like Tom Kerridge) but even he struggled to find the winning formula. In 2003 it was announced that he was parting company with Sodexo, the catering firm that financed his various restaurant enterprises, and Rhodes in the Square closed its doors for the last time in May that year, once again leaving a legacy of some memorable nights but an underperforming profit and loss sheet.

Just about the time Rhodes started his Dolphin Square adventure, another of its residents – Conservative MP Iain Mills – was ending his. In doing so, he played a significant part in the demise of John Major's premiership and ushered in the last days of some eighteen years of continuous Tory rule. It was a death peculiarly emblematic of the Square itself – a collision of an individual's sad personal circumstances and their place in public life. The sort of personal tragedy that makes headlines and shapes wider fates in a way that simply does not happen in many other places, and certainly with nowhere near such regularity.

Mills had been born in 1940 in Scotland but spent a chunk of his childhood in southern Africa. Having returned to Britain, he became the MP for Meriden in the West Midlands in 1979 and served as Norman Tebbit's parliamentary private secretary in the Thatcher years but his own career stalled on the back benches. He was not one of his party's socialites, by no means clubbable in the way that many of his contemporaries were and with few close friends in Westminster.

There had been concerns about his drinking for a while. In April 1996, he was arrested for drunkenness after he was found prone on Great Smith Street, close to the Houses of Parliament and Conservative Central Office. He spent almost five hours in custody before he was released with a warning. He said he had fallen as he carried a pile of books and papers from the Commons back to the Square, but colleagues were not so sure.

Mills' body was discovered in his Dolphin Square flat on 16 January 1997, found by a fellow Dolphinite and senior government whip, Derek Conway. He had seen Mills drinking in the Commons on Monday, 13 January but noted his absence from a crucial vote in the House the following night and decided to go in search of him two days later. Through the window of Mills' ground-floor flat, Conway saw the figure of his colleague lying face down on the bed. With the help of a security guard, the front door was forced open but it was too late and he was certified dead at the scene a short while later. He was 56 and left behind a wife, Gaynor. At the inquest, acute alcohol intoxication was identified as the cause of death and the coroner recorded a verdict of misadventure, commenting that the MP's alcohol level was 'astonishingly high'. Afterwards, Conway told reporters, 'We were encouraging

Iain to try and get a grip … We knew he was drinking, but we had no idea it was in the order found by the pathologist.'[16]

Conway was a political pragmatist. Jeremy Paxman wrote in his book, *The Political Animal*,[17] that when Conway lost his Shrewsbury and Atcham seat at the 1997 election, he blamed financier James Goldsmith and his anti-European Referendum Party for splitting his vote. Goldsmith died of pancreatic cancer a short while afterwards and Paxman quotes Conway as saying, 'I hear it's the most painful of deaths. I'm so pleased.'

Even as he must have felt pity for Mills and his sad end, Conway would also have been acutely aware that the loss of this MP meant that the government had lost its majority. A couple of months earlier, the Conservative MP for Wirral South, Barry Porter, had also passed away. In the resulting by-election a few weeks after Mills' death, Porter's seat was taken by Labour, heaping more pressure on Major and his government as a general election loomed into view. The Tory glory days of the 1980s seemed a very long time ago. But aside from its political ramifications, Mills' passing was another Dolphinite death laced with pathos. As the coroner put it, 'It is … a sad story that nobody noticed that Iain Mills wasn't so much around.'[18]

20

FALSE ACCOUNTS

By the turn of the twenty-first century, Westminster Council was increasingly under pressure to review how the Square was run. It had come to public attention that the Dolphin Square Trust had kept rents artificially low over many years. An article in *The Guardian* in 1999 had disclosed that some residents were paying as little as £62 per week for a two-bed apartment, while standard council tenants up the road were paying £90 and the market rate stood somewhere around £320. According to the Trust's own figures, only some £7,400,000 of £12,400,000 in theoretical rental income was being collected. In addition, the Trust did not operate a straightforward waiting list scheme for potential new tenants but ran an admissions process that critics categorised as a 'someone like us' policy favouring well-to-do professionals and individuals with social status and influence. An internal Westminster report labelled 'not for publication' admitted 'awkward anomalies' between Dolphin Square and other council-owned properties in the area.[1]

The Trust kicked back against council pressure, arguing that as a non-profit-making entity, it could sanction rebates to residents. Meanwhile, the private sector was sniffing around this prime slab of real estate. *The Guardian*'s revelations followed a move by the freeholder, Friends Provident, to purchase the lease outright from the council for some £50 million ahead of its lapsing in 2034. Legal advisors to Friends Provident had noted, 'The trust's current letting policy, especially in the context of its control by Westminster, is unusual, probably unique and, in the present environment, difficult to justify.' Westminster Labour councillor Paul Dimoldenberg said of the potential deal, 'Thousands of Westminster tenants are being forced to live in inadequate housing and if the Council can secure £50m or more to improve conditions that must be good news.'

In the event, Friends Provident did not secure the buyout. By August 2003, there was talk of another bid worth £200 million from a consortium led by a member of the Cadbury family. In a report from that time, the *Daily Telegraph* memorably observed, 'if anywhere could be said to be home to the British Establishment, then Dolphin Square is it'.[2] Finally, in 2005, a deal was agreed to sell the lease to an American private equity firm, Westbrook Associates, for £176 million. As part of the deal, the company offered individual tenants a choice of either agreeing to higher rents or accepting a one-off payment to give up their flat. It was an offer laden with unforeseen consequences for several MPs who lived in the Square.

Whereas the 1980s had largely been the decade of the Conservatives, the noughties felt very much like Labour's time. In the early part of the century, Blair had enjoyed popularity and authority akin with Thatcher in her pomp. One impact of Labour's resurgence was a dramatic upturn in the number of female MPs – a phenomenon encapsulated in the phrase, 'Blair's Babes'. The 1997 election saw 120 women elected to the Commons, 101 of them from Labour – and twice the number elected at the previous election in 1992. This was a fact reflected in the make-up of the Square, where several of the new intake took up residence. Among them was Anne Begg, the Labour MP for Aberdeen South between 1997 and 2015, and one of the very few wheelchair users ever to sit in the Commons – although she could look to a Dolphinite predecessor from the Square's earlier days, Lady Viola Apsley, who took up her husband's place in the House and cut an instantly recognisable figure in Westminster in her wheelchair in the 1940s.

Another of the 'Dolphinite Babes' was Estelle Morris, who in 2002 resigned from her position as Education Secretary and in doing so did a remarkable thing for a politician – she publicly considered the idea that maybe she wasn't the best person for the job. With certain government targets on literacy and numeracy having been missed, she wrote to Blair:

> I have learned what I am good at and also what I am less good at. I am good at dealing with the issues and in communicating to the teaching profession. I am less good at strategic management of a huge department and I am not good at dealing with the modern media. All this has meant that with some of the recent situations I have been involved in I have not felt I have been as effective as I should be or as effective as you need me to be.[3]

It was a brave gesture and one whose example a number of her fellow Dolphinites ought perhaps to have followed over the years.

Hazel Blears, the MP for Salford (and later, Salford and Eccles), held several ministerial posts under both Blair and his successor, Gordon Brown. However, her resignation from Brown's Cabinet in 2009 came amid a number of high-profile departures and after she had gently mocked a YouTube video the prime minister had put out, all of which was considered to have weakened his premiership. On the day of her resignation, she was also spotted wearing a brooch that provocatively said, 'Rocking the boat'. She selected the piece, she explained, as a response to several weeks of media scrutiny regarding her expenses claims.

In 2009, the subject of politicians' expenses raged like a wildfire through the British political landscape. It all began with a legal battle over a freedom of information request to disclose parliamentarians' expenses claims. In April that year, with a High Court ruling on the matter imminent, the parliamentary authorities announced that they would release the data but with some redactions. However, before they could, the information was leaked and large amounts of it published by the *Daily Telegraph*.

The public were incensed by what they read. There were headline-grabbing peculiarities, such as the MP who'd attempted to claim for a duck island in his back garden, but what really concerned people was the sheer scale of – if not abuses – limit pushing. It seemed that the political class had routinely been using the expenses system as a de facto salary top-up. In particular, there was widespread bemusement at how politicians took public money in relation to second homes. 'Flipping' entered the lexicon of public discourse, as it was exposed how individuals could repeatedly redesignate homes in order to secure public funding for financing and renovating private properties and to avoid paying capital gains tax.

This all had particular implications for several of the forty-plus MPs who lived in or had recently left the Square. In particular, the pressure descended upon those who'd accepted a pay-off from Westbrook in 2005. Among them was Andy Burnham, who had entered Parliament as the Member for Leigh in 2001 and served as Chief Secretary to the Treasury and as Secretary of State for Health and for Culture, Media and Sport under Gordon Brown. In due course, he would twice fight for the party leadership before becoming mayor of Greater Manchester.

Burnham was found to have accepted some £18,200 from Westbrook, which was disclosed to and accepted by the parliamentary authorities so that he did not have to pay capital gains, which might have exceeded £6,000. However, this lump sum was allowed to run alongside his normal second-home allowance, so in effect he was able to claim over £32,000 in a single year, despite the usual threshold standing at less than £22,000. This after he had claimed over £90,000 for rent and bills over the previous five years, having nominated his flat in the Square as his second home.

He used a significant part of his windfall to purchase and renovate another London flat. It transpired that he had been in negotiations with the Commons' fees office for several months over the issue, having had his claim rejected three times before it was at last accepted. Burnham defended the claim, saying:

> It is complete nonsense to suggest that I set out to avoid capital gains tax. My file shows I made arrangements to pay over this money in full to the fees office, and all arrangements were signed off by them. At no stage did I make any personal profit on this transaction.[4]

Several MPs avoided a similar furore by rejecting Westbrook's offer. The former Minister of Transport, Tom Harris, turned down £10,000 on offer to leave and Brian Iddon, the Labour MP for Bolton South

East from 1997–2010, rejected around £11,000. Iddon, though, was not afraid to court a little controversy. Having earned a doctorate in organic chemistry, he was a knowledgeable advocate for the legalisation of cannabis, a subject that always threatened push-back.

While Harris and Iddon were doubtless relieved at their choices, others took the Westbrook money and paid the price. Several hailed from the Liberal Democrats, notably John Barrett, Sandra Gidley, Paul Holmes and Richard Younger-Ross, who received payments of between £8,000 and £18,750 and were deemed to have made 'serious misjudgements' in relation to the matter by John Lyon, the parliamentary standards commissioner. Each was made to pay back several thousand pounds and to write a letter of apology to the Commons. Younger-Ross was also reported to have claimed £1,200 for mirrors to furnish his apartment and almost £1,500 on a chest of drawers. These were both paid despite being in excess of the informal 'John Lewis List' arrangement that laid out 'reasonable' costs for such items.[5]

Also caught up in the expenses fiasco were Dolphinite Lib Dem bigwigs, Menzies Campbell (party leader from 2006–07) and Alan Beith (deputy leader from 1992–2003). Both accepted payments of £5,000 to give up succession rights on their tenancies – actions that Lyon said constituted further misjudgements, though less serious than in the cases of the other party members. Both rejected potentially higher payments and were not found to have breached the Commons code. Nonetheless, Beith's case came under further scrutiny as his wife, Diana, a former MP and by then in the House of Lords, had also made expenses claims for overnight stays in the Square. New guidance suggested only one of a married couple could claim for a second home. In the period 2001–08, the couple claimed over £175,000 jointly in second-home and overnight-stay allowances.

In total, fifteen MPs took Westbrook's offers. Others included Rosemary McKenna, the Labour MP for Cumbernauld, Kilsyth and Kirkintilloch East, who received around £15,000. Also involved was Michael Mates, the Conservative MP for East Hampshire and a man somewhat familiar with scandal, having resigned from the Northern Ireland Office in 1993. On that occasion, it was his ties to controversial businessman Asil Nadir, the CEO of the FTSE 100-listed Polly

Peck, that caused problems. Polly Peck had collapsed in 1990 while under investigation by the Serious Fraud Office but Nadir fled the country before he could face charges of false accounting and theft. He did not face trial until 2010, when he was convicted of theft of some £23 million and sentenced to ten years in prison. When the case was in its infancy in the 1990s, Mates had sent Nadir, a prominent Conservative donor, a watch inscribed 'Don't let the buggers get you down'.

Back to 2005, Mates was offered somewhere around £40,000 to give up his apartment after some thirty years in the Square. He then invested the money, with permission from the Commons fees office, in another London property, which he subsequently put up for sale at a price that would have earned him in excess of £100,000 profit. Mates stood down as an MP in 2010, having stated two years earlier that he would then consult with the Commons authorities as to whether any of his Dolphin Square money ought to be paid to Parliament. However, he was yet to have any such consultation a full two and a half years after he left the House.

Dolphinite and Deputy Speaker of the Commons, Alan Haselhurst also found himself under scrutiny, particularly for claims for £12,000 for gardening services at his Essex farmhouse between 2004 and 2008 (as well as a claim for cleaning his chimney). The question was posed as to whether these services complied with the regulatory demand that expenses be 'wholly, necessarily and exclusively' incurred to enable parliamentarians to carry out their parliamentary work. 'The gardener does eight hours a week, he does all the heavy work which I don't have the opportunity to do when I'm in London,' Haselhurst said. 'People will judge how far these things are necessary; quite a lot of people would regard even the existence of the allowances as something they are not sure MPs should have. My view is that it should have been dealt with through salary which is taxable.'

Ian Gibson, the Labour MP from Norwich North, was another who emerged from the scandal battered and bruised. He was accused of claiming nearly £80,000 over four years towards expenses on a flat in Barons Court that had actually served as the principal home of his grown-up daughter and her boyfriend for several years. Gibson then sold the property to his daughter in 2008 at significantly below the market value, moving briefly into a hotel and then into a Dolphin Square flat. When the affair came to light, he was blocked by the Labour Party from standing at the 2010 general election, so he chose instead to resign from the Commons, causing a 2009 by-election that the Conservative Chloe Smith won and still retains.

Lord John Taylor, a long-term Dolphin Square resident, meanwhile went to prison for his abuse of the expenses system. A barrister by profession, he was sent to the Lords by John Major in 1996 when he was just 44, making him one of the youngest members of the House and one of the very few of Afro-Caribbean origin. He was a tabloid-friendly figure, at one stage embarking on a twenty-four-day marriage that saw him spend his wedding night at a hotel near the Hanger Lane gyratory in West London before honeymooning at Disneyland Paris. He was accused of falsely claiming £11,277 in expenses and was one of only eight Members of Parliament who faced criminal conviction during the expenses scandal. In court, he suggested that fellow lords had told him that the various allowances were there in lieu of a salary. With this in mind, he made various claims for journeys he never made and accommodation he never used. He was sentenced to twelve months' imprisonment and disbarred from practising as a barrister.

Arguably the highest-profile ex-Dolphinite caught up in the expenses scandal was the then Chancellor of the Exchequer, Alistair Darling, who received criticism as a serial flipper – nominating three different properties as his second home, flipping them four times in as many years, even when he had his Downing Street grace and favour flat as Chancellor. The future leader of the Liberal Democrats, Vince Cable, said Darling had been 'caught with his fingers in the till'. 'His moral authority,' he said, 'has vanished. He must go, now.'[6] In the event, though, Darling paid back £700 for a separate claim that he said had been made in error and remained in No. 11 until the end of Brown's tenure. It was not, though, a good look for a man who in his day job was seeking to find a path out of the global financial crisis that had recently taken hold.

Sir Christopher Kelly, a civil servant who'd been appointed chair of the Committee on Standards in Public Life in 2007, drew up guidelines for the future of parliamentary expenses in light of the scandal. Among his many recommendations, he proposed that no longer should MPs expect to have swanky properties in prime locations paid for from the public purse but that instead they should look at renting cheaper properties in disparate locations throughout the capital. He could hardly have made the message any clearer, stating, 'MPs do not have to live in Dolphin Square.'[7]

21

ANY OTHER BUSINESS

In December 2013, some 150 of Dolphin Square's cleaners, concierges and caretakers went on a one-day strike in protest at low pay. Their salaries were as low as £9,850, at a time when the average salary across the country was something approaching three times that. Beverley Hughes, who was the Home Office minister in charge of immigration and had herself lived in the Square since 1997, said: 'I am very concerned to hear about the low pay-rates for people living in London and working in an expensive area. I think most of the tenants would want them to be as well paid as possible and I will be investigating this and discussing the issue with my colleagues.'[1] On the other hand, Bill Morris, the general secretary of the Transport and General Workers' Union, commented, 'This is a case of *Upstairs, Downstairs* syndrome. It is symptomatic of a lot that is wrong with society.'[2]

Back in 2001, the Square had lost 81-year-old former Labour MP Maurice Miller. His was not the most high profile of political careers but for those convinced that those in the political class all led charmed lives, he doubtless could have provided evidence that Westminster was not always a land of milk and honey. Miller was a medical doctor who over the years had treated many of his colleagues, giving him a unique insight into the medical and psychological strains that a career in politics can cause. Perhaps most memorably, in the 1970s he was medicating fellow Labour MP John Stonehouse for anxiety and depression shortly before Stonehouse staged his own death in Florida in one of the strangest episodes in late-twentieth-century British politics (Stonehouse would be discovered in Australia a few months later, and was later revealed as having been a Czech spy to boot). From Ellen Wilkinson through to Iain Mills, Dolphin Square offered ample proof of lives ravaged at least in part by the pressures of inhabiting the Westminster goldfish bowl.

Nonetheless, the expenses scandal highlighted once more the concern that the powerful and well-to-do were benefitting from a gamed system. It was a suspicion that reared its head with regularity in Dolphin Square as the new century progressed – a hunch that there was an entitled section of society playing entirely by its own rules. On 25 July 2015, Dolphin Square was struck by the sort of scandal that felt like it belonged to an earlier age – maybe those days when Sid James and Barbara Windsor were tearing it up around Pimlico. At first sight, it had all the elements of the cheeky chappy sex farce, but there was something more serious at stake: the fear that there were different rules for 'them' and 'us'. *The Sun* ran a story that a 69-year-old, married Dolphinite member of the House of Lords, Baron John Sewel, had been secretly filmed in his flat cavorting with 'a pair of £200-a-night hookers' and sniffing a white power that the newspaper claimed was cocaine.[3]

Sewel was an academic who had been elevated to the House of Lords by Tony Blair and served as an Under Secretary at the Scottish Office at the time when plans for devolution were being honed. He even gave his name to a parliamentary motion regarding the circumstances in which the UK Government could legislate on an issue over which the Scottish Parliament would normally have say-so. At the time of the *Sun*'s exposé, Sewel was Deputy Speaker of the Lords and had played a role in drawing up a code of conduct that demanded peers conduct themselves with 'selflessness, integrity, accountability, openness, honesty and leadership'.

The Sun therefore had claim to legitimate public interest in the story – that of an authority figure and regulator of other's behaviour who himself misbehaves. They reported how he had paid the two sex workers £200 each, while complaining about the challenges of living off a lords' daily allowance of £200 per day ('I do spend it on wine and different things,' he commented). There were also embarrassing comments about the then prime minister, David Cameron ('the most facile superficial prime minister') and former Dolphinite and leader of the Scottish National Party Alex Salmond ('a silly pompous prat'). And as well as the powder-sniffing caught on camera (at one stage, he sniffed it from one of the women's breasts), Sewel was also shown sitting back, wearing an orange bra and leather jacket and dragging on a cigarette. He could hardly have been a more obliging fall guy for a tabloid sting. 'I just want to be led astray,' he told his companions on the night – although he did thoughtfully turn over a photo of his wife that sat on a nearby table before engaging in his infidelity.[4]

The story had arrived at the desk of *The Sun* journalist Stephen Moyes several months earlier. One of the sex workers had phoned the news desk late one night while inebriated and given some details of her regular dealings with Sewel (it would be claimed he had met one of the women in a strip club several years earlier). By the next morning, the woman was no longer willing to pursue the matter so Moyes decided to put it on the back burner. But over several months, he gained her trust as well as establishing the public interest basis for the story and ironing out potential compliance and legal issues. A surveillance operation of this type was not undertaken lightly. Then, when the footage had been secured, Sewel was told that the story was about to appear and given a right to reply. As Moyes tells it, Sewel was 'very gentlemanly. A polite guy. We had an open and robust conversation … It's interesting that I've never seen him do a "mea culpa" afterwards, which one often sees in these instances, where they do an interview with *The Guardian*, or somewhere, to try and get their career back on track. Interesting that that hasn't happened.'[5]

Sewel resigned as chairman of committees in the Lords on 26 July 2015 and gave up his position in the House altogether two days later. 'The question of whether my behaviour breached the Code of Conduct is important, but essentially technical,' he wrote to the clerk of parliaments. 'The bigger questions are whether my behaviour is compatible with membership of the House of Lords and whether my continued membership would damage and undermine public confidence in the House of Lords.'[6] But he did not eschew the limelight altogether afterwards. He subsequently defended the UK Government's right to legislate on Brexit despite the lack of support from the Scottish Parliament in accordance with his eponymous consent motion – in the process, no doubt once more upsetting Dolphinite Alex Salmond in particular.

Just a short while before the story was published, Sewel had written in the *Huffington Post* in his role as chairman of the Privileges and Conduct Committee, 'The actions of a few damage our reputation. Scandals make good headlines.'[7] But it was the poet Pam Ayres who summed up the whole sorry saga best:

All hypocrites should take due care,
When snorting Coke in Dolphin Square,
An orange bra is not so cute,
And best left on the prostitute.[8]

Back in March 2003, another Dolphinite, Baron Mackenzie of Framwellgate – a 59-year-old Labour peer who served as an advisor to the Home Office and was previously president of the Police Superintendents' Association – had also found himself in trouble for an association with a prostitute, although he insisted it was all a set up by journalists.

The *News of the World* reported that Mackenzie had been sitting in the House of Commons' Sports and Social Club a few days earlier when he had struck up conversation with a barmaid, a 32-year-old French-Algerian woman called Salima Kebache. The following day, he had given her a tour of the House of Lords. 'She seemed very interested in the workings of the building,' Mackenzie elaborated, 'and I agreed to give her a tour of the building with a description of the architecture and procedures.' Then, by his own account, she rang him at about a quarter to midnight in a distressed state and wanting someone to talk to. He invited her to his flat in Dolphin Square, where she stayed until about 2 a.m. According to the newspaper, she told a friend that the pair had had sex, but Mackenzie denied this and refuted any claim that money had changed hands. Instead, he said, they had discussed subjects including Parliament and the Iraqi war.

Mackenzie did not consider a libel action, saying, 'It would be very difficult to prove what did or didn't happen. Probably the best is to leave it and let it die a death.' He did, however, intend to discuss with the parliamentary authorities as to whether the incident raised any security concerns, including the vetting process for people employed within Westminster.[9]

Mackenzie pulled off the rare trick, even for the Dolphinite political class, of making headlines for scandals separately involving sex and money. After the Kebache affair, in 2009 it was reported that the peer had been paid over £600,000 by Inter TV, a company owned by a Russian oligarch in exile. There was some confusion at the time as to whether this money was paid for his involvement as a consultant, or whether he was in fact a director of the company – a position that ought to have been registered with the parliamentary authorities.[10] Then, in 2013, Mackenzie was one of three Labour peers caught up in yet another journalistic sting. On this occasion, journalists posed as representatives of a solar energy company offering financial retainers in return for the lords lobbying on their behalf, in defiance of parliamentary rules.[11]

Mackenzie, for instance, suggested that he could arrange for parties on the House of Lords terrace by requesting a colleague host them on his behalf. On learning of newspaper involvement, he declined to resign the party whip, insisting that he had broken no rules. He said no financial arrangement had been agreed upon and that, in the event 'when I went back to my office I checked the codes of conduct and I decided that it was getting a bit near the mark and I decided to decline the offer'. Nonetheless, the House of Lords Committee for Privileges and Conduct did eventually rule that he had breached the code of conduct in relation to the incident.[12]

The same journalists attempted to ensnare one of Mackenzie's Dolphin Square neighbours in the same episode – Baron Cunningham of Felling (known as Jack Cunningham when a Cabinet minister in the early Blair years). Cunningham's father had been a prominent Labour figure in the north-east before he was given a three-year jail sentence in the 1970s for his part in the Poulson scandal, in which it was revealed how architect John Poulson had bribed assorted public figures over several years in return for the awarding of contracts. But Jack's career had been largely taint-free until he found himself embroiled in claims of lobbying. He, though, argued that he had suspected that he was being set up even as he requested £12,000 per month from the purported energy company. 'Knocking on doors, introductions and getting to see the people, including if necessary the ministers – this is part of the package,' he was said to have promised. But Cunningham insisted that he 'quickly became suspicious' and 'sought to test my suspicions during the meeting'. 'What the article does not make at all clear,' he said, 'is that I told the undercover journalists that I always stick to the rules and declare any interests,' he said in a statement. 'The article also fails to properly acknowledge the important fact that I informed them the next day that I wanted nothing more to do with them.' Cunningham was suspended from Labour pending investigations but was cleared of breaching parliamentary standards and had the whip restored.[13]

Before the expenses scandal exploded in 2009, one of the Square's national party leaders, Alex Salmond, faced his own accusations of financial misconduct. Twice leader of the Scottish National Party (from 1990–2000 and 2004–14), he was also Scotland's First Minister from 2007–14, during some of which time he held a flat in Dolphin Square. Indeed, it was his Pimlico pied-à-terre that caused him problems. Records showed that for the months covering May 2007 to March 2008, Salmond claimed £116,000 for his MP expenses, even though he had only attended Westminster sittings six times in that period. This included £14,000 for rent on his Dolphin Square apartment, which works out at £2,333 for each usage.

To make matters worse in the eyes of some observers, he also used hotels for much of his First Minister business in London, costing Scottish taxpayers a further £1,100 between May and December 2007 when he could, in theory at least, have used his Pimlico flat. In his defence, a spokesperson said:

These were the occasions when the First Minister was in London on official ministerial business, with the support of a full civil service team and back-up. The hotels were used for many business meetings, as well as for accommodation. This would not have been possible in the rented flats at Dolphin Square.

But at a moment when politicians and their expenses were hot news, it cannot have been comfortable for Salmond.[14]

Salmond gave notice on his flat in October 2007 and left at the end of the year, completing a two-year stint in the Square. A Labour spokesperson was moved to note: 'He may have given up his flat but that doesn't alter the fact that £14,000 of taxpayers' money was spent on a flat he hardly used. He should admit he cannot do three jobs – MP, MSP and First Minister – and quit as an MP.'[15]

Yet, all this paled when compared to the scandal that engulfed Salmond from late 2017, when the SNP first received allegations of serious sexual misconduct against him. In January 2019, he was charged with thirteen sexual offences, including two of attempted rape, and one of breach of the peace relating to 2013–14 when he was still First Minister (although no longer a resident of Dolphin Square). He denied the charges (one of which was dropped pre-trial) but resigned from the SNP. In court, it was admitted that the married Salmond did have sexual contact with two of the complainants but in March 2020 he was found not guilty of twelve charges, with a 'not proven' verdict on the thirteenth.

All the while, there were inquiries into the response to the original complaints by the Scottish Government and its First Minister (and Salmond's former friend and deputy), Nicola Sturgeon. Salmond claimed that the government's response had been seriously flawed. The resulting Parliamentary Committee on the Scottish Government Handling of Harassment Complaints concluded that Sturgeon had misled the committee, while a separate inquiry decided that she had not breached the Ministerial Code. The affair threatened to wreak serious havoc in the SNP and certainly did the party few favours as it narrowly failed to achieve a majority in elections to the Scottish Parliament held shortly afterwards. It all made questions over his hotel bills over a decade earlier seem rather inconsequential by comparison.

In 2012, the Square was struck by a scandal that involved not a politician but a man of the cloth. A Catholic priest, Michael Seed, found himself in the firing line after details emerged of his attempt to sell a papal knighthood to an Israeli arms dealer, Hezi Bezalel, in return for a £45,000 donation to charity. Seed, a Franciscan friar, already had a significant public profile for his dealings with famous people. He was ecumenical advisor for over twenty-five years to two archbishops of Westminster, Cardinal Basil Hume and then Cormac Murphy-O'Connor. In this role, he was widely considered to have facilitated the Catholic conversions of several public figures, including the politician Ann Widdecombe and the Duchess of Kent. Perhaps most notably, he performed mass for the Blair family when Tony Blair was prime minister, and shortly after leaving office Blair confirmed his conversion. Seed was also said to be living in a Dolphin Square flat rent-free at the discretion of another papal knight.

The friar was always a sociable figure, known to get along well with journalists. He was exuberant, too. At the time of the cash-for-honours scandal, he was on leave from his religious order after it was said he celebrated the twenty-fifth anniversary of his ordination by hosting a champagne party at a night club at which the entertainment was a troop of men dressed as nuns. Previously, in 2006, he'd held the launch for his book *Sinners and Saints: The Irreverent Diaries of Britain's Most Controversial Priest* at Stringfellows nightclub. Then the following year he published his biography, *Nobody's Child*, which detailed his upbringing in Manchester with a stepfather who abused him, an adoptive mother who committed suicide and time spent at the notorious Knowl View School where Cyril Smith abused boys.

Even after his troubles over the knighthoods, Seed regularly returned to the limelight. In 2016, it was reported that he had held private meetings with Prince Andrew, although neither party disclosed details of what they discussed. Subsequently, Seed was appointed chaplain to the Italian-based Dignitatis Humanae Institute, which has strong links to the prominent 'alt-right' figure and key advisor to Donald Trump before and during his presidency, Steve Bannon.

For a while back in 2007, the attention was less on knights and more on the question of whether the Square was about to get a royal prince. An article in the Square's regular newsletter speculated that the then 24-year-old Prince William, grandson of Queen Elizabeth II, was to follow in his Aunty Anne's footsteps and take up a lease.[16] In the event, though, the gossip mill seems to have got it wrong or perhaps William had a change of heart in a year when scandal and drama was not in short supply in Pimlico. For example, long-standing resident Lord Desai was unwittingly cast into an academic and political scandal in 2007 that played out over a number of years. Desai, an Indian-born economist and academic, was notably connected to the London School of Economics. In 2003, he retired as director of the LSE's Centre for the Study of Global Governance – a school he had founded some eleven years previously – but in 2007 he was asked to review a PhD thesis submitted by Saif al-Islam Gaddafi, son of the Libyan dictator, Colonel Muammar Gaddafi. There were concerns that the thesis was not up to scratch, so its author was subjected to a two-and-a-half-hour oral examination. Subsequently, a revised version of the work was accepted and the doctorate awarded. That was not to be the end of the story, though. Over time, there were increasing concerns that Gaddafi may have plagiarised whole sections of his thesis – several passages bear striking resemblances to other published works. Moreover, in 2009 the LSE voted to accept a donation set to be worth £1.5 million from the Gaddafi International Charity and Development Foundation, chaired by Saif al-Islam Gaddafi.

Ties between the university and the Libyan regime continued to grow. The donated money was used to fund a 'North Africa Programme' at the university and Saif al-Islam Gaddafi even gave the Ralph Miliband memorial lecture at his alma mater in 2010. There were also plans to develop a programme in which several hundred hand-picked 'future leaders' of Libya would receive education and training in the UK. Then, in 2011, the Arab Spring arrived. Across North Africa and the Middle East, popular protests demanded democratic reforms. But the Libyan regime took a predictably hard line, meeting the protests with violence. In February that year, Saif al-Islam Gaddafi broadcast to the nation, warning of 'thousands of deaths' and that 'rivers of blood' would 'run through Libya'. His father, he insisted ominously, would 'fight until the last man, the last woman, the last bullet'. Desai was left to observe that Gaddafi Jr 'was not behaving as if he had had an LSE education'.[17] In 2020, the Dolphinite also broke off relations with the Labour Party after an almost fifty-year association in protest at former leader Jeremy Corbyn's readmission to the party amid concerns about his handling of antisemitism in the Labour ranks during his tenure.[18]

Dolphin Square had earlier played its part in a saga of the state policing of political protests rather closer to home. In 1998, the Blair Government had established the Saville Inquiry to look into the events of 'Bloody Sunday', when in 1972 British troops fired on protesters marching in Derry against the policy of internment without trial. Fourteen protesters, all Catholics, died from gunshot wounds as the incident became a defining moment in the Troubles.

The inquiry lasted for twelve years and in 2002 temporarily relocated from the Guildhall in Derry to Westminster Central Hall amid concerns that British soldiers would be the target of attacks if forced to testify in Northern Ireland. A number of people related to the inquiry were put up in apartments in Rodney House, including members of victims' families. Sir Ronnie Flanagan, Chief Constable of the Police Service of Northern Ireland (formerly the Royal Ulster Constabulary), also had a flat in the Square at that time. Accounts suggest that relations between the two sides were generally cordial as they mingled in the Square's bar. Flanagan, incidentally, was said to be related to the Sergeant Major Flanagan, whose name Bud Flanagan had once appropriated.

The year 2007 also saw the tragic death of Rodney McKinnon, a 64-year-old judge and a former member of Westminster Council, who died in June from head injuries suffered after he fell from the window of his third-floor flat in Drake House onto the concrete path below. McKinnon had lived in the Square for a decade, during which time he had been appointed a circuit judge. 'Everybody is completely devastated that something so awful could have happened in our midst,' said fellow resident Patricia McVicar, while Brendan Martin, the chair of the tenants' association, described McKinnon as 'very well-known and well liked, particularly among the older residents'.[19] At the inquest, it emerged that the judge had been suffering with depression for several months. There was a footprint on a chair in his apartment and it was suggested that he would have needed to clamber across his desk on to a narrow parapet to propel himself away from the building.

But McKinnon's brother, Warwick – who was sworn in as a judge on the same day as his brother – expressed doubts. He believed that his brother's death was the result of some sort of accident, convinced that Rodney would have left a letter of explanation if he had decided to take his own life. He also suggested that the depression – and he did acknowledge his brother had been in a low mood in the days before his death – had been exacerbated by the medication he was taking for high blood pressure. Warwick even wrote to the coroner, Paul Knapman, to remind him that a verdict of suicide demanded evidence 'beyond all reasonable doubt'. A demand, it turned out, that Knapman believed had been met.[20]

While McKinnon's death was premature, news broke in 2012 of the passing of Charlie Florman, who had lived a rich and varied life that stretched over ninety-two years. A gourmet, he'd lived in Keyes House until 2003 and was celebrated for, among other things, having eaten in all but one of the three-Michelin-star restaurants that there had ever been. Despite being a mostly non-political figure, his life fitted the classic Dolphinite blueprint, combining wealth, excitement, some controversy and not a little eccentricity.

The Swedish-born son of Carl Florman – the founder of the airline that evolved into Scandinavian Airlines – as a young man during the Second World War, Charlie secretly flew to Britain to supply armaments and then set himself up in London to co-ordinate a programme of further clandestine flights between Sweden and the UK. After a stint helping his father grow his airline business overseas in the post-war period, he then moved into magazine publishing, working on prestigious titles including *Life*, *Time* and *Fortune*. And having been introduced to the world of fine dining as a teen by his father, he now had a sufficiently expansive expense account to indulge his culinary passions more regularly.

By the mid-1970s, he was living in London in Chester Square with his wife, Madeleine. Alone in the house one night, she heard the intercom ring. The voice that greeted her was so incoherent that she refused to answer the door and the caller eventually went away. It turned out that it was the father of a school friend of the Flormans' daughter, and he left bloodstains on the steps of the Chester Square residence. He was Lord Lucan, and earlier in the evening he had bludgeoned to death his children's nanny, Sandra Rivett, in the basement of his nearby Lower Belgrave Square home. Florman could thus claim the rare distinction of Dolphin Square arguably being only the second most notorious address at which he had lived.

In 2018, the Square said goodbye to another of its long-term residents who could also claim to have lived a full life and then some. Sir Alan Dawtry, 102 when he died, was a solicitor by training, although his career as a lawyer with Sheffield City Council was interrupted by the Second World War. During active service, he became stranded in France as the German Army invaded, necessitating a daring dash across the country to Cherbourg, where he arrived to find a single ship left in the harbour. Worse still, its captain was drunk and incapable, so Dawtry arrested him and took control of the vessel, navigating it safely back to Britain. Under his command on this trip was a young man, Iain Macleod, a future Conservative Government minister (including a brief stint as Chancellor of the Exchequer in 1970). As a young man in the war, Macleod was known for a hedonistic lifestyle and his aplomb as a serious bridge player. On one memorable evening, Dawtry refused to play him at cards on account of Macleod's drunkenness. The irate Macleod responded by emptying his revolver into Dawtry's room.

Dawtry had many other wartime adventures, serving in North Africa and Italy, finishing up as a lieutenant colonel. While in Milan, it was he who ordered that the bodies of Mussolini and his mistress Clara Petacci were cut down after they had been strung up for public display. After the war, Dawtry became an important figure in local government, including a long stint as town clerk for Westminster Council. Among his many achievements in that job was to oversee the introduction of the first parking meters and, more importantly, his part in the reorganisation of London into thirty-two boroughs in accordance with the London Government Act of 1963. A Yorkshireman by birth, London came to flow through his veins, and Dolphin Square was where his heart lay. Indeed, he helped shape its culture over his very long tenancy. He got married for the first time at the age of 81, to Sally, and died as something of a Dolphin Square legend.

Another Dolphinite of notable longevity is Lord Mereworth, who entered his tenth decade in the course of the new century. Mereworth is not, by any stretch, the most political of the Dolphin Square peers, but he is nonetheless intriguing. A hereditary peer, in 2002 he succeeded his father who died at the age of 100 having never made a speech in the Lords. In 2010, when he was 81, Lord Mereworth was said to have formed a close relationship with 28-year-old Sara Al Amoudi, who claimed to be the estranged daughter of a billionaire Saudi sheikh. However, doubt has persisted as to her true identity. Five years later, Al Amoudi won a High Court battle against two property magnates, Ian Paton and Amanda Clutterbuck, who claimed she had fraudulently persuaded them to sign over six London properties to her. In court, it was argued by the tycoons that she was in fact an Ethiopian who had previously worked in the sex industry. The presiding judge, however, concluded that while her true identity remained unknown, it was not relevant to the case anyway.

Lord Mereworth – a follower of the Bahá'í faith who can trace his family line directly back to Henry VII – was involved in his own legal battle back in 1999, when he led a group of some seventy hereditary lords who considered an action for compensation for the forced removal of all but ninety-two hereditary peers from the House of Lords under the terms of the House of Lords Act 1999. Although it came to nothing, he did not let the matter lie. In 2011 he unsuccessfully sought a hearing in the High Court against the Ministry of Justice on the grounds that he had been denied 'A Seat, Place and Voice in Parliament's Public Assembly and Councils' as set out in the letters patent that created the peerage to which he had acceded. His argument, though, was rejected on the grounds that composition of the House was a matter for Parliament and not the courts. At least he was not short of nearby parliamentarians whose ears he could bend back in Pimlico.

Yet another of the Square's peers who did not allow age to wither him was Baron Jenkin of Roding, who, as Patrick Jenkin, served variously as Minister for Energy (under Ted Heath) and then as Margaret Thatcher's Secretary of State for Social Services, then Industry and, finally, Environment. Elevated to the Lords in 1987, arguably his finest moment came in 2013 when he was well into his ninth decade, on the occasion of a debate on the right of same-sex couples to marry. It was a contentious issue at the time and few had marked Jenkin, an old-school Conservative, as the man for the moment. But his speech was considered, moving and helped to allay the fears of several of those wavering in their support for the Bill. 'Last year,' he said, 'my wife and I celebrated our diamond wedding anniversary, and I have to say that it has been a marriage with mutual comfort and support. Is this Bill going to redefine that marriage? I cannot see how that could possibly happen.'[21]

The Bill was subsequently passed into law (his MP son Bernard Jenkin also voted in favour) and Jenkin was nominated at the PinkNews Awards that year for speech of the year. In early 2015 he took advantage of the recently passed House of Lords Reform Act to retire from the Upper House and died, aged 90, the following year. He was a figure emblematic of the changing times. A Dolphinite whose heyday was in an era when homosexuality was still widely considered an affliction and when the House of Lords was peopled by hereditary peers with a job for life, he cast off his mortal coil in a new age when gay people can freely marry and where the majority of lords are appointed in adulthood and can, for the first time, retire or resign at will.

If that was a landmark piece of legislation, surely the defining legislative act in twenty-first-century British life so far has been Brexit – and it is perhaps inevitable that the Square should also feature in a cameo in its story. Principally, the Square has been called home by two of the pivotal figures in the movement to take the UK out of the European Union. It has served as the long-time home to the West German-born Gisela Stuart, who moved to the UK in 1974 when she was 19 and sat as the Labour MP for Birmingham

Edgbaston between 1997 and 2017. Going against the official line of her own party, she served as chairperson of the Vote Leave Campaign Committee ahead of the decisive 2016 in/out referendum on EU membership, gaining a public profile as a key ally to leading Conservative Brexiteers including Boris Johnson and Michael Gove. While Johnson became the chief political beneficiary of Brexit, its spiritual leader was Nigel Farage, who also briefly took a flat in the Square after the referendum was over. Perhaps wary of being cast as living among the Establishment of which he has been so insistent over the years that he is not a part, he has done little to play up his time in Pimlico, commenting, 'I lived there for ease and convenience and it being two minutes to the office in Westminster. There were more Chinese students than Establishment figures in my block.'[22]

His latter observation is perhaps particularly pertinent. Since the Square came under new ownership in 2005, its demographics have changed. Large numbers of the old guard have died off or moved on. The admissions procedure and rent structure have fallen increasingly in line with other commercial letting properties. While plenty of politicians, including one of the authors of this book, continue to make a home there, it is slowly but surely becoming less the bastion of the British Establishment that it once was. Even in Farage's Britain, where patriotic pride has often been held up as among the ultimate virtues, Dolphin Square is defiantly becoming increasingly international.

Not everything changes, though. Intriguingly, there is the suspicion that the Square's traditional reputation for espionage continues. A former lettings manager, for instance, reveals that among the many international renters he encountered, he spent a week dealing with a group of prospective Chinese customers who were not like the usual students and young professionals that Farage encountered. Instead, they were, the lettings manager said, 'suited and booted, they were a bit bizarre'. They were only interested, too, in rooms in the south of the building that had direct views on to a local embassy. So concerned was the manager that he passed the negotiation to the Square's security team and in the end the various individuals opted to move elsewhere.[23] But it served as a reminder that Dolphin Square remains a place where all is often not quite as it might first seem.

22

'CREDIBLE AND TRUE'

In December 2014, Detective Supt Kenny McDonald of the Metropolitan Police made a public appeal for information in relation to allegations of historical sexual abuse by prominent people. He was a lead officer on what was called Operation Midland and among the sites where the alleged abuse had taken place in the 1970s and '80s was Dolphin Square. The police were examining claims that abusers had murdered three children. Much of the evidence came from a witness known at the time only as 'Nick'. McDonald said that officers who had heard Nick's story considered his claims to be 'credible and true'.[1]

It was arguably the defining moment in moulding public perceptions of the Square. It seems likely that Dolphin Square will forever be associated with allegations that a murderous paedophile ring of powerful Establishment figures wrought its havoc within Pimlico. When Dolphin Square is mentioned, the public at large shall not think first of Mosley or Vassall, Keeler or Princess Anne. They will remember instead the horror of children abused and killed, the crimes against those innocents carried out and assisted by people close to the levers of power. But we now know that there is a problem with that narrative. Nick was lying.

The 'Nick' episode wrought enormous damage on all those directly involved. To those he falsely accused, it turned lives upside down and destroyed reputations overnight – in some cases, not to be restored while the principals involved or their loved ones were still alive. The credibility of the police and other public figures who urged that 'Nick' be taken seriously was also battered. 'Nick' – the name chosen to protect the accuser's identity – is actually Carl Beech, a former nurse now serving eighteen years in prison for perverting the course of justice, fraud and his own paedophile offences. Moreover, the effect of his falsifications has been to render impossible calm public debate about the possibility that paedophiles historically operated in the Square. This is unfortunate, not least in giving a ready-made 'get out clause' to those who might have a case to answer. The subject has simply become too toxic for the public arena. Anyone who suggests that all was not always well at Dolphin Square is brushed off as a fantasist, a disturbed mind, a conspiracy theorist. But take away the sound and fury that constantly surrounds the subject and there remain questions that are unresolved and deserve, at the very least, to be examined coolly and respectfully. So, how did it come to this?

The 'Nick' allegations must be seen in the context of the Jimmy Savile case. In 2012, Savile was exposed as an abuser on an industrial scale, seemingly protected by public institutions – including the BBC – and prominent individuals who turned a blind eye to his activities or played deaf when told of his exploits. In the aftermath of the investigation into Savile, several other high-profile names from the world of entertainment were also convicted of historical abuse. The public and the authorities were of a like mind – the time had come to take seriously accusations of abuse, historical and current, without fear or favour in regard to those accused.

In 2012, Beech approached police in Wiltshire alleging he was himself a victim of Savile, and that he had also been abused by his stepfather, who had been in the army, and other individuals. Wiltshire Police, however, discontinued investigations after failing to find supporting evidence. Beech subsequently appeared in a documentary about the Savile case and also used the internet to outline and discuss claims of historical abuse. In 2014, journalists at Exaro, an investigative news website, became aware of Beech's blogs and made contact with him. Over a period of time, Beech told Exaro that in the 1970s and '80s he had been a witness to and victim of abuse by a ring of paedophiles that included prominent public figures. The abuse, he said, took place at several locations including Dolphin Square, and three children had been killed. In particular, the police explored possible links to the murder in 1981 of 8-year-old Vishal Mehrotra, abducted in London on the day of Princess Diana's marriage to Prince Charles, and the disappearance off the streets of London of Martin Allen in 1979.

As we have seen, allegations of abuse at Dolphin Square had been in the public domain for many years, as had claims of a 'VIP vice ring'. In 2014, the Metropolitan Police picked up on Exaro's coverage and launched Operation Midland. In 1983, Conservative MP Geoffrey Dickens had presented Home Secretary Leon Brittan with a dossier containing allegations of abuse against public figures, including the diplomat Peter Hayman. Beech now named some of those he said were part of the ring that he said had abused him. They included Brittan himself, former Prime Minister Edward Heath, former MPs Harvey Proctor and Lord Janner, former Chief of the Defence Staff Lord Bramall, former MI6 Director Maurice Oldfield and former MI5 Director General Michael Hanley.

Several politicians commented publicly on Beech's claims, with Tom Watson, a future deputy leader of the Labour Party, describing Brittan as 'close to evil'.[2] Fellow MP Zac Goldsmith told the House in November 2014:

> There can no longer be any doubt at all that powerful people have done terrible things and that they have been protected by the Establishment and we know that some of the key figures are alive today. The measure of success for the police investigations is that those people face justice before they die.[3]

Meanwhile, another MP, John Mann, passed a dossier to police detailing allegations against twenty-two public figures.

There were very public raids on the homes of a number of those accused by Beech but it was not long before the investigation began to unravel. Where an appeal for witnesses in the Savile case had generated hundreds of leads, there was now no such public response. In truth, the police were confronted by an utter lack of credible corroborative evidence. Moreover, there was also an absence of due diligence done on Beech himself. For a long time, the Met were not even aware that he had previously gone to Wiltshire Police. Doubts grew over inconsistencies in his story and there were suggestions that he might have actively researched elements of his narrative using other sources. In short, the police came to the realisation that there was no substantial case beyond Beech's own testimony and after fourteen months the investigation was closed.

The police were vilified for wasting time and resources and putting intolerable strain on the accused. They were accused of being intent on believing the complainant at virtually any cost. Commentators spoke of an over-correction in light of the Savile case, with the accuser too readily believed and the accused assumed guilty by a police force stung by Savile criticism, a political class trying to make good with the public after the expenses scandal and a media reeling from its own damaging phone-hacking practices. But now Beech was to become the focus of police inquiries. In 2018, he was charged with a string of offences, most shockingly a number of paedophile offences, many committed while Operation Midland was ongoing. He was tried and found guilty in 2019, receiving eighteen years for his crimes.

That, then, seemed to be that. All the talk of VIP paedophiles at Dolphin Square that had permeated down the years was, some were saying, hogwash. While other individuals have gone public with their own allegations, none have been tested in court. The all-important corroborative evidence has never been put before the public, no compelling forensics. Often, accusers do not make for the best witnesses either. Not uncommonly, their lives may be chaotic, their stories inconsistent, memories potentially distorted by time and the mind's own attempts to protect the self from revisiting trauma of one type or another.

But for all that, it is difficult to give Dolphin Square an entirely clean bill of health in regard to historical sexual abuse. Was there a paedophile network operating out of the Square, run by a cabal of Illuminati, plotting to rape and murder? We can assume not. Has paedophilia been practised in the Square at various times? The weight of evidence would suggest that it has. How organised was it? It is impossible to tell. Organisation implies a power hierarchy directing events in a premeditated fashion. But organisation can happen after the fact. It may amount, rather, to a cover-up. An unwillingness to poke the bear in case it turns on you.

We have ample evidence that, historically, individuals have been able to get away with abuse despite figures of power and authority either knowing of their crimes or having good grounds to suspect them. Jimmy Savile, Cyril Smith, Peter Morrison, to name just three.

Meanwhile, Dolphinite Alan Beith originally won his seat in a by-election after the previous MP Antony Lambton was caught up in a prostitution scandal. Lambton, we now know, was the subject of police intelligence passed to MI5 in 1973 concerning 'an alleged video recording that showed [him] involved in sexual activities with a boy'.[4] We know, too, that party whips were long used to maintaining 'dirt books' recording the misdemeanours of politicians that their parties helped to cover up. This was done so that MPs could then be compelled to toe the party line as and when required. Conservative Chief Whip Tim Fortescue even allowed himself to be filmed for a documentary in 1995, saying:

> Anyone with any sense, who was in trouble, would come to the whips and tell them the truth, and say now, 'I'm in a jam, can you help?'. It might be debt, it might be … a scandal involving small boys, or any kind of scandal in which … a member seemed likely to be mixed up in, they'd come and ask if we could help and if we could, we did.[5]

Where, then, is the evidence of abuse in relation to Dolphin Square? There is, for starters, the testimony of David Ingle detailed elsewhere in this book. But there is much else besides. We know, for instance, that Roddam Twiss frequented the Square over many years. The son of Admiral Sir Frank Twiss – who served as the former Second Sea Lord and Chief of Naval Personnel, as well as Black Rod in the House of Lords – Roddam Twiss was a teacher jailed for three years in 1967 after being accused of stripping, tying up and beating children as young as 11. According to an article in the *Daily Mail* based on interviews with two retired police officers, Twiss had been banned by his father from entering the Palace of Westminster (a claim Roddam denies) and that he was known to visit Dolphin Square. However, the former vice squad officers also say that when, in the late 1970s, they attempted to investigate suspicions that Twiss might be involved in the supply of 'rent boys' to 'VIPs', their investigations were ended by their superior officers. This, they claimed, happened after they had seen Cyril Smith take a male sex worker to Twiss's home – a claim Twiss also denies.

One of the officers stated:

> We went to the police station in Belgravia, and found a file that said Twiss had been banned by his father from entering the Palace of Westminster. He also went to Dolphin Square late at night. We thought he could be procuring boys for bigger figures from pimps at the Meat Rack. Well-to-do people would not want to be seen somewhere like that. We also followed him to the Meat Rack. Our superiors called it off. We assumed it was to protect VIPs.[6]

Twiss, who now lives under a different name, told a journalist from the *Daily Mail* of how the Piccadilly Meat Rack worked in the 1970s and '80s. 'Rent boys looking for customers,' he said, 'would lean on the railings and men looking for boys would go and see if they fancied anyone. But it was dangerous. Most of the boys just wanted to rob you for drugs. It was much safer to pick up one in one of Soho's gay drinking clubs. They would all say they were over age but some were more like 14 or 15.' He also acknowledged that public figures were among those he knew to be using male sex workers but could not recall any names and would not disclose them even if he could, although he did note, 'There were more Tories than Labour.'[7]

He also acknowledged being a regular visitor to Dolphin Square, where he visited his friend, Mervyn Greenway. Greenway was renowned as a charmer and playboy, a City trader of the pre-Big Bang era, who wined and dined, gambled, played sport to a good standard and was a mostly unsuccessful owner of racehorses but a successful owner of greyhounds. In short, he was a bon viveur, who worked and played equally hard. Professionally, he was particularly known for working as the stockbroker of corporate wheeler-dealer Tiny Rowland. Greenway is also remembered for his sometimes outrageous behaviour. On one occasion, he is said to have arranged for porn actress Linda Lovelace to attend a City luncheon that was traditionally more straight-laced than Lovelace. And his obituary in *The Telegraph* included the following passage:

> Each year, Greenway arranged a match between the Lords & Commons and the girls' school Roedean, an occasion he always keenly anticipated. On one occasion he had a heart seizure while at the wicket. Opening his eyes to see a cluster of 17-year-old girls looking down at him, Greenway proclaimed, before being taken off to hospital, that he had gone to heaven.[8]

One of Greenway's neighbours in the Square, meanwhile, remembers him as an 'oddball', often to be found sunbathing – 'bald-headed' and 'stretched out in a skimpy costume' – on one of the lawns.[9]

Twiss said of Greenway that he 'knew everyone in high places' and 'I met them through him'. As for Dolphin Square, 'If you knew the right porter, you'd leave a few pounds and they would allow your guests in with no questions asked.' Twiss described how parties typically began in a flat before spilling 'outside into the square on balmy summer evenings'. It was, he said, 'a den of iniquity for 30 years' where residents' 'mistresses and prostitutes' circulated among guests.[10]

At the Independent Inquiry into Child Sexual Abuse (IICSA) – established by then Home Secretary Theresa May in 2014 to examine institutional responses to claims of sexual abuse in light of the Jimmy Savile scandal – a former Met officer called Paul Holmes was probed on the surveillance of Twiss. In his evidence, he confirmed that Twiss was seen visiting the West End and walking around the area of the Meat Rack and its environs, he had 'conversations with a number of males of varied ages' and he went to Dolphin Square on at least one occasion. He also confirmed that Dolphin Square was considered significant because 'it had previously appeared in a number of vice-related operations and intelligence reports'.[11]

Moreover, Ian Graham – the first officer at the scene of Michael Shepley's murder in 1975 – went on to include Dolphin Square on his beat for several years. He describes it variously as a 'Pandora's box' and 'the sort of place you lived if you didn't want anyone to know your business'. He remembers how difficult it was to attempt to impose any police authority in the Square, with even parking tickets discouraged from a senior level within the force. On the rare occasions that crime sheets were submitted, he recalls, they were customarily returned with the advice that 'no further action' was necessary. He remembers, too, the common sight of teens – often aged just 14 or 15 – entering the Square in the company of older men who, when challenged, were typically asserted to be the 'uncle' of the youth.

At the time of the original police inquiries into Carl Beech's allegations, a long-term Square resident was among those to be interviewed. Today, that resident says that they think 'there were a number of people who were involved in something. Perhaps not as bad as has been made out.' They recalled the response of a fellow Dolphinite who 'got very hot under the collar when he discovered the police had been to see me'. 'He was in a terrible state,' the resident continued, 'asking me what I said to them. He was worried, and wanted to see me straight away … I put him off and saw him the next day and he told me not to speak to the police again, which I refused to do.' This is not to suggest that the individual described was in any way involved in abuse, but rather to highlight that there was long-standing tension over even discussion of the subject.[12]

The same resident also made the claim that one of the boys Beech suggested as a potential murder victim, Martin Allen, had concrete associations with the Square. 'He [Nick] named one of these boys and the police say he got the name of one of these boys from a list of missing children,' the resident says. But the resident says that Allen used to clean cars at the Square, adding, 'That pulls the rug from underneath the idea that this was a random choice.' The story is seemingly confirmed by a passage in the Henriques Report. In 2016, in the aftermath of the collapse of Operation Midland, Judge Richard Henriques was invited by Metropolitan Police Commissioner Sir Bernard Hogan-Howe to review the Met's handling of allegations of historical sexual offence allegations involving people of public prominence. Three officers criticised in the report – Deputy Assistant Commissioner Rodhouse, Detective Superintendent McDonald and Detective Chief Inspector

Tudway – were given the opportunity to respond to specific criticisms. In relation to Martin Allen, they said:

> Martin Allen's father worked at the Australian High Commission as a chauffeur. The Embassy had retained flats at Dolphin Square. Martin Allen used to wash cars at Dolphin Square. Martin had been found by police in May 1978 frequenting Piccadilly Circus, a location popular with rent boys. Officers had spoken to chauffeurs at Dolphin Square and received anecdotal evidence of collecting clients in company with young boys and, in one case, a description of pool parties involving young boys at Dolphin Square.[13]

William van Straubenzee is another name linked to the Square suspected of sexual offences against children. David Weeks, the former Westminster Council leader, has described how before being granted his Dolphin Square flat in 1970 he had to be interviewed by the Square's general manager, a retired colonel. Weeks was confident he would pass muster with the colonel because he knew van Straubenzee, the solicitor for the Dolphin Square Trust and someone who went on to become Conservative MP for Wokingham. Straubenzee had told Weeks that he should mention his name to the colonel.[14] While Straubenzee did not live in the Square himself – he had a grace and favour flat at Lambeth Palace thanks to his involvement with the Church of England – he nonetheless clearly wielded significant influence in the Square as a legal advisor and quasi-gatekeeper. In evidence provided to IICSA by MI5, it was stated: 'In 1982, MI5 received information that suggested that William van Straubenzee engaged in sexual activities with young boys whilst in Northern Ireland [he had been Northern Ireland Minister between 1972 and 1974]. This information was shared with the Cabinet Office, who shared it with the Prime Minister.' MI5 confirmed that if this intelligence had been received today, under current policy it would be passed to the police.[15]

In July 2014, Lord Tebbit, who served in various Cabinet positions under Margaret Thatcher, appeared on *The Andrew Marr Show* and answered questions related to allegations of historical abuse. Tebbit acknowledged that 'there may well have been' a 'big political cover-up' of abuse in the 1980s that needed to be understood in the context of the 'atmosphere of the times'.[16] IICSA, which specifically did not look into the claims of Carl Beech but did investigate 'Allegations of child sexual abuse linked to Westminster', threw up other significant evidence in relation to the Square. Of Dolphinite David Steel, for example, and his failure to act on his assumption formed in 1979 that his Liberal Party colleague Cyril Smith was guilty of child sexual abuse, the inquiry said, 'In our view, rather than give primacy to the protection of children, he yielded to considerations of political expediency and failed to launch a formal internal inquiry into Smith's alleged activities.'[17]

Among the most incendiary evidence of wrongdoing at Dolphin Square came in a statement taken from a former police officer identified only as GB. It was entered into evidence only at the end of the last day of hearings in IICSA's Westminster investigation and the witness did not appear in person to give evidence, nor were they seemingly provided with questions by the inquiry to which GB would have been legally obligated to give answers. The statement adduced in evidence dated from 20 December 2016 and was given as part of Operation Winter Key, the Metropolitan Police's investigation into allegations of non-recent abuse.[18]

GB's statement was wide ranging. It included allusions to surveillance of a London MP who was suspected of hosting young people overnight in his constituency office. But it also included significant detail of police operations concerning Dolphin Square in the 1990s. GB talked about how he had joined the Met's Paedophile Unit so that the force could 'have a response to child abuse' because a lot of the existing expertise was in 'dirty books' (i.e. child pornography) instead. At one point, the transcript of the interview notes, '(Discussion on lack of ability of Met to deal with child abuse.)'

GB was asked by the Winter Key interviewers about his knowledge of an operation codenamed Mileshogue (MH). His redacted reply reads:

MH was ... an intelligence gathering operation revolved around a guy called [NAME REDACTED] ... He had been a rent boy himself, living in Greenwich at that time. He had a series of young boys. One was [WM-A118] another was [WM-A119] and another 5 or 6. Those boys I interviewed on tape several times. [GB suggested that these children were thirteen or fourteen when they were speaking to them but that their abuses had started when they were as young as 8.]

They claimed one another had been abused by other people, were taken to parties and things by [NAME REDACTED] himself he was like a modern day Fagan [*sic*]. He also had them doing robberies and burglaries but he was also an informant for the police, inform on them and then turn up as their appropriate adult. These were kids all from local Children's Home. He would befriend them and take them out ... The problem was the kids would never say anything about their own abuse, only ever talk about others abuse and if they were present when others were abused. They would never talk about their own abuse, there was never any direct evidence ...

Going back to [NAME REDACTED] he would take kids round to various addresses, there was a core group of about 5 people's homes, 5 suspects that were names. There were others, the boys were taken to what they call the Dolphin Place, we thought that was Dolphin Square. They used to talk about a big dolphin there ... They knew of a network of other children who were abused. We were told that one of [NAME REDACTED]'s boys had been beaten up in Trafalgar Square, had serious brain injuries. From what the boys say this lad was going to inform the police, tell them everything. [NAME REDACTED] got hold of him, beat him up, he was left brain dead.

GB was then asked what information the attacked boy was going to give. He said:

Around people [NAME REDACTED] was taking them to see. More Dolphin Square, it was to do with Dolphin Square. He was a young [Withheld Under Data Protection Act] lad at the time about 14. He started young. He was about 10 when he started to be abused. He had moments of clarity talking about being abused, talked about

[NAME REDACTED] taking him places, talked about a Dolphin, the Dolphin place and going on a boat. I never got the whole conversation. I interviewed him and took a day to get to know him so he would speak to me. Then a couple of days trying to interview him. I tried it on tape but he was not having that. If he saw cameras he would freak ...

I didn't speak to him before he was attacked. He was in the secure unit for his mental health after being beaten up. [WM-A118] and [WM-A119] told me about their friend who was going to tell and this was what happened to him and this [was] why [WM-A118] and [WM-A119] were afraid to talk about anything to do with the guy who was running it.

GB was next asked what information WM-A118 and WM-A119 gave about Dolphin Square. GB responded:

There was someone in the Navy that they had met there. Supposed to be a politician involved that they had met but no name. Things they were told by [NAME REDACTED]. Half the time when they were taken to these places they were drunk out of their brains. They would top them up with more alcohol and they would be abused. There was no one specific person from the meetings or on the boat they named. They said a politician, someone in the Navy ... no names of prominent people. Any prominent people I would have remembered, noted it. There were nicknames and bits and pieces. It will all be in the intelligence files. I meticulously recorded everything.

When asked how they had identified the venue as Dolphin Square, GB said:

Didn't particularly, they said there were Dolphins and it was near Westminster Bridge. They used to call it the place with Dolphins.

GB then referred to the 'Fagin-figure', saying, 'He also mentioned Dolphin Square he had been there as a child himself, been abused.'

GB discussed how they had made requests for additional investigative resources to senior officers but their requests were repeatedly refused or bounced back as it was 'too difficult to do at this time' and 'we weren't regarded as a priority'. Of the Paedophile Unit at that time, GB said, 'They didn't want to know about a mass operation with loads of kids to interview. They didn't know how to deal with it.'

During the IICSA Inquiry, those who claimed to be victims of abuse at the hands of public figures were characterised as 'false complainants' by the son of one of the accused, Greville Janner (a Leicestershire MP for Labour for twenty-seven years up to 1997). His son, Daniel Janner, a QC, spoke of 'the infamous – this is quite an easy one to jump on; Dolphin Square – Dolphin Square rumours' and of 'false accusers' who were 'all, or nearly all, in care homes as youngsters. Here is the thing: not one made any complaint, when in care, against my late father. Not one.'[19] Daniel Janner reiterated a commonly held conception in the post-Beech environment: that the rumours about Dolphin Square are the product of a few testimonies from witnesses whose reliability is often difficult to gauge. Yet the inquiry received information relating to no less than thirty-three alleged victims of his father.

In October 2021, IICSA chair, Professor Alexis Jay, concluded: 'Despite numerous serious allegations against the late Lord Janner, police and prosecutors appeared reluctant to fully investigate the claims against him. On multiple occasions police put too little emphasis on looking for supporting evidence and shut down investigations without pursuing all outstanding enquiries.'[20] In response, Simon Cole, Chief Constable of Leicestershire Police which handled a number of allegations over many years and several investigations, said: 'It is fair and correct to say that the allegations could and should have been investigated more thoroughly, and Lord Janner could and should have faced prosecution earlier than 2015 [when he was due to stand trial before being ruled unfit to plead].'[21]

Regardless of the innocence or guilt of Janner himself, there is much more evidence of wrongdoing in the Square by others. We know that there were individuals associated with the Square who were actively abusive, and we know of others living there who turned a blind eye to abuse. We have firm evidence of an association between the Square and the Piccadilly Meat Rack going back decades, and it may be safely assumed that there was not a robust age-checking system in practice for those working the Meat Rack. There are long-term residents who harbour suspicions that abuse took place within the Square, while we know that other residents urged non-co-operation with police investigations. We know that chauffeurs working at the Square were accustomed to transporting individuals with underage companions. And then we have the evidence of multiple police sources, which together build a picture of an address routinely the subject of intelligence reports, subject to surveillance and regularly vacillating between being actively investigated and then 'un-investigated' on orders from above. Carl Beech lied. There is no disputing that. But Carl Beech does not represent the whole picture and it is a non sequitur to suggest that because he deceived, all other evidence regarding abuse at Dolphin Square is untrue, too. The very idea is, surely, a form of self-deception.

Several of the IICSA Westminster Investigation Report's conclusions are instructive on the matter. Its findings relate to Westminster as a whole but must be seen in the context of the Square as well. The report's conclusions begin with a rejection of the idea of a 'VIP paedophile ring' of the type suggested by Beech, but an acceptance that abuse did occur:

> There is ample evidence that individual perpetrators of child sexual abuse have been linked to Westminster. However, the Inquiry has found no evidence to support the most sensational of the various allegations of child sexual abuse made over recent years that there has been a powerful paedophile network operating within Westminster. There is no evidence to suggest an organised network of abusers in Westminster, or that individuals with a Westminster connection who sexually abused children were part of a coordinated, organised group.[22]

The report then confirms the assumption that abuse has taken place and been covered up:

It is clear that there have been significant failures by Westminster institutions in their dealing with, and confrontation of, allegations of child sexual abuse. This has included not recognising it, turning a blind eye to it, actively shielding and protecting perpetrators, and covering up allegations of child sexual abuse.[23]

There has been, it continues, 'institutional complacency about child sexual abuse and indifference to the plight of victims. We found, in particular, that institutions regularly put their own reputations or political interests before child protection.'[24]

This complacency extended to the police, who have often historically been at pains not to upset prominent public figures. In the words of the report:

We heard evidence of overt and direct deference by police towards powerful people, such as a conscious decision not to arrest or investigate someone because of their profile or position … A second form of deference we have heard about is a more internal kind within institutions themselves, such as where junior police officers did not challenge senior officers' questionable decisions during investigations of the powerful for fear of harming their own career prospects.[25]

The report's authors also highlighted a reluctance to probe an individual's sexual behaviour for fear of being considered illiberal. In particular, there was a period in the 1960s and '70s when organisations such as the Paedophile Information Exchange (PIE) – an organisation founded in 1974 with the aim of lobbying for the removal of the age of consent – were able to gain support from various civil society organisations. The report talks of how:

… in some circles there was an unwillingness to challenge efforts to make 'paedophilia' acceptable or to ask difficult questions about proposals to reduce the age of consent which seemed to be borne of inappropriate attitudes, for fear of being seen as old fashioned, buttoned-up or out of touch with the times. Child welfare and protection yielded to self-serving ideas of sexual liberation.[26]

The report also pays attention to the fact that there was a power imbalance that impacted the treatment of accusers and accused:

> This investigation has provided striking evidence of how wealth and social status insulated perpetrators of child sexual abuse from being brought to justice to the detriment of the victims of their alleged abuse ... We heard in a particularly stark way in this investigation how the poverty and disadvantaged position of victims led to their allegations of child sexual abuse not being taken seriously. The evidence of Paul Holmes about the difficulties in getting help for boys being sexually exploited around Piccadilly Circus was a vivid account of this problem. These boys were often runaways from damaged backgrounds who were known as 'street rats' by many police officers ... A consistent pattern that has emerged from the evidence we have heard is a failure by almost every institution to put the needs and safety of children who have survived sexual abuse first.[27]

The moment that Carl Beech's untruths were labelled 'credible and true' by the police responsible for investigating them, an unpalatable but significant strand of the Dolphin Square story was skewed, perhaps forever. There was, all the evidence suggests, never an organised network of 'VIP paedophiles' plotting the murders of children. But there were, it is fair to conclude from a wealth of evidence, powerful individuals who did abuse children in Dolphin Square and who got away with it because of who they were and who they knew: in other words, they abused because they knew they could.

AFTERWORD AND ACKNOWLEDGEMENTS

What is next for Dolphin Square? Now into its tenth decade, the estate, in material terms, is not what it was. The original mod cons that once drew residents to the new apartments are now historical artefacts. The plumbing could do with an overhaul. Some of the brickwork needs attention. But for the time being, it seems to have fended off the threat that it might be knocked down to make way for a new, modern high-rise. Instead, the structure that Costains launched on an unsuspecting world back in the 1930s – when it was an exemplar of modernity itself – is scheduled for a comprehensive programme of works over the next several years. While regeneration is the watchword, it is also an act of preservation. If the Square was once an emblem of the potential of the contemporary, it now also serves as a monument to the past.

Dolphin Square undoubtedly has a role to play in the modern world. Its geographical location and its enduring aesthetic appeal ensure that it remains a destination residence. Moreover, a rich history – both light and dark – adds its own appeal. But the Square now has an opportunity to recalibrate, to prepare itself to remain relevant for perhaps another ten decades. That mix of residents from the fields of politics and commerce, espionage and the military, sports and entertainment and many other areas besides has ensured Dolphin Square a unique role in the story of modern British life. But it has been a double-edged sword. At times, a culture of entitlement and a policy of 'people like us' have held the place back and may even have fostered the atmosphere necessary for some of the episodes that not only brought ignominy on those involved but were damaging to the Square and even the nation as a whole. Dolphin Square was intended to serve a certain class of people – the movers and shakers discussed earlier in the book – but in doing so, it inevitably became something of an exclusive club with its own rules and traditions. It is within this club context that many of the events related in these chapters must be understood. And perhaps now the time has come to open up the club and revise its regulations.

But what a run it's had so far. When we embarked upon this book, we knew we would not be short of stories to tell. But we did not quite realise just how much material we would discover and how many tales we'd have to leave out. One of the authors here has had scandals of his own and political experience that qualify him well for co-writing the book. Expense irregularities, sexual dalliances, tabloid stings and serious false allegations against him. It could, and might one day, fill a book in its own right.

We have had numerous stories related to us that were either too incredible to quite believe or, more commonly, we were just not able to corroborate. Rumours of residents who lived undercover, or who buried deep family secrets here. Allegations of criminal activity, not least, of course, in relation to abuse (but by no means exclusively). Every now and then, we have been quietly warned off pursuing particular lines of research. A gentle reminder here and there not to believe everything we hear (and, for the record, we don't). On one occasion, a short missive from a member of the House of Lords telling us that they knew one or two people who'd lived in the Square and nudging us to remember that Carl Beech's allegations had been discredited and he was now serving a long prison sentence for voicing them. When we assured the member of the Upper House that we knew Beech was not a credible witness and invited them to chat instead about their own knowledge of the Square, they promptly retreated, claiming that they couldn't recall anyone who'd lived there after all. A curious exchange.

Putting together the book has often been a case of joining together dots, cross-referencing various sources and building a picture. Part of the character of Dolphin Square is undoubtedly its secretiveness.

As A.N. Wilson once said, reflecting on his 1977 novel *The Sweets of Pimlico* and its Dolphin Square setting, 'I was drawn to the secrecy of the place. It seemed the ideal for such a morally ambivalent character as the hero of the novel.' But the writing of this book would not have been possible without the help of a great many people who have generously shared their memories of Dolphin Square, both good and bad. Some have requested that they remain anonymous, such is the sensitivity of the material they have shed light upon. They know who they are and they have our thanks.

Among those we can name, the authors express their sincere gratitude to the following who agreed to be interviewed about their knowledge and experience of the Square. Their openness and, in several cases, courageousness, was vital to the writing of this volume. They are: Bob Donovan; Christine Forrest; Craig Douglas; David Ingle; David Weeks; Decia Stephenson; Deirdre Marshall; Des Barrit; Gareth Heald; Gloria Askew; Ian Graham; Jan Prebble; Jane Salt; Jo Gurnett; Mikey Georgeson; Councillor Paul Dimoldenberg; Nicholas Crawley; Nigel Farage; Roger Bradshaw; Rosemary McKenna; Sally Dawtry; Sally Tooth; the Shepley Family; Stephen Moyles; Stephen Pound; Tessa Somerville; Tom Harris; Tommy Foster; Lord Tom Pendry; Wendy and Alan Perriam; and William Gingles.

Thanks also to several institutions on whom we relied for access to much information. These include the British Library, Westminster Libraries, the National Archives, Westminster Archive and the National Association of Retired Police Officers. Others who have given us their time and expertise are: Amanda O'Neill; Brendan McParland; Dan Jukes; David Profumo; David Tang; Debra Kelly; Duncan Craig OBE; Katie Osborne; Lisa Wade; Mark Conrad; Michael Meadowcroft; Nick Thomas-Symonds; Nicole Barchilon Frank; Patrick Strudwick; Paul Angelo; Paul Barchilon; Paul Cahalan; Peter Nutt; Richard Hargrave and the Hargrave family; Sam Holden and Simon Walters.

We also wish to express our gratitude to our agent, Andrew Lownie, and to Mark Beynon and his team at The History Press. Thanks for finding and giving this book a good home. Dan would also like to say a special thanks, as ever, to Rosie, Charlotte, Ben and the rest of the family for their support.

NOTES

Introduction

1   Terry Gourvish, *Dolphin Square: The History of a Unique Building*, p.38.

1. Movers and Shakers

1   Gourvish, *Dolphin Square*, p.16.
2   Ibid., p.82.
3   Ibid.
4   'Admirals All', *Truth*, 26 December 1952.
5   Hansard (HC, Vol. 351, 2 September 1939).
6   Nobelprize.org: The Nobel Peace Prize 1934 citation.
7   Madge Dresser, 'The tale of Bristol's fascist-sympathising, disability rights-promoting first woman MP', *The Bristol Cable*, www.thebristolcable.org/2020/01/the-tale-of-bristols-fascist-sympathising-disability-rights-promoting-first-woman-mp
8   *The Stage*, 20 June 1963, p.22.
9   *Dundee Courier*, 7 December 1938, p.7.

2. The Mirror Crack'd from Side to Side

1   *Chelsea News and General Advertiser*, 14 July 1939, p.5.
2   *The Scotsman*, 8 December 1937, p.20.
3   *Shepton Mallet Journal*, 21 October 1938, p.7.
4   *The People*, 12 April 1942, p.3.
5   *Daily Mirror*, 20 October 1938, p.1.
6   *Daily Herald*, 20 October 1938, p.11.

7   Ellen Wilkinson, Hyde Park, 1 November 1936.
8   *The Manchester Guardian*, 1 March 1947. p.3.

3. The Gathering Storm

1   *John Bull*, 4 March 1931, p.21.
2   Charles Stuart (ed.), *The Reith Diaries*, pp.142–43.
3   *Pontypridd Observer*, 18 September 1937, p.4.
4   'The opera-loving sisters who "stumbled" into heroism', *BBC News*,
     www.bbc.co.uk/news/uk-england-tyne-38732779
5   Ibid.
6   Joan Miller, *One Girl's War*, p.48.
7   Ibid., p.49.

4. The Square at War

1   *Chatham News*, 21 July 1939, p.15.
2   *London Gazette*, 29 June 1915.
3   Miller, *One Girl's War*, p.57.
4   *Chelsea News and General Advertiser*, 19 October 1945, p.3.
5   *The Tatler*, 12 August 1942, p.12.
6   *Chelsea News and General Advertiser*, 5 March 1943, p.4.
7   Christine Froula, *Virginia Woolf and the Bloomsbury Avant-garde*, p.10;
     Katie Roiphe, *Uncommon Arrangements: Seven Marriages in Literary London
     1910–1939*, p.210.
8   *Sunday Express*, 19 August 1928.
9   Michael Baker, *Our Three Selves: A Life of Radclyffe Hall*, p.345.

5. 'M' is for Mosley

1   Hastings William Sackville Russell, 12th Duke of Bedford, *Is this Justice?:
     An Examination of Regulation 18B*, p.16.
2   Diana Mosley, *A Life of Contrasts: The Autobiography*, p.167.
3   'Diana Mosley, Hitler's angel, dies unrepentant in Paris', *The Guardian*,
     13 August 2003, www.theguardian.com/politics/2003/aug/13/obituaries.uk
4   Christopher Andrew, *The Defence of the Realm: The Authorized History of
     MI5*, p.192.
5   *Belfast Telegraph*, 21 February 1942, p.4.
6   Morris Beckman, *The 43 Group: Battling with Mosley's Blackshirts*, pp.52–53.

6 Doves, Hawks, Heroes and a Government in Exile

1   William L. Shirer, *Rise and Fall of the Third Reich: A History of Nazi Germany*, p.615.
2   'Who We Are', Hansard Society, www.hansardsociety.org.uk/about/who-we-are/our-history
3   'What we do', Hansard Society, www.hansardsociety.org.uk/about/who-we-are/what-we-do
4   *Truth*, 17 January 1940.
5   *Truth*, 6 August 1940.
6   For a full account, see John Humphries, *Spying for Hitler: The Welsh Double-Cross*.
7   Nigel West and Oleg Tsarev, *The Crown Jewels: The British Secrets at the Heart of the KGB Archives*, p.317.
8   Gourvish, *Dolphin Square*, p.101.
9   André Gillois, *Histoire secrète de Français à Londres de 1940 à 1944*, p.171.
10 Jacques Barchilon, 'An (Almost) Unknown Moment in the Life Of General De Gaulle, by Jacques Barchilon', *Open Hands Open Heart*, https://open-heart-open-hands.com/2018/11/04/an-almost-unknown-moment-in-the-life-of-general-de-gaulle-by-jacques-barchilon/
11 National Archives, KV 2/2418.
12 Michael John Hargrave, *Bergen-Belsen 1945: A Medical Student's Journal*, entry for 3 May 1945.

7. Life Resumes

1   Francis Watson, 'The Death of George V', *History Today*, 36 (1986), pp.21–30.
2   Bud Flanagan, *My Crazy Life*, p.10.
3   *Newcastle Evening Chronicle*, 14 March 1960, p.12.
4   Michael Millgate, 'Angus Wilson, The Art of Fiction No. 20', *The Paris Review*, www.theparisreview.org/interviews/4848/the-art-of-fiction-no-20-angus-wilson
5   Gourvish, *Dolphin Square*, p.109.
6   *Chelsea News and General Advertiser*, 19 December 1952, p.3.
7   Antonia Fraser, *My History: A Memoir of Growing Up*, extracted in the *Daily Mail*, 2 January 2015, www.dailymail.co.uk/news/article-2894966/My-exquisitely-eccentric-father-couldn-t-boil-kettle-Lord-Longford-s-brilliant-historian-daughter-Lady-Antonia-Fraser-written-enchanting-account-childhood-delightfully-dotty-dad.html

8. In the Shadows

1 Nigel Starck, 'Sex after death: The obituary as an erratic record of proclivity', *Mortality*, 14:4 (2009), pp.338–54.
2 *Chelsea News and General Advertiser*, 23 May 1952, p.7.
3 *Aberdeen Evening Express*, 21 March 1952, p.6.
4 *Chelsea News and General Advertiser*, 21 February 1947, p.2.
5 *Aberdeen Press and Journal*, 10 September 1948, p.1.
6 *Chelsea News and General Advertiser*, 10 July 1953, p.2.
7 *Aberdeen Evening Express*, 25 September 1952, p.8.
8 Marcel Berlins, 'A Chief Justice got away with murder', *The Independent*, 22 October 2011, www.independent.co.uk/voices/a-chief-justice-got-away-with-murder-1169087.html

9. Champagne and Princesses

1 *Sunday Sun*, 1 April 1956, p.1.
2 *Sunday Pictorial*, 24 June 1956, p.5.
3 *Aberdeen Evening Express*, 5 January 1959, p.5.
4 *Chelsea News and General Advertiser*, 28 August 1959, p.7.
5 Thanks to Shar Daws, author of *Bombshells: Five Women Who Set the Fifties on Fire*, for this quotation.
6 *The Manchester Guardian*, 15 May 1959, p.7.
7 Quoted by Adrian Bingham in his article, 'Swinging – only pampas grass is quite as suburban – and as British' in *The Independent*, 4 December 2011.

10. 'You have to play it cool, real cool, man'

1 Hansard (HC, Vol. 670, 23 January 1963).
2 Rachel Trethewey, *The Churchill Girls: The Story of Winston's Daughters*, p.212.
3 *Belfast Telegraph*, 6 September 1961, p.4.
4 Angela Lambert, 'A Rose that Refuses to Wilt', *The Telegraph*, 2 January 2001, www.telegraph.co.uk/culture/4720871/A-rose-that-refuses-to-wilt.html
5 *Daily Mirror*, 31 October 1960, p.9.
6 Gourvish, *Dolphin Square*, p.271.
7 *Jewish Telegraphic Agency Daily News Bulletin*, 6 September 1972, http://pdfs.jta.org/1962/1962-09-06_172.pdf

11. Bringing Down the House: A Drama in Two Acts

1 *Aberdeen Evening Express*, 9 October 1962, p.5.
2 Ibid.

3   *Newcastle Journal*, 23 October 1962, p.8.

4   *Birmingham Daily Post*, 1 February 1963, p.11.

5   *Sunday Pictorial*, 25 May 1952, p.6.

6   John Vassall, *Vassall: The Autobiography of a Spy* (Sidgwick & Jackson, 1975).

7   Alistair Horne, *Harold Macmillan, Vol. II: 1957–86* (Penguin, 1989) p.461.

8   *Daily Mirror*, 23 October 1962, p.10.

9   *The Sunday Mirror*, 28 April 1963, p.7.

10 *Sunday Pictorial*, 11 November 1962, p.9.

11 *Daily Herald*, 24 January 1963, p.10.

12 *Birmingham Daily Post*, 8 November 1962, p.29.

13 Gourvish, *Dolphin Square*, p.274.

14 *Belfast Telegraph*, 30 January 1963, p.1.

15 'Report of the Tribunal appointed to Inquire into the Vassall Case and Related Matters', 1963, pp.62–63.

16 *Sunday Mirror*, 9 June 1963, p.1.

17 Margarette Driscoll, 'My mother Christine Keeler was raped at knife point...', *The Telegraph Magazine*, 8 May 2021, pp.16–23.

18 Phillip Knightly and Caroline Kennedy, *An Affair of State*, pp. 101–02.

19 Ibid.

20 *Tatler*, 24 January 1962, pp.8–9.

21 Hansard (HC, Vol. 674, 22 March 1963).

22 *The People*, 4 August 1963, pp.10–11.

23 Lord Alfred Thompson Denning, Lord Denning's Report, p.16.

24 Mandy Rice-Davies and Shirley Flack, *Mandy*, p.78.

25 This claim was included in a review of the film *Scandal*, in *Time* (1989).

26 John Finch, *Granada Television: The First Generation*, p.259.

12. All Change

1   Elizabeth Wilson, 'Gayness and Liberalism' in *Hidden Agendas: Theory, Politics and Experience in the Women's Movement*, pp.139–47.

2   *The Stage*, 21 July 1966, p.7.

3   *Tatler*, 2 July 1966, p.36.

4   *Daily Mirror*, 23 July 1960, p.10.

5   *Chelsea News and General Advertiser*, 15 December 1967, p.4.

6   Margaret Thatcher, *The Downing Street Years* (1993), p.3.

7   Simon Hoggart, 'Another Pint of Claret', *New Humanist*, 31 May 2007, https://newhumanist.org.uk/articles/590/another-pint-of-claret

8   Michael Brown, 'They take risks - and How ... ', *Daily Telegraph*, 29 May 2006, www.telegraph.co.uk/comment/personal-view/3622729/They-take-risks-and-how-which-is-why-we-need-our-gay-MPs-and-their-scandals.html

9   Sally Tooth, interviewed by the authors, 6 January 2021.
10 Lord Tom Pendry, interviewed by the authors, 27 February 2021.

13. Crimes and Misdemeanours

1   See Bobby Teale, *Bringing Down the Krays* (2013) and David Teale, *Surviving the Krays* (2021).
2   *Chelsea News and General Advertiser*, 1 April 1960.
3   A Peter F. Worley was resident in Ashford at the time of the trial.
4   *Reading Evening Post*, 28 June 1966, p.1.
5   *Chelsea News and General Advertiser*, 12 January 1968, p.7.
6   See especially Hallie Rubenhold, *The Five: The Untold Lives of the Women Killed by Jack the Ripper* (2019).
7   David Seabrook, *Jack of Jumps*, pp. 107–10. (NB: Another Hammersmith Murders victim, Frances Brown, had previously given evidence for the defence alongside former Dolphinites Christine Keeler and Mandy Rice-Davies in the trial of Stephen Ward.)
8   Dick Kirby, *Laid Bare* (2016), p.42.
9   *Daily Mirror*, 27 November 1969, p.7.

14. Carry On Up the Dolphin

1   Barbara Windsor, *All of Me: My Extraordinary Life*, pp.171–72.
2   Windsor, *All of Me*, pp.178–79.
3   *Marylebone Mercury*, 30 December 1977, p.11.
4   *The People*, 17 January 1971, p.7.
5   Gloria Askew, interviewed by the authors, April 2021.
6   *Sunday Mirror*, 5 March 1967, p.22.
7   Craig Douglas, interviewed by the authors, 18 March 2021.
8   David Hughes, 'A Personal History of the British Record Business 66 – Bunny Lewis 4', *Vinyl Memories*, 9 April 2018, https://vinylmemories. wordpress.com/2018/04/09/a-personal-history-of-the-british-record-industry-66-bunny-lewis-4
9   'The Nobel Prize in Physics 1948', Nobelprize.org, www.nobelprize.org/ prizes/physics/1948/summary/
10 Vasili Mitrokhin and Christopher Andrew, *The Mitrokhin Archive: The KGB in Europe and the West*, pp.526–27.
11 Kim Sengupta and Paul Lashmar, 'Widow of MP denies he spied for Russia', *The Independent*, 14 September 1999, https://archive. ph/20130731103717/http://www.highbeam.com/doc/1P2-5013666.html
12 Gourvish, *Dolphin Square*, pp.295–96.

13 Marcus Scriven, 'The Satanic Marquess: She flushed three kilos of his cocaine away, but the wife of John Hervey still couldn't save him from self-destruction', *Daily Mail*, 16 November 2009, www.dailymail.co.uk/femail/article-1228109/The-Satanic-Marquess-She-flushed-kilos-cocaine-away-wife-John-Hervey-save-self-destruction.html

14 *Daily Mirror*, 8 January 1975, p.5.

15 Interview with the authors, April 2021.

16 Ben Lawrence, 'How Toyah Lost Her Punk Virginity', *Daily Telegraph*, 18 October 2017, www.telegraph.co.uk/films/0/toyah-willcox-lost-punk-virginity-making-derek-jarmans-jubilee/

15. Murder Comes to the Square

1 *Chelsea News and General Advertiser*, 10 July 1970, p.3.

2 Tommy Foster, interview with the authors, 9 March 2021.

3 'Profile: Dolours Price', *Sunday Times*, 30 September 2012, www.thetimes.co.uk/article/profile-dolours-price-tlfpnd2lbvp

4 Tommy Foster, interview with the authors, 9 March 2021.

5 *Chelsea News and General Advertiser*, 18 June 1971, p.7.

6 *Daily Mirror*, 24 June 1975, p.2.

7 Private family correspondence shown to the authors, April 2021.

8 *Daily Express*, 24 June 1975, p.9.

9 Private family correspondence shown to the authors, April 2021.

10 Victim was interviewed by authors in March 2021.

11 See *The Telegraph*, 29 May 1976 (p.5) and 8 June 1976 (p.5).

16. Political Blues

1 *Marylebone Mercury*, 8 September 1978, p.12.

2 *The Spectator*, 19 April 1986, p.43.

3 An undated cutting from *Harpers & Queen*, preserved in Nicholas Crawley's personal scrapbook.

4 *News of the World*, 24 November 1986.

5 '1974: Minister's wife survives bomb attack', *BBC On This Day*, http://news.bbc.co.uk/onthisday/hi/dates/stories/october/28/newsid_2477000/2477645.stm

6 David Steel, *Against Goliath* (1989), p.223.

7 Leader's speech, Llandudno 1981, www.britishpoliticalspeech.org/speech-archive.htm?speech=42

8 *Aberdeen Press & Journal*, 8 December 1984; *Sunday Mirror*, 9 December 1984.

9   Evidence to IICSA Inquiry, 13 March 2019, www.iicsa.org.uk/
    key-documents/9810/view/public-hearing-transcript-13-march-2019.pdf,
    pp.126–27

10 IICSA, 'Allegations of child sexual abuse linked to Westminster
    Investigation Report', p.xi, www.iicsa.org.uk/key-documents/17579/
    view/allegations-child-sexual-abuse-westminster-investigation-report-25-
    february-2020-amends-may-2020.pdf

11 *Newcastle Journal*, 5 March 1985, p.2.

12 Paul Dimoldenberg interview with the authors, 6 April 2021.

13 Andrew Hosken, *Nothing Like a Dame*, p.291.

14 Obituary of Dame Simone Prendergast, *Daily Telegraph*, 30 August 2012,
    www.telegraph.co.uk/news/obituaries/politics-obituaries/9509808/
    Dame-Simone-Prendergast.html

15 John Magill, *Westminster City Council: Auditor's Report*, paragraph 53(2)(d)
    (v), 1996.

16 Magill v. Porter, UKHL 67, 13 December 2001.

17 Statement by Colin Barrow, leader of Westminster City Council,
    27 November 2009, https://web.archive.org/web/20100423195938/;
    http://www.thisislondon.co.uk/standard/article-23775862-westminster-
    chief-were-sorry-for-dame-shirley-and-homes-for-votes.do

18 David Weeks interview with the authors, 14 January 2021.

17. The End of the Party

1   John Warden, 'Top Tories may not serve under Mrs Thatcher', *The Herald*,
    12 February 1975, p.1.

2   'Tory MP attacks Thatcher', *The Herald*, 24 June 1989, www.heraldscotland.
    com/news/11920128.tory-mp-attacks-thatcher

3   Ibid.

4   Obituary of Sir Anthony Meyer, *Daily Telegraph*, 10 January 2005, www.
    telegraph.co.uk/news/obituaries/1480801/Sir-Anthony-Meyer.html

5   Ibid.

6   John Campbell, *Margaret Thatcher (Vol. 2)*, p.695.

7   *Daily Mirror*, 24 July 1981, p.15.

8   John Osborne, *Almost a Gentleman: An Autobiography, 1955–66*, p.259.

9   *Liverpool Echo*, 20 December 1985, p.22.

10 Hunter Davies, 'The Hunter Davies Interview', *The Independent*,
    5 October 1992, www.independent.co.uk/life-style/the-hunter-davies-
    interview-sir-nicholas-too-sexy-for-his-trews-i-still-get-emotional-over-
    those-trials-he-said-tearfully-scotland-s-former-solicitorgeneral-holds-
    forth-on-advocacy-infidelity-golf-and-other-natural-1555729.html

11 Document CAB000161 (Cabinet Office File) adduced into evidence
    at the Independent Inquiry into Child Sex Abuse, www.iicsa.org.uk/
    key-documents/9914/view/.pdf

12 Carole Cadwalladr, 'Ann Leslie, Queen of the frontline', *The Guardian*, 5 April 2009, www.theguardian.com/lifeandstyle/2009/apr/05/ann-leslie-journalist

13 Dani Garavelli, 'Call for inquiry into Scots historical sex abuse', *The Scotsman*, 17 August 2014, www.scotsman.com/news/opinion/columnists/call-inquiry-scots-historical-sex-abuse-1999957

14 Vic Rodrick, 'Scots former prosecutor remanded over charges of historical child sex abuse', *Daily Record*, 24 November 2020, www.dailyrecord.co.uk/news/scottish-news/scots-former-prosecutor-remanded-over-23062092

15 Jeffrey Gordon interview with the authors, February 2021.

18. David Ingle

1 Police report viewed by the authors.

2 Harrison explained this in a witness statement entered into evidence at the coroner's inquiry.

3 Email to David Ingle from Detective Sergeant James Townly, 25 March 2015.

4 Coroner's verdict recorded at Louth Magistrates, Lincolnshire, on 16 May 2007.

5 Letter to David Ingle from Detective Superintendent Richard Hatton, 7 June 2018.

6 Something, it ought to be noted, that the authors were able to do with relative ease, although without discovering anyone with any obvious connection to David's case.

7 David Ingle interview with the authors, 12 February 2021.

19. Caned

1 *Sunday Mirror*, 23 September 1990, pp.1, 4–5.

2 John Blashford-Snell, correspondence with the authors, 6 May 2021.

3 Jessamy Calkin, 'Col John Blashford-Snell: the last of the great adventurers', *Daily Telegraph*, 5 December 2015, https://s.telegraph.co.uk/graphics/projects/john-blashford-snell/index.html

4 Ibid.

5 Gordon Tooth. Tooth and Denis Thatcher were both enthusiastic rugby referees and were active in the referee's union.

6 *Irish Independent*, 9 February 1993.

7 *Daily Mirror*, 16 April 1993, p.3.

8 Deidre Marshall interview with the authors, 26 January 2021.

9 *Daily Mirror*, 20 August 1992, pp.1–3.

10 Sebastian Faulks, 'Anne's Passport to Pimlico', *The Guardian*, 6 February 1993, p.25.

11 *Irish Independent*, 24 September 1999, p.10.
12 Ibid., 22 October 1999, p.20.
13 Ed Carty and Sarah Stack, 'Mahon: Corruption continued in Irish politics because no one shouted stop', *Irish Independent*, 22 March 2012, www.independent.ie/irish-news/mahon-corruption-continued-in-irish-politics-because-no-one-shouted-stop-26835032.html
14 Colin Hughes, 'Just William', *The Guardian*, 4 July 1998, www.theguardian.com/politics/1998/jul/04/conservatives.uk
15 *Aberdeen Press and Journal*, 25 January 1997, p.10.
16 'Tory MP drank himself to death alone in his flat', *The Independent*, 23 October 2011, www.independent.co.uk/news/tory-mp-drank-himself-to-death-alone-in-his-flat-1280827.html
17 Jeremy Paxman, *The Political Animal: An Anatomy* (2003), location 4601 in e-book edition.
18 'Tory MP drank himself to death alone in his flat', *The Independent*, 23 October 2011, www.independent.co.uk/news/tory-mp-drank-himself-to-death-alone-in-his-flat-1280827.html

20. False Accounts

1 Kevin Maguire, '£62 a week for one of London's best addresses. £90 for a council flat', *The Guardian*, 5 November 1999, www.theguardian.com/uk/1999/nov/05/kevinmaguire
2 Edward Simpkins, 'Establishment fights for its rights as developers circle Dolphin Square', *The Telegraph*, 31 August 2003, www.telegraph.co.uk/finance/2861785/Establishment-fights-for-its-rights-as-developers-circle-Dolphin-Square.html
3 Estelle Morris's resignation letter, 23 October 2003.
4 Steven Swinford and Jon Ungoed-Thomas, 'Commons officials helped culture secretary beat tax', *The Sunday Times*, 24 May 2009, www.thetimes.co.uk/article/commons-officials-helped-culture-secretary-beat-tax-z5hjmxbqmnv
5 'Lib Dem MPs criticised after second home rent probe', *BBC News*, 19 March 2010, http://news.bbc.co.uk/1/hi/uk_politics/8576304.stm
6 Joe Churcher, 'Cabinet ministers defend Darling', *The Independent on Sunday*, 23 October 2011, www.independent.co.uk/news/uk/politics/cabinet-ministers-defend-darling-1693689.html
7 Sam Coates, 'MPs to be forced into one bedroomed flats under expenses revolution', *The Times*, 4 November 2009, www.thetimes.co.uk/article/mps-to-be-forced-into-one-bedroomed-flats-under-expenses-revolution-w09kwtgfh9b

21. Any Other Business

1 Robert Mendick and Claire Newbon, 'Class war erupts in Dolphin Square', *The Independent*, 31 December 2013, www.independent.co.uk/news/uk/home-news/class-war-erupts-in-dolphin-square-184222.html

2 Ibid.

3 Stephen Moyes, 'Lord Coke: Top peer's drug binges with £200 prostitutes', *The Sun*, 25 July 2015, www.thesun.co.uk/archives/news/100018/lord-coke-top-peers-drug-binges-with-200-prostitutes/

4 Ibid.

5 Stephen Moyes interview with the authors, 5 January 2021.

6 Rose Troup Buchanan, 'Lord Sewel resigns after "drugs" video', *The Independent*, 28 July 2015, www.independent.co.uk/news/uk/politics/lord-sewel-resigns-after-drugs-video-house-lords-member-s-resignation-letter-full-10420535.html

7 George Parker, 'Lord Sewel quits over drugs scandal', *Financial Times*, 26 July 2015, www.ft.com/content/2cedd026-338e-11e5-bdbb-35e55cbae175

8 Pam Ayres, 'All hypocrites should take due care, When snorting coke in Dolphin Square, An orange bra is not so cute, And best left on the prostitute.' [Twitter post], 6.55 p.m., 27 July 2015, https://twitter.com/pamayres/status/625726093136404480?lang=en

9 '"I didn't have sex with vice girl" insists Lord Mackenzie', *Northern Echo*, 17 March 2003, www.thenorthernecho.co.uk/news/7038549.i-didnt-sex-vice-girl-insists-lord-mackenzie/

10 Coreena Ford, 'Lord hits back at claims of sleaze', *Chronicle Live*, 8 February 2013, www.chroniclelive.co.uk/news/north-east-news/lord-hits-back-claims-sleaze-1449339

11 Jonathan Calvert and Heidi Blake, 'Cash for Access: Lords Exposed', *The Sunday Times*, 2 June 2013, www.thetimes.co.uk/article/cash-for-access-lords-exposed-jb9k89ptfd5

12 House of Lords, Committee for Privileges and Conduct: 9th Report of Session 2013–14, 'The conduct of Lord Mackenzie of Framwellgate', p.5 para. 4.

13 Rajeev Syal, 'Labour peers stripped of party whip over lobbying allegations', *The Guardian*, 2 June 2013, www.theguardian.com/politics/2013/jun/02/labour-peers-stripped-whip-lobbying-claims

14 'First minister's London hotels cost £1000 while he also claimed for rented flat', *The Herald*, 27 September 2009, www.heraldscotland.com/default_content/12612990.first-ministers-london-hotels-cost-1000-also-claimed-rented-flat/

15 Dave King, 'Alex Salmond claimed £116K expenses for just six Westminster visits', *Daily Record*, 27 March 2008, www.dailyrecord.co.uk/news/scottish-news/alex-salmond-claimed-116k-expenses-972571

16 'William to Move into His First London Bachelor Pad', *Hello!*, 28 May 2007, www.hellomagazine.com/royalty/2007/05/28/prince-william-house/

17 'Londoner's Diary', *London Evening Standard*, 22 February 2011, http://londonersdiary.standard.co.uk/2011/02/desai-tells-lse-not-to-disown-gaddafis-son.html

18 'Lord Meghnad Desai resigns from Labour Party over racism'. *The Hindu*, 20 November 2020, www.thehindu.com/news/international/lord-meghnad-desai-resigns-from-labour-party-over-racism/article33143318.ece

19 Fred Attewill, 'Judge dies in fall from fourth-floor flat', *The Guardian*, 25 June 2007, www.theguardian.com/uk/2007/jun/25/1

20 'Judge killed in 50ft fall from flat "was suicide", inquest hears', *London Evening Standard*, 5 September 2007, www.standard.co.uk/hp/front/judge-killed-in-50ft-fall-from-flat-was-suicide-inquest-hears-6611270.html

21 Nick Duffy, 'A hero of the equal marriage debate has died', *Pink News*, 21 December 2016, www.pinknews.co.uk/2016/12/21/a-hero-of-the-equal-marriage-debate-has-died/

22 Nigel Farage statement to the authors, 23 April 2021.

23 Interview with the authors, 2 February 2021.

22. 'Credible and true'

1 'Child abuse inquiry: Police investigate three alleged murders', *BBC News*, 18 December 2014, www.bbc.co.uk/news/uk-30534235

2 Tom Watson, *Sunday Mirror*, 24 January 2015, www.mirror.co.uk/news/uk-news/tom-watson-leon-brittan-child-5038130

3 Hansard (HC, Vol. 588, 27 November 2014).

4 IICSA Westminster Investigation, 'Witness Statement of Security Service Witness', www.iicsa.org.uk/key-documents/9774/view/INQ004032.pdf, p.14.

5 Fortescue was a whip in the government of Edward Heath between 1970 and 1973. He was interviewed for the documentary, *Westminster's Secret Service*, broadcast on BBC2 on 21 May 1995.

6 Simon Walters, and Paul Cahalan, 'Pervert son of a former Black Rod ...', *The Mail on Sunday*, 12 May 2018, www.dailymail.co.uk/news/article-5721973/Pervert-son-former-Black-Rod-quizzed-police-investigating-Westminster-child-sex-abuse-claims.html

7 Ibid.

8 Mervyn Greenway Obituary, *Daily Telegraph*, 18 April 2001, www.telegraph.co.uk/news/obituaries/1316423/Mervyn-Greenway.html

9 Anonymous witness interview with the authors, December 2020.

10 Walters and Cahalan, 'Pervert son of a former Black Rod ...'.

11 IICSA Westminster Inquiry, Public Hearing, 7 March 2019, p.110, www.iicsa.org.uk/key-documents/9697/view/public-hearing-transcript-7-march-2019.pdf

12 Anonymous witness interview with the authors, December 2020.

13 Independent Review of the Metropolitan Police Service's handling of non-recent sexual offence investigations alleged against persons of public prominence (Sir Richard Henriques), 31 October 2016, www.met.police.uk/SysSiteAssets/foi-media/metropolitan-police/other_information/corporate/mps-publication-chapters-1---3-sir-richard-henriques-report.pdf

14 David Weeks interview with the authors, 14 January 2021, p.168.

15 IICSA, 'Allegations of child sexual abuse linked to Westminster: Investigation Report', February 2020, www.iicsa.org.uk/key-documents/17579/view/allegations-child-sexual-abuse-westminster-investigation-report-25-february-2020-amends-may-2020.pdf, p.19.

16 Ibid., p.2.

17 Ibid., p.152.

18 IICSA, 'Operation Winter Key', 20 December 2016, www.iicsa.org.uk/key-documents/11271/view/OHY005576.pdf

19 IICSA, (Preliminary) Janner Investigation, Public Hearing, 24 September 2019, pp. 47–48, www.iicsa.org.uk/key-documents/14241/view/preliminary-hearing-transcript-24-september-2019.pdf

20 IICSA, 'Report finds multiple failings in responses to child sexual abuse claims against Lord Janner QC', 19 October 2021, www.iicsa.org.uk/news/report-finds-multiple-failings-responses-child-sexual-abuse-claims-against-lord-janner-qc

21 'Lord Janner: Police shut down MP child abuse investigations - report', *BBC News*, 19 October 2021, www.bbc.co.uk/news/uk-england-leicestershire-58932593

22 IICSA, 'Allegations of child sexual abuse linked to Westminster: Investigation Report', p.148.

23 Ibid.

24 Ibid., p.148.

25 Ibid., p.150.

26 Ibid.

27 Ibid., p.151.

BIBLIOGRAPHY

Andrew, Christopher, *The Defence of the Realm: The Authorized History of MI5* (Penguin, 2010)

Atkinson, Kate, *Transcription* (Black Swan, 2018)

Baker, Michael, *Our Three Selves: A Life of Radclyffe Hall* (Hamish Hamilton, 1985)

Beckman, Morris, *The 43 Group: Battling with Mosley's Blackshirts* (The History Press, 2013)

Bedford, Duke of, *Is this Justice?: An Examination of Regulation 18B* (Steven Books, 2005)

Bell, Mary Hayley, *What Shall We Do Tomorrow?: An Autobiography* (Cassell & Co., 1968)

Bresler, Fenton, *Lord Goddard: A Biography* (Harrap, 1977)

Campbell, John, *Margaret Thatcher: Vol. 2: The Iron Lady* (Jonathan Cape, 2003)

Cullen, Pamela, *A Stranger in Blood: The Story of Dr Bodkin Adams* (Elliott & Thompson, 2004)

Dalley, Jan, *Diana Mosley: A Life* (Faber & Faber, 1999)

Daly, Anthony, *The Abuse of Power* (Mirror Books, 2019)

De-la-Noy, Michael, *The House of Hervey* (Constable, 2001)

Denning, Lord Alfred Thompson, *Lord Denning's Report* (HMSO, 1963)

Dimoldenberg, Paul, *The Westminster Whistleblowers* (Politico's Publishing, 2006)

Dorril, Stephen, *Black Shirt: Sir Oswald Mosley and British Fascism* (Penguin Books, 2007)

Dundy, Elaine, *Finch, Bloody Finch: A Biography of Peter Finch* (Holt Rinehart & Winston, 1980)

Farndale, Nigel, *Haw-Haw: The Tragedy of William and Margaret Joyce* (Pan Books, 2006)

Finch, John, *Granada Television: The First Generation* (Manchester University Press, 2003)

Flanagan, Bud, *My Crazy Life* (Frederick Muller, 1961)

Fraser, Antonia, *My History: A Memoir of Growing Up* (Nan A. Talese, 2015)

Froula, Christine, *Virginia Woolf and the Bloomsbury Avant-garde* (Columbia University Press, 2005)

Gillois, André, *Histoire Secrete des Français a Londres de 1940 à 1944* (Hachette, 1973)

Goodwin, Cliff, *Sid James: A Biography* (Century, 1995)

Gourvish, Terry, *Dolphin Square: The History of a Unique Building* (Bloomsbury, 2014)

Green, Shirley, *Rachman* (Michael Joseph, 1979)

Hargrave, Michael John, *Bergen-Belsen 1945: A Medical Student's Journal* (Imperial College Press, 2013)

Hemming, Henry, *Maxwell Knight: MI5's Greatest Spymaster* (Arrow Books, 2017)

Hosken, Andrew, *Nothing Like a Dame* (Granta, 2007)

Howell, Denis, *Made in Birmingham: The Memoirs of Denis Howell* (Queen Anne Press, 1990)

Humphries, John, *Spying for Hitler: The Welsh Double-Cross* (University of Wales Press, 2012)

Irving, Clive, Wallington, Jeremy, and Ron Hall, *Scandal '63: The Profumo Sensation* (Mayflower-Dell, 1964)

Jackson, Julian, *De Gaulle* (Allen Lane, 2018)

Janvrin, Isabelle, and Catherine Rawlinson, *The French in London: From William the Conqueror to Charles de Gaulle* (Wilmington Square Books, 2016)

Kay, Ernest, *Pragmatic Premier: An intimate portrait of Harold Wilson* (Leslie Frewin, 1967)

Keeler, Christine, and Douglas Thompson, *Secrets and Lies* (John Blake, 2012)

Kenny, Mary, *Germany Calling: A Personal Biography of William Joyce, Lord Haw-Haw* (New Island Books, 2003)

Kirby, Dick, *Laid Bare: The Nude Murders and the Hunt for 'Jack the Stripper'* (The History Press, 2016)

Knightley, Phillip, and Caroline Kennedy, *An Affair of State: The Profumo Case and the Framing of Stephen Ward* (Jonathan Cape, 1987)

Lane-Smith, Roger, *A Fork in the Road* (Icon Books, 2014)

McConnell, Brian, *Found Naked and Dead* (New English Library, 1974)

McKay, Sinclair, *The Lost World of Bletchley Park* (Aurum Press, 2013)

Masters, Anthony, *The Man Who Was M.: Life of Charles Henry Maxwell Knight* (Wiley-Blackwell, 1984)

Miller, Joan, *One Girl's War: Personal Exploits in MI5's Most Secret Station* (Brandon Book Publishers, 1986)

Mitrokhin, Vasili, and Christopher Andrew, *The Mitrokhin Archive: The KGB in Europe and the West* (Penguin, 2000)

Morris, K.F., *A History of Dolphin Square* (Dolphin Square Trust Ltd, 1995)

Osborne, John, *Almost a Gentleman: An Autobiography, 1955–66* (Faber & Faber, 1991)

Paxman, Jeremy, *The Political Animal: An Anatomy* (Penguin, 2007)

Pendar, Kenneth W., *Adventure in Diplomacy: Our French Dilemma* (Dodd, Mead & Co., 1945)

Pendry, Tom, *Taking it on the Chin* (Biteback Publishing, 2016)

Pincher, Chapman, *Treachery: Six Decades of Espionage Against America and Great Britain* (Random House, 2009)

Prebble, Jan, *Forty-Two Years a Secret Mistress* (Author House, 2013)

Prebble, Jan, *Square Tales: A Short History of Dolphin Square* (Blue Dolphin Tenants Association, 2016, 4th ed.)

Prebble, Jan, *Wartime in Dolphin Square* (privately published, 2011)

Profumo, David, *Bringing Down the House: A Family Memoir* (John Murray, 2006)

Reed, Jeremy, *The Dilly: A Secret History of Piccadilly Rent Boys* (Peter Owen, 2014)

Report of the Tribunal appointed to Inquire into the Vassall Case and Related Matters (HMSO, 1963)

Rice-Davies, Mandy, and Shirley Flack, *Mandy* (Michael Joseph, 1980)

Roberts, Glenys, *Metropolitan Myths* (Victor Gollancz, 1982)

Roiphe, Katie, *Uncommon Arrangements: Seven Marriages in Literary London 1910–1939* (Virago, 2009)

Scriven, Marcus, *Splendour and Squalor* (Atlantic Books, 2010)

Seabrook, David, *Jack of Jumps* (Granta Books, 2006)

Seed, Michael, *Nobody's Child* (John Blake Publishing, 2008)

Shirer, William L., *Rise and Fall of The Third Reich: A History of Nazi Germany* (Arrow Books, 1991).

Snow, C. P., *The Masters* (Macmillan, 1951)

Souhami, Diana, *The Trials of Radclyffe Hall* (Quercus, 2013)

Stuart, Charles (ed.), *The Reith Diaries* (Collins, 1975)

Summers, Anthony, and Stephen Dorril, *Honeytrap* (Coronet Books, 1987)

Teale, Bobby, *Bringing Down the Krays* (Ebury Press, 2013)

Teale, David, *Surviving the Krays* (Ebury Press, 2021)

Thatcher, Margaret, *The Downing Street Years* (HarperCollins, 1993)

Trethewey, Rachel, *The Churchill Girls: The Story of Winston's Daughters* (The History Press, 2021)

Vassall, John, *Vassall: The Autobiography of a Spy* (Sidgwick & Jackson, 1975)

Wallis, Keith, *And the World Listened: The Biography of Captain Leonard F. Plugge – A Pioneer of Commercial Radio* (Kelly Publications, 2008)

West, Nigel, *The Cross: MI5 Operations, 1945–72* (Stein and Day, 1984)

West, Nigel, and Oleg Tsarev, *The Crown Jewels: The British Secrets at the Heart of the KGB Archives* (HarperCollins, 1998)

West, Rebecca, *The Vassall Affair* (Sunday Telegraph Books, 1963)

Wilson, A.N., *The Sweets of Pimlico* (Penguin, 1983)

Wilson, Elizabeth, and Angela Weir, *Hidden Agendas: Theory, Politics and Experience in the Women's Movement* (Routledge, 1986)

Windsor, Barbara, *All of Me: My Extraordinary Life* (Headline, 2012)

Ziegler, Philip, *Wilson* (Harper Collins, 1995)

INDEX